SPORT
PSYCHOLOGY
A complete introduction

To Mairéad – with all my love

Teach® Yourself

SPORT PSYCHOLOGY
A complete introduction

Dr John L. Perry

First published in Great Britain in 2015 by Hodder & Stoughton. An Hachette UK company.

Copyright © John Perry 2015, 2016

Database right Hodder & Stoughton (makers)

The *Teach Yourself* name is a registered trademark of Hachette UK.

British Library Cataloguing in Publication Data: a catalogue record for this title is available from the British Library.

Library of Congress Catalog Card Number: on file

Paperback ISBN 978 1 47360 846 7

eBook ISBN 978 1 47360 847 4

2

Cover image © Shutterstock

Typeset by Cenveo® Publisher Services.

Printed and bound in Great Britain by CPI Group (UK) Ltd., Croydon CR0 4YY.

John Murray Learning policy is to use papers that are natural, renewable and recyclable products and made from wood grown in sustainable forests. The logging and manufacturing processes are expected to conform to the environmental regulations of the country of origin.

Hodder & Stoughton Ltd
Carmelite House
50 Victoria Embankment
London EC4Y 0DZ
www.hodder.co.uk

Contents

About the Author

Dr John L. Perry CSci CPsychol is a lecturer in sports coaching and performance at the University of Hull. After achieving a degree and master's degree in sport and exercise science and psychology, John began lecturing and completed a PGCE in doing so. He went on to gain a PhD in psychology and now has more than ten years' experience in lecturing in sport psychology. John's main research areas are mental toughness, coping with stress, sportspersonship and statistical methods. His research has been published in a host of international journals, he has also presented at many conferences and worked with athletes from a wide range of sports. John is a chartered psychologist, a chartered scientist, an accredited sport and exercise scientist, a fellow of the Higher Education Academy and an associate fellow of the British Psychological Society. He also proudly supports Grimsby Town Football Club and likes drinking tea.

How to use this book

This Complete Introduction from *Teach Yourself®* includes a number of special boxed features, which have been developed to help you understand the subject more quickly and remember it more effectively. Throughout the book, you will find these indicated by the following icons.

 The book includes concise **quotes** from other key sources. These will be useful for helping you understand different viewpoints on the subject, and they are fully referenced so that you can include them in essays. The book also includes motivational quotes from respected sportspeople.

 The **case study** is a more in-depth introduction to a particular example. There is at least one in most chapters, and hopefully they will provide good material for essays and class discussions.

 The **key ideas** are highlighted throughout the book. If you only have half an hour to go before your exam, scanning through these would be a very good way of spending your time.

 The **spotlight/nugget** boxes give you some thought-provoking additional information that will enliven your learning.

 The **fact-check** questions at the end of each chapter are designed to help you ensure you have taken in the most important concepts from the chapter. If you find you are consistently getting several answers wrong, it may be worth trying to read more slowly, or taking notes as you go.

 The **dig deeper** boxes give you ways to explore topics in greater depth than we are able to go to in this introductory level book.

Introduction

Think about your favourite sport. Now ask yourself the following question:

How much of success in my favourite sport is down to physical skills and how much is because of mental skills?

No doubt you will have apportioned a percentage to each. Perhaps you went for a 50/50 split? Maybe a 60/40 either way? Maybe 80/20 either way? Regardless, you have just acknowledged that mental skills contribute to a significant proportion of success. Now ask yourself this:

Do you know how to train mental skills?

Many people know that physical skills are vital for performance and understand about training them. We know that some sports require people to be fast or strong or have excellent stamina. So it is normal to see fitness trainers plying their trade to improve these. We accept that many sports require good technical skills and tactics. So it is normal to see coaches and managers working with individuals and teams to help improve these. We know that psychology is important, because we always hear all of the above plus commentators, performers and pundits talking about mental toughness, coping with pressure and staying focused. But what people do to actually understand and train in this area is more unfamiliar.

In this book you will learn about how the mind works and how that has an impact on sporting performance. More than that, you will learn what sport psychologists actually do to improve a performer's psychological skills and mindset.

This book is designed to help you to teach yourself sport psychology. This includes understanding what it involves, the scientific theory behind sport psychology, how people become sport psychologists, and what they do.

The book is structured into two main parts: understanding psychology and applying sport psychology.

FIVE MYTHS ABOUT SPORT PSYCHOLOGY

Before we begin, it is worth setting a few things straight. Sport psychology is often misunderstood by performers, coaches, journalists and commentators. Below are some of the common misunderstandings about what sport psychology is *and* isn't. Hopefully, I can clear some of these up.

▶ Myth One: Using a sport psychologist means that you have a problem

Sport psychology is about training your mind to reach your potential. It is not about solving problems. People don't only use a coach when there is a problem with their technique; they understand that no matter how good their technique is, there is always room for improvement. Well, it's the same with a sport psychologist. No matter how confident, assured, focused, etc. an athlete may be, there is always room for improvement.

▶ Myth Two: Sport psychology is just for elite athletes

It is not. In the same way that coaching or using a physiotherapist is not purely for top athletes, sport psychology can help to improve everybody's performance.

▶ Myth Three: Sport psychologists have a magic wand

Sport psychologists teach skills. Skills take time and effortful practice to master. This means that spending time with a sport psychologist does not 'cure' problems. Over time, with effort, performers will improve their mental performance and achieve better results, but there is no Jedi mind trick, magic wand or voodoo that a sport psychologist can perform for significant performance gains overnight. You will see small improvements fairly quickly, but larger improvements take time.

▶ Myth Four: Sport psychology is about mental illness

Clinical psychology is a strand of psychology that diagnoses and treats mental disorders. Psychiatry is a strand of medicine that does likewise. Sport psychology is not about fixing things that are broken – it is about enabling people to increase the probability that they will reach their potential.

▶ **Myth Five: Having been there and done it means that you know best**

In the past, some famous sports stars have wondered how a sport psychologist who has never performed at their level can tell them about how to perform under pressure. The fact is that any sport performance is personal to the individual. Two people in the same team in the same match could have an entirely different experience of the situation because they are different people with their own minds, their own perceptions and their own strengths. Therefore, just because someone has a personal experience, it does not mean that others have that same experience. As such, you do not have to have performed at the top level to help others do so.

Part One: Understanding sport psychology

The first half of this book focuses on the theoretical side of sport psychology. This means understanding how the mind works and conducting research to find out more about the thought and emotional processes a sports performer goes through.

Before we can help to improve an athlete's performance by applying sport psychology methods, we need to understand what motivates people, or makes them anxious, or why some people can handle pressure and others can't. We need to understand what mental toughness is, or how emotions affect our behaviour. On topics like these, there have been many fascinating pieces of research. This book will explain some of this while signposting you to others. This research has been vital in establishing applied methods to help sports performers and beyond.

Sport is a great stage for developing and testing psychological theories. Take stress and coping, for example. If we are trying to better understand what happens when people are anxious and how they cope with that, then sport is a perfect playground for researchers. The unique sporting environment with high amounts of pressure and scheduled fixtures means that we can locate when and where people will experience stress. Moreover, at an elite level, this amount of stress could be huge. It could be the culmination of many years' training. This means that the things we learn can be extremely helpful not just in sport, but we can apply this outside of sport too.

Part Two: Applying sport psychology

The second half of this book focuses on how we use the theories explained in the first part to improve sports performance. This includes understanding what a sport psychologist actually does when they are working with clients, who may be individuals or teams, coaches or players, elite athletes or amateurs, adults or children.

Most of the people a sport psychologist works with are interested in one main goal – improving their performance. In the second part of this book you will learn about how to assess an athlete's needs and identify areas where they can improve. We also consider a host of methods to improve mental toughness, cope better with stress, concentrate for longer, become more confident and motivate people to train harder.

A sport psychologist's toolkit consists of a wide variety of techniques and interventions. Things like goal-setting, using imagery and visualization, positive thinking and self-talk, and concentration techniques are covered. The focus of this part is not just to discuss them, but to show you how to do them – that's what makes this an applied section.

For all the techniques and interventions that sport psychologists use, though, the biggest way to effect a change in a person is to understand them. Building relationships with clients, reflecting on your own performance, and knowing where to find support are crucial for any would-be sport psychologist. Throughout this part, advice on how to develop the necessary skills to become an effective sport psychologist is provided.

Part One

Understanding sport psychology

I thought for a long time about what to include in this section. The purpose is to provide you with an overall view of some of the key theoretical pieces of knowledge that inform modern sport psychology. As such, I have not included an overview of the history of sport psychology, nor have I included a chapter on what sport psychology is. Rather, I have identified some of the most active areas of recent research in the area and tried to explain them with historical and current research.

The result is a discussion of what I consider to be front and centre of sport psychology at the moment: understanding people, stress, mental toughness, confidence, motivation, emotion, character and measurement. That does not mean that this is an exhaustive list. There are many other areas of sport psychology and a full encyclopaedic discussion of these is simply not feasible for an introductory book. The areas I have discussed are all current and developing areas. Some have longstanding theories behind them that we are still developing and testing, others are much newer and take different approaches towards understanding mental performance in sport.

1

Understanding people: psychology of sport

In this chapter you will learn:

▶ *psychological approaches to understanding people*
▶ *what we mean by personality*
▶ *about the big five personality traits*
▶ *what the dark personality triad is*
▶ *if we can change our personality*

Understanding people is integral to sport psychology because, ultimately, that is what sport performers fundamentally are: people. It is important to remember that their sporting performance is one aspect of their life – typically their occupation. Behind that, all of the psychological theories that we use to understand the person hold true to sport psychology.

Since the beginnings of psychology and Sigmund Freud's interpretation of the human mind, researchers have been striving to better understand people. In this time there have been many different approaches adopted by psychologists. Freud's approach is referred to as **psychodynamic theory** or **psychoanalysis**. If you are new to psychology, you may have an image of a client (or 'patient') lying on a couch while the psychologist interprets their deepest unconscious desires. This is derived from Freud's work but is very different from most approaches used in sport psychology.

In contrast to the psychodynamic approach to psychology there is **behaviourism**. The behaviourist approach became the primary method of exploring psychology between the 1920s and 1950s. Very briefly, a behavioural approach assumes that behaviour is a response to a stimulus. Perhaps the most famous behavioural study is that of Pavlov's (1897) classical conditioning study, where he conditioned dogs to salivate upon hearing a bell. The bell (stimulus) is ordinarily completely unrelated to salivation (response). However, by ringing a bell before feeding dogs, Pavlov was eventually able to remove the food and the stimulus–response (S–R) association continued.

Key idea: Classical conditioning

A process of behaviour modification in which an often necessary and typically innate response to a stimulus becomes an automated response to a previously neutral stimulus.

A more complicated version of classical conditioning is **operant conditioning**. This was initially developed by Edward Thorndike (1901) and popularized by B. F. Skinner (1938). The key distinction between classical and operant conditioning is that operant conditioning includes both positive and negative conditioning. Specifically, it looks at the role of rewards and punishment as reinforcement, leading to learned behaviour. Skinner refers to the learned behaviour in response to a stimulus as **operant behaviour**.

The aim of this chapter is not to discuss every approach (sometimes called a paradigm) to psychology, as there are many excellent resources on these that you may wish to read. It is worth considering, though, that all theories discussed throughout the book have in some way derived from one or more of these approaches, including cognitive, behavioural, social, biological, evolutionary and humanist.

Personality

In trying to understand people, we often refer to **personality**. There are many, many definitions of personality. Often, these are very complex or contradict each other, which isn't surprising really when you think about it because people are very complex and often contradict each other. Because of this, one of my favourite definitions of personality is the suitably broad: 'The characterization of individual differences' (Wiggins, 1996). That is essentially what we try to do by researching personality; we try to explain what it is that makes each of us different... and we are *very* different.

To manage the complexity of personality, most theoretical approaches group typical behaviours and responses as personality traits. A **trait** is often explained as an enduring, relatively stable characteristic that is resistant to change. The great thing about understanding personality traits is that it makes people more predictable and the goal of most human science is to be able to predict. If we can predict the future, we can change the future.

The notion of examining personality, particularly in the form of traits, was first presented by Gordon Allport and his brother (1921). In the early 20th century, psychoanalysis and behaviourism existed as the two main schools of psychology. Allport was uncomfortable with both approaches and proposed that personalities, in the eye of the observer, can be **nomothetic** (traits observable across people) or **idiographic** (specific to the individual). In particular, he identified levels of centrality of traits. **Cardinal traits** refer to ruling passions, such as altruism (selflessness and concern for others) (Allport, 1937). Allport noted that not everybody had cardinal traits, but were recognizable by them if they did have them. **Common traits** were the typically recognizable ones such as honesty and aggression. In the absence of cardinal traits, these traits were considered to shape someone's personality. Finally, Allport identified **secondary traits**, which were more situation-specific, such as being nervous before a job interview.

Personality traits were further developed and popularized by Eysenck (1967), who identified personality by assessing two main traits: **extroversion** and **neuroticism**. Extroversion refers to the extent to which people are naturally inclined or pre-disposed to direct their attention outwards, while the opposite, the introverts, typically direct their attention inwards. In practice, this means that extroverts focus on other people and the environment. Extrovert behaviour is to be sociable, outgoing and active, while introvert behaviour is to be more quiet and reserved. Neuroticism refers to the extent that an individual is typically emotionally stable or unstable (neurotic). Emotionally stable individuals are normally even-tempered, while neurotic people are more liable to mood swings.

Key idea: A personality trait

A relatively stable and enduring personal characteristic that influences typical behaviour.

Thinking about personality traits like this can help us to understand individual differences but is perhaps overly simple. In reality, incredibly few people would consider themselves to be entirely introvert or entirely extrovert. We are on a continuum between the two. This raises a very important question related to personality though; do we stay the same or does personality change over time? And so begins an important argument...

Once upon a time, psychologists would categorize human characteristics into traits and states. We know that a trait is enduring and resistant to change. Conversely, a state is a feeling or behaviour that is often determined by a situation, which lasts for a period of time. An easy way to think about it is to think of an emotion, like anger. If someone was an angry person, we would be making a comment on some kind of relatively enduring characteristic (a trait). However, if someone was angry as a result of an occurrence and this feeling passed after an hour or two, we would be making a comment on their emotional state. It is frequently explained with reference to the difference between climate and weather. England has a relatively cool and wet climate, but still has warm and dry weather at times. Or consider how a person may normally be thoughtful and giving (trait), but selfish at times (state).

But is anything truly a trait? Is there any characteristic that you could confidently say lasts a lifetime? In reality, all psychological constructs lie on a continuum from trait to state. Extroversion for example, would be towards the trait end and fear would be towards the state end. In between, however, are many other constructs. Mental toughness, for example, has a genetic component, meaning that it must be fairly trait-based, but we also know that this is affected by the environment. We could refer to this as a 'statey-trait'. Anxiety is heavily dependent upon the situation, but is strongly influenced by more stable personality characteristics like pessimism. Therefore we could refer to this as a 'traity-state'.

Five-factor model

A five-factor model (FFM), sometimes known as 'The big five' personality traits, has emerged over time. Most notably, these traits were defined by Digman (1990). The idea of the big five personality traits is that they can account for differences in personality without too much overlap. Underneath them is a whole host of smaller, more specific traits. The big five are commonly remembered using the acronym OCEAN, and are:

- ▸ Openness
- ▸ Conscientiousness
- ▸ Extroversion
- ▸ Agreeableness
- ▸ Neuroticism.

This is in no way the last word on personality. I am sure that as time and research progress, we will no doubt be presented with a superseding model. For the time being though, this is the dominant model in understanding personality and, as such, I will explain it here.

OPENNESS

Openness refers to one's intellectual curiosity – perhaps through an appreciation of art or emotion, or general openness to new experience. Generally, people with a high degree of openness to experiences display a preference for a variety of activities. Your friend who always orders a different meal when they eat out, for example, is open to new experience. To aid your understanding of openness, the figure below lists a set of adjectives associated with the factor and scales taken from a common psychometric assessment, the NEO Personality Inventory (Costa, McRae & Dye, 1991).

Adjectives	Scales
• Artistic	• Fantasy
• Curious	• Aesthetics
• Imaginative	• Feelings
• Insightful	• Actions
• Original	• Ideas
• Wide interests	• Values

Openness is associated with positive wellbeing, intelligence, and social and political liberalism. Glisky, Tataryn, Tobias, Kihlstrom & McConkey (1991) were interested in the association between openness, absorption (into one's own mental imagery), and how easily people can be hypnotized. After questioning 724 participants in a research study, they found that there are moderate relationships with openness and hypnotizability. With this in mind, sport psychology consultants tend to like to work with people high in openness, as they are more prepared to try new strategies.

In sport, openness could be seen as a beneficial trait because it is closely associated with creativity and ingenuity. There are many examples of the creative little number 10 in football with the ability to unlock a defence, the gymnast who can provide the most novel floor routine or the tennis star who stays at the top because they are always prepared to learn new skills. Being open to new experience is fundamental if a performer is going to learn from others. Think about the whole coaching process. Performers surround themselves with those who are more experienced. For the experiences of others to be truly beneficial, the performer needs to be prepared to listen and try new things. Even the most talented need to keep improving in order to stay ahead.

But openness to experience is not always great. Imagine an athlete who is offered performance-enhancing drugs, or a young performer who finds themselves with much attention and money. Perhaps such a high level of curiosity and willingness to try new things could lead them astray. Although research in sport doping and personality remains limited, openness has been associated with the use of recreational drugs (Flory, Lynam, Milich, Leukefeld & Clayton, 2002). Openness is also associated with a wide range of interests. However, to reach your potential at something, the amount of time required to dedicate to this means that performers often need to focus very specifically on few things.

Key idea: Openness

An individual's intellectual curiosity and openness to new experiences. It is characterized by undertaking a variety of activities.

CONSCIENTIOUSNESS

Conscientiousness is best characterized by an individual's desire to perform a task well. Conscientious people tend to be very well organized and plan their activities in advance rather than being spontaneous. They are often thorough, careful and vigilant. Your friend who is the organizer of parties, who meticulously plans each detail and has good self-discipline can be said to be conscientious. The figure below outlines general adjectives and scales related to conscientiousness.

Adjectives	Scales
• Efficient	• Competence
• Organized	• Order
• Planful	• Dutifulness
• Reliable	• Achievement striving
• Responsible	• Self-discipline
• Thorough	• Deliberation

Conscientiousness is often associated with perfectionism, which is not necessarily a healthy thing but in sport it is easy to see how it can be a sign of a hard trainer. Stoeber, Otto and Dalbert (2009) measured this association on 214 adolescents and found that as well as conscientiousness being positively related to perfectionism, it was a lasting association, which they confirmed eight months later using the same individuals.

In sport, conscientiousness is often seen as a positive personality trait. A coach or a sport psychologist who has a performer who can take responsibility for their own performance is invaluable. Sometimes, performers may view it as the job of another person to make them as good as they can be. To get there, they need to see it as *their own job* and view the roles of others as being there to facilitate their development. This would be an example of a conscientious performer.

Elite-level sport requires great self-discipline. Swimmers spend much of their career getting up at 4 a.m. for training and many of them then go on to school or work. You simply could not do this if you were not conscientious. This level of discipline is also seen as a duty. This makes our conscientious performer a great team player – someone who values their duty to a team and carries out performances meticulously. It is for these reasons that coaches often love conscientious performers – they can be relied upon.

So does this mean that if someone is not conscientious then they cannot be successful in sport? Well, no. People who are highly conscientious are generally less spontaneous. This can make them predictable. If your opponent is predictable, it makes it easier for you to come up with tactics to defeat them. Planning can be great but many sports require those plans to be flexible. Plan B, Plan C and beyond are often required to find a way to win.

Key idea: Conscientiousness

An individual's desire to perform a task well. Those exhibiting this tendency are often very organized and meticulous and like to plan ahead.

EXTROVERSION

Extroversion refers to the extent to which an individual is comfortable in social situations, displaying outgoing behaviour, is talkative and presents great energy in groups. The opposite of extroversion is introversion, where individuals tend to prefer being on their own or in smaller groups. Your friend who likes to be the centre of attention and enjoys telling stories to large groups is more extrovert, whereas your friend who talks more in one-to-one situations but becomes more withdrawn in larger groups is more introvert. The figure below outlines general adjectives and scales related to extroversion.

Adjectives	**Scales**
• Active	• Warmth
• Assertive	• Gregariousness
• Energetic	• Assertiveness
• Enthusiastic	• Activity
• Outgoing	• Excitement seeking
• Talkative	• Positive emotions

Extroverts also tend to score highly in openness to new experiences. Extroversion is normally associated with behaviours in social settings but has also been shown to predict other things. Rentfrow & Gosling (2003), for example, found that extroverts demonstrated a general preference for more upbeat music than introverts.

In sport, there is no general consensus over whether it is beneficial to be more introverted or more extroverted. There are clearly some benefits to being an extrovert though. Most sports require high amounts of energy. Even in sports where physical movement is limited, such as target sports like archery and shooting, energy is required to concentrate and play with the right amount of intensity. In more explosive sports, the energy brought by extroverts can be infectious. A team needs some extroverts, as they bring a zest to the dressing room. Many captains are extrovert because it is a role that requires somebody to be happy being the centre of attention. This person needs to be communicative and inspire others. It is also important that they can be assertive, which is a common trait of extroverts.

But imagine a team full of extroverts. It would be a nightmare! Everyone would be competing for attention, talking over one another, trying to be assertive, and feeling unhappy when they are unable to exert enough influence over the rest of the group. It just wouldn't work. We need introverts also. Introverts are measured in their thinking and consider things carefully before they say them. They are less interested in being the centre of attention and think more about their own performance. This can be every bit as useful as the benefits delivered by extroverts.

Key idea: Extroversion

The extent to which an individual is comfortable in social situations. Extroverts are characterized by outgoing behaviour and enjoyment of group settings.

AGREEABLENESS

Agreeableness is the extent to which an individual values cooperation, a person who is generally kind and sympathetic towards others. Highly agreeable individuals are typically seen as warm and considerate. The friend who always remembers your birthday and is the one you can trust with anything is likely to be high in agreeableness. The figure below highlights some general principles related to agreeableness.

Adjectives	Scales
• Appreciative	• Trust
• Forgiving	• Straightforwardness
• Generous	• Altruism
• Kind	• Compliance
• Sympathetic	• Modesty
• Trusting	• Tender-mindedness

Someone high in agreeableness is likely to be a decent, kind person. Agreeableness is often associated with things like trust, empathy and altruism. In 2002, Laursen, Pulkkinen & Adams presented findings from an astoundingly lengthy study on agreeableness. They measured 194 people in 1974 aged 8 and again 25 years later aged 33. They found that highly agreeable children presented fewer disobedience and concentration problems than their less agreeable counterparts. A quarter of a century later, the agreeable people reported fewer problems with alcoholism and depression, had fewer arrests and had more stable careers.

In sport, highly agreeable people make very good coaches because they enjoy working hard to help others but are less interested in taking accolades themselves. They also have good powers of forgiveness, which is important when trying to develop others. Agreeable performers are generally very appreciative of support they receive, which is likely to aid their cause with their coach. Agreeable performers are likely to be seen as very professional.

Those who are less agreeable are generally less concerned with how others see them. This can be useful in sport. There is a tendency in many sports for former top athletes to become coaches. While this makes sense from some aspects, such as understanding high level competition and how technique can become unpicked at a top level, it has always struck me as a fundamentally flawed progression because of the agreeableness requirements. As much as it is helpful for a coach to be altruistic (that is, giving without receiving), performers are generally taught to be very inward-facing. We encourage great reflection on personal performance and matters. Performers spend their entire careers focusing on themselves and then step into a job where it is essential to put others first. It's no wonder that many top performers fail to become top coaches when you think about it.

Key idea: Agreeableness

The value an individual places on cooperation with others. It is characterised by warmth and sympathy towards others.

NEUROTICISM

Neuroticism is essentially emotional instability. The opposite of emotional stability, neuroticism is characterized by moodiness, fear, anxiety, jealousy and frustration. You may find yourself 'treading on eggshells' around more neurotic individuals because they have a tendency to overreact. Emotionally stable people are less jealous and more level-headed. Typical adjectives and scales of neuroticism are presented below.

Adjectives	Scales
• Anxious	• Anxiety
• Self-pitying	• Hostility
• Tense	• Depression
• Touchy	• Self-consciousness
• Unstable	• Impulsiveness
• Worrying	• Vulnerability

Neurotic individuals often seek instant gratification. A way of examining this is to test the extent to which someone is capable of delaying gratification. That is, how long can someone resist something that they want for more fruitful long-term gains?

The Stanford Marshmallow Experiment

How good are you at resisting temptation? In 1970, Mischel and Ebbesen of Stanford University conducted a study on delayed gratification. This is an individual's ability to wait for something that they want. In total, 600 nursery school children took part. Each was individually led to a room with a marshmallow on a table.

The children were told that they could eat the marshmallow but if they resisted for 15 minutes, they would be rewarded with a second marshmallow. Overall, only a third of children were able to successfully delay gratification long enough to get a second marshmallow.

A consistent area of interest in personality research is the differences between genders. Generally, women tend to exhibit higher levels of conscientiousness, extroversion, agreeableness and neuroticism than men. This finding was confirmed by Schmitt, Realo, Voracek & Allik (2008), who measured the big five personality traits of 17,637 men and women from 55 different countries. They found that results were consistent across nations. Although women were more neurotic than men, the difference is no more than moderate.

In sport, neuroticism is much more evident than in everyday life. This is because the intensity of the emotions experienced can become greater when in a pressure situation. Sport contrives to constantly produce pressure situations. This means that neurotic traits are brought to the fore in sport, and are often unwelcome. Look at the adjectives in the earlier figure. Clearly, these are not words that we would use to describe a good sporting performance. Rather, we would use opposite terms, which would be terms related to emotional stability. We want performers who are assured and controlled. The reality of it is though that many are not and it is the sport psychologist's job to help with this.

Key idea: Neuroticism

The emotional instability of an individual. It is characterized by moodiness, fear, anxiety, jealousy and frustration

Combining traits

In this chapter I have presented a simple overview of personality, which can be made much more complex. Each of the big five traits discussed have their sub-traits, which are plentiful. Without wishing to overcomplicate things, we will now consider how these traits can be combined to provide roles within teams. This is by no means intended to be an exhaustive description of all roles and trait combinations. It is merely illustrative to get you thinking about what other roles combine traits.

THE CLUB CAPTAIN

All teams and clubs have leaders. Indeed, most social circles do in an informal way. A captain is a person who organizes, makes difficult decisions and is prepared to tell others what they should be doing. This personality type is typically conscientious, since it likes assuming responsibility and organizing. Captains must also be extrovert though, as they are required to take centre stage regularly. Difficult decisions can arise in terms of assigning roles within a team. A captain who is low in agreeableness will find this much easier than someone more highly agreeable. Highly agreeable people do not like to upset others for fear that they will be disliked. Finally, our captain should be emotionally stable. Passion is a positive thing but overall, neurotic traits in a captain can create enormous uncertainty throughout a team.

THE DEDICATED PROFESSIONAL

Our dedicated stalwart of the team; they never miss a training session. They help the younger performers and they are a genuine role model. Our dedicated pro looks after themselves in the off-season and even trains extra hard. Their dedication is a clear sign that they are highly conscientious. They rarely fall out with their teammates and are liked by the whole squad. They are likely to be high in agreeableness.

THE JOKER

Every club has one. The joker wants to be liked by everybody and will perform in order to please others. This is a clear sign of someone who is highly agreeable. They tend to be open to new experiences, as they seek new adventures to avoid boredom. They are clearly extroverted and love the attention of others. They may be conscientious when necessary but are more likely to prefer spontaneity and impulsiveness, seemingly performing random behaviours in order to amuse.

The big one

The big five personality traits presents the most common understanding of personality in psychology research. However, some researchers (e.g., Musek, 2007) have recently argued that there exists a higher, overarching general factor of personality. Essentially, this factor is a low score in neuroticism (i.e., high emotional stability), and high scores in the other four factors. Indeed, Rushton & Irwing (2011) went as far to say that this represented a 'good' personality, whereas the opposite was a 'difficult' personality. There is some disagreement in the literature on this subject but van der Linden, te Nijenhuis & Bakker (2010) conducted a large meta-analysis, which grouped together 212 studies on personality and found support that a general factor of personality exists. While the jury remains out for the moment, there is certainly some interesting evidence in favour of the idea of a big one personality that predicts how content, healthy and socially desirable an individual is.

The dark triad

Recently, interest in personality research has turned towards what is known as the **dark personality triad**. The dark personality triad refers to three personality traits that have malevolent qualities. That is, they are more sinister and less socially desirable than other personality traits. The dark triad are narcissism, Machiavellianism and psychopathy. Let's explore these a little here.

NARCISSISM

The term **narcissism** derives from the Greek myth about Narcissus, who fell in love with his own reflection in a pool of water. Narcissism, then, is the pursuit of gratification from vanity. It is an egoistic admiration of the self and is characterized by grandiosity and a lack of empathy. In short, it is about being overly self-involved and not thinking of others.

Although narcissism is clearly not a desirable trait, it is one likely to be found in sports performers, since a level of self-involvement beyond the norm is required to continuously push to get better. That said, there is no empirical evidence to suggest that sport performers are more or less narcissistic than non-sport performers.

MACHIAVELLIANISM

This term derives from the 16th-century Italian Renaissance diplomat and writer Niccolò Machiavelli and describes the employment of duplicity for personal gain. Said differently, it is about manipulating and exploiting others. It is characterized by a disregard for morality, as the individual seeks only to benefit themselves. A Machiavellian will deliberately manipulate people around them to gain what they want.

PSYCHOPATHY

Psychopathy is seen in enduring antisocial behaviour. Psychopaths are often self-centred and impulsive but show little or no remorse for their actions, regardless of the consequences to others.

The dark personality triad is a growing area of research and is yet to be fully explored in connection with sport. A recent study by Onley, Veselka, Schermer & Vernon (2013) found that Machiavellianism and psychopathy were both negatively associated with mental toughness, which we know to be a useful attribute in sport. So at this stage we don't know if people participating in sport, or certain sports, or at different levels are more likely to have dark personality traits. It is likely that because personality is so varied within successful sports performers that there will be some dark personalities that play sport and some that don't. There is no rationale to suggest that there should be a relationship with sport performance in a positive or negative sense.

Sadist trolls

In a recent study, Buckels, Trapnell & Paulhus (2014) sought to examine dark personality types of Internet trolls. Trolls are Internet commenters who harass others and have made headlines with abuse aimed at various people in recent times.

The researchers explored trolling in 1,215 participants and compared this to the dark personality tetrad (which is the dark triad, plus sadism; gaining pleasure in seeing others in discomfort). The results were startling. All forms of dark personality were significantly higher in individuals who troll on the Internet. Of these, sadism was the strongest association.

Are champions born or made?

Now let us pick up our earlier state versus trait argument and take it a little further: to what extent are sports performers identified by similar personality traits? If there were a host of similar traits that were present in most successful performers, we could argue that champions are largely born, not made. However, if we cannot find such consistency, then perhaps there is no more successful personality and the environment is the key determinant of success. If this were true, we could argue that champions are made, not born. This is commonly referred to as the **nature versus nurture** argument.

'Genius is one per cent inspiration, ninety-nine per cent perspiration.'
Thomas Edison, US inventor

In the early days of psychology, researchers would search for personality traits or profiles of successful performers. The one-size personality that is going to be a world champion – that is the golden ticket. We could identify them when they are young and invest our efforts. But this one-size personality doesn't exist. We know that because there are many very different personalities that are equally successful in sport. There is clearly a strong biological basis for success. For example, if you are born with many fast-twitch muscle fibres in your body, you will likely be a better sprinter than someone who has predominantly slow-twitch muscle fibres. Perhaps in some sports the biological basis is more prominent than others.

> *'Hard work beats talent if talent doesn't work hard.'*
> Nigel Adkins, English football manager

There have been several proponents of hard work over the years. One of the more vociferous campaigners for hard work over natural talent is journalist and former British table tennis number one, Matthew Syed. After competing at two Olympic Games, Syed explained that he felt he had choked at Sydney 2000. He went on to explore what really makes a champion. After reviewing many fascinating stories around people who had been honed for success through parenting, dedication or social factors, Syed produced his book *Bounce: The Myth of Talent and the Power of Practice* in 2011. Syed's main contention was that so much of success is generated by deliberate practice.

Case study: Practice makes perfect

K. Anders Ericsson, a renowned scholar on expertise, worked with his colleagues Chase & Faloon (1980) to explore the extent to which memory skill was acquired. Short-term memory is our ability to recall recent events and was thought to be severely limited in capacity.

Ericsson and colleagues sought to test this by taking one undergraduate student (S.F.) with average memory recall skills and average intelligence for a student. S.F. was read random digits at the rate of one digit per second and recalled the sequence. If he remembered all of the digits in the correct order, the sequence was increased by one digit. At the start of the testing, S.F. could recall seven digits.

By practising one hour per day, three to five days per week, S.F.'s performance improved rapidly. After 20 months, he could recall 79 digits on average.

In total, S.F. practised this skill for 230 hours. Many involved in expertise development talk about 10,000 hours of practice to become elite, yet here S.F. had gone from barely remembering a phone number to being capable of performing at a world-class level within a fraction of this time.

That Ericsson was able to show how something so widely considered as restricted in capacity as memory recall could be developed so rapidly with deliberate practice supports the notion that much success is made and not born.

So it doesn't matter what you're born with, it's how hard you work. Well, that makes sense until you consider this: what if the ability to work hard is genetic? You may think that someone without natural talent has become successful by sheer hard work, but perhaps their ability to work hard is a natural talent. This makes perfect sense really, as working hard requires the brain to uptake particular hormones more than others, which helps us to stay positive and concentrate. One key hormone is dopamine. This helps to control the brain's reward and pleasure centres. To test the genetic impact on hard work, Ravel & Richmond (2006) used gene therapy on monkeys. Specifically, they suppressed the level of dopamine uptake in the brain.

Normally, monkeys, a lot like humans, procrastinate when a reward is a long way off and work less hard. When the reward is imminent, they increase their work rate. Richmond et al (2004) trained monkeys to release a lever when a spot on a computer screen changed colour. When they completed the task, they received a reward. Towards the end of each trial, the monkeys made fewer errors, as the reward was closer, so they were working harder. However, when the dopamine levels were suppressed, they lost the balance between effort and reward. The outcome was that they could not judge when a reward was coming so they went from being fairly lazy at the start to consistently working hard. This supports the notion that there is a genetic basis for hard work.

Last-minute assignments

If you are a student, just imagine if you could have your dopamine suppressed a month before an assignment was due – you would work as hard as you do the night before the deadline all the time. You'd be unstoppable!

Dig deeper

Collins, J. (2001), *Good to Great*. London: Random House Business.

Coyle, D. (2010), *The Talent Code: Greatness isn't Born. It's Grown*. London: Arrow.

Epstein, D. (2014), *The Sports Gene: Talent, Practice and the Truth About Success*. London: Yellow Jersey Press.

Peters, S. (2012), *The Chimp Paradox: The Mind Management Programme to Help You Achieve Success, Confidence and Happiness*. London: Vermilion.

Syed, M. (2011), *Bounce: The Myth of Talent and the Power of Practice*. London: Fourth Estate.

1 People who like being in groups are...?
   a introvert
   b extrovert
   c neurotic
   d conscientious

2 People who are meticulous are...?
   a open
   b extrovert
   c conscientious
   d Machiavellian

3 The opposite of neuroticism is...?
   a emotional stability
   b psychopathy
   c agreeableness
   d openness to experience

4 Altruism and modesty indicate an individual high in...?
   a Machiavellianism
   b psychopathy
   c openness
   d agreeableness

5 A charismatic manager is likely to be high in which personality traits?
   a conscientiousness and agreeableness
   b openness and psychopathy
   c extroversion and narcissism
   d extroversion and conscientiousness

6 Vanity is an example of...?
   a openness
   b narcissism
   c Machiavellianism
   d sadism

7 Machiavellianism is characterized by...?
  a taking pleasure in others' pain
  b manipulating others for personal gain
  c self-centredness and impulsivity
  d self-involvement

8 General factor of personality suggests it is beneficial to have high...?
  a conscientiousness
  b openness
  c emotional stability
  d all of the above

9 The brain's reward centre is controlled by...?
  a dopamine
  b adrenaline
  c steroids
  d serotonin

10 Perfectionism is most closely related to which personality trait?
  a openness
  b conscientiousness
  c agreeableness
  d psychopathy

2

Stress in sport

In this chapter you will learn:

▶ *what are common stressors for sports stars*

▶ *what stress, arousal and anxiety are*

▶ *how stress can impact sporting performance*

▶ *about individualized zones of optimum functioning*

▶ *the difference between cognitive and somatic anxiety*

▶ *what a stress appraisal is*

▶ *about sources of stress in sport*

A cruel game

Sport is designed to be stressful. First of all, we set an objective and encourage people to really want to achieve it, and then we make it difficult for them by adding rules. Take golf, for example. The objective is to get the ball from the tee to the hole in as few shots as possible. That sounds easy enough so we make it harder... let's put some trees in the way... and sand bunkers... maybe a lake... we could even make the greens slope so once someone manages to get close to their objective they realize they can still fail. As if this wasn't stressful enough, we add opponents to the mix. But not just any opponents. We use leagues or seeding systems to match people up against opponents of similar ability. This adds uncertainty over the outcome. Once we add all this together – the desire to achieve something that is made difficult and the possibility that we might fail – we create stress.

The extent to which we manufacture this stress in sport could almost be considered cruel but it is also what makes the achievements greater and the entertainment better. The purpose of this chapter is to gain an understanding of what stress is and how it affects sport performance.

Stressors in sport

There are so many things going on during a sporting competition that can cause stress. We call these things **stressors**. For example, during an important match a tennis player has the following potential stressors.

▶ The opponent's performance

▶ Serving percentage

▶ Match score

▶ Tactical considerations

▶ Public expectation

▶ Coach/parent expectation

This is nowhere near an exhaustive list either; you can probably think of many other stressors in tennis. But a stressor itself is non-directional. The list above does not necessarily mean that concern about failure should be higher or lower, it is merely information for the performer. How the performer then appraises this is vital and is discussed in the latter part of this chapter.

Stress, arousal and **anxiety** are three terms that are used regularly and sometimes interchangeably. This can often be very confusing when trying to learn about them, so here I will clearly define them:

▶ Stress represents an imbalance between a demand and perceived response capacity.

▶ Arousal refers to the level of physiological and psychological activation.

▶ Anxiety is the negative emotional state characterized by nervousness and worry.

So these related topics are quite different. In this chapter, each of these is discussed in greater depth.

To understand stress, consider a see-saw with a demand on one side and perceived resource on the other. The demand is what the situation requires, such as winning a race, sinking a putt, scoring a penalty, etc. Our perceived resource (or response capacity) is how capable we consider ourselves to be at the task. If the demand is much easier than our perceived resources, then there is little stress. However, when the see-saw is evenly balanced, then we are less sure about the outcome, which represents significant levels of stress.

Arousal is a type of bodily energy, which is reliant upon the sympathetic nervous system and several key hormones. A level of heightened arousal therefore is not necessarily positive or negative.

Anxiety, on the other hand, is a label that we use to understand arousal as an emotion. In effect, anxiety is negatively interpreted arousal.

Stress

Sport psychology often overlooks theory on stress and goes straight on to talking about arousal and anxiety. These are born out of stress though, so it is important to gain a sound understanding of this before moving on. The first point to understand is the difference between stress and a stressor. Stress is the process of adjusting to circumstances, while a stressor is the event or situation to which people must adjust. So a stressor is the thing that happens and stress is how we adjust to it.

Stressors can be large, significant or even catastrophic events. A bereavement or a natural disaster are examples of enormous stressors that have an immediate and profound impact. Stressors could also be at a much lower level though. Lower level stressors that are chronic (ongoing) can also have a significant impact. Imagine living directly under a busy flight path or commuting through busy traffic every day. Although these events are relatively minor, the persistence of them takes a toll.

Stress is our adaptive response to a stressor. While stressors are external, stress is internal. It is mediated by appraisal (which is discussed a little later in this chapter) and stress responses include cognitive, emotional, physical and behavioural aspects.

Cognitive stress responses include poor decisions, poor concentration and forgetfulness. Anyone who drives down country roads will, all too often, spot the poor decisions made by drivers as cognitive stress responses. They get stuck behind a vehicle driving slower than they desire (stressor) and cognitively adapt by deciding to overtake at a dangerous spot in the road.

Physical stress response is seen in galvanic skin responses (sweat), cardio responses (heart rate), reduced efficiency of the immune system, gastrointestinal and digestive problems, and hormonal activity. Much research on stress focuses on the hormone cortisol, which is a steroid hormone. It is strongly associated with stress responses. Most notably, peak daily cortisol levels increase with greater stress, which leads to visible ageing effects. From a behavioural perspective, stress responses include absenteeism from work and education. If something makes us feel uncomfortable, it is often easier to stay away from it. This forms part of avoidance coping, which is discussed in Chapter 13.

GENERAL ADAPTATION SYNDROME

General adaptation syndrome (GAS) was originally described by Hans Selye (1936, cited in Selye, 1976). It describes the body's short- and long-term reactions to stress. Selye's GAS model had three stages and focused entirely on the endocrine and nervous systems. The endocrine system consists of all glands in the body, which are responsible for producing and secreting hormones. The nervous systems coordinate all voluntary and involuntary actions in the body by transmitting signals. The three stages of the GAS model are: alarm reaction, stage of resistance and stage of exhaustion.

The **alarm reaction** stage is our immediate reaction to the stressor. This is where our sympathetic nervous system is activated, which releases adrenaline from the adrenal glands. Adrenaline is a hormone and hormones are essential chemical messengers. The message from adrenaline is to increase the heart rate, which in turn pumps more oxygen-carrying blood around the body, quicker. This is commonly referred to as a 'fight or flight' response, preparing the body for some sort of physical activity.

Key idea: Fight or flight

This is a physiological response to a perceived threat that is characterized by a variety of emotions.

Next after alarm is a **stage of resistance**. Essentially, this is about adaptation. It is where we draw on coping strategies to adapt to the stressor in an attempt to minimize any negative consequences. These adaptations occur at many levels in the body. In doing so, we divert our energy resources to defence. For example, if the stressor was something of impending physical threat, our resources go on defending ourselves, either through avoidance or attack. If the stressor is a milder, more persistent source, such as the requirement to reach a certain performance level, we continuously seek assurance and cognitively adapt to feel like we can be successful.

Resisting stress is effortful and fatiguing. It is easy to visualize this when considering the stressor to be a physical threat. If our stress response was to run away, this would become exhausting. The third stage of the GAS model is the **stage of exhaustion**. Whether this is exhaustion of the body's immune system to disease, our cardio-respiratory system to physical fatigue, or our ability to maintain cognitive effort when demand is high, eventually, we will reach exhaustion. At this final stage, we must relent.

'Stress should be a powerful driving force, not an obstacle.'
Bill Phillips, entrepreneur and author

Arousal

Arousal is an old theory that has routinely been taught to students of sport psychology for many years. It is quite a simple construct that is often now considered to be outdated. To genuinely understand anxiety though, it is helpful to first learn about arousal.

You may have heard of some old arousal theories such as **drive theory** (Hull, 1943; Spence & Spence, 1966) and **inverted-U theory** (Yerkes & Dodson, 1908). Rather than discussing out-of-date theories, in this chapter we are going to focus on newer theories that have evolved from these earlier theories. That is not to say that these theories are wrong, but as time goes on more research is conducted and newer theories develop.

Arousal is effectively a physiological state. It is the extent to which the body is reacting to a situation or thoughts. Think of a time when you felt nervous. You might have thought about having butterflies, a dry throat, trembling hands, sweating or feeling weak. All of these are physiological responses to stress. It is good to think about this as on a continuum from completely relaxed to extremely aroused. When playing sport we need to be somewhere between these two extremes to perform at our best.

The sport makes a difference though. We don't see target shooters psych themselves up, jumping and pounding their chest in the same way that a boxer might before entering the boxing ring. A shooter needs to be very relaxed. A very tiny movement in the fingertip can be enough to make the shooter miss their main target. This could be the difference between a gold and a silver medal. The shooter must be so controlled that they try to fire in between heart beats, as the blood pumping through the fingers could be enough to cause an error. So our shooter needs to lower their heart rate to expand the gaps between each beat. This means being very relaxed. Our boxer, on the other hand, needs to channel their energy and aggression towards moving quickly and being as alert as possible. If they are too relaxed, they may move too slowly.

This is the core of inverted-U theory (Spence & Spence, 1966), which describes how the relationship between arousal and performance is curvilinear. This means that it is not a straight line (which would be linear). Inverted-U suggests that as arousal increases, performance also increases up to a certain point. However, after this point, continued increases in arousal will lead to a detriment in performance.

So we can start to see how the sport has an impact on optimum arousal level and someone could be 'under-aroused', meaning that they are too relaxed for the event, or 'over-aroused', meaning that they are too active and need to relax. But some people are naturally very active and on edge while others are naturally very relaxed and chilled out. Some people might have to try really hard to psych themselves up to reach the right arousal level. Others might naturally be very aroused, so need to relax to reach their optimum level. This effect was first described by Hanin (1997, 2000), who explained that each athlete has an **individualized zone of optimal functioning** (IZOF).

IZOF explains that some athletes perform best when they have low levels of arousal, some with a moderate level of arousal and some when highly aroused. This can be thought of as being 'in the zone'. Figure 2.1 illustrates what it means to be in the zone for varying individuals.

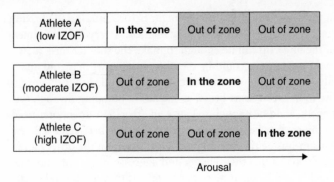

Figure 2.1 Individualized zones of optimal functioning

Anxiety

Anxiety is more complicated than arousal. As stated earlier, it is the negative interpretation of arousal. However, while arousal mainly considers only physiological states, anxiety also focuses on thoughts. There are two main components of anxiety: cognitive and somatic.

Cognitive anxiety is worry, doubt or concern. It includes negative thoughts. Some common examples in sport are thoughts like 'am I good enough?', 'what if I mess up?', 'I'm going to let my team down' and 'I can't afford to miss this'. All of these represent a negative outcome and can be detrimental to performance. **Somatic anxiety**, on the other hand, is physiological. This is like our examples of arousal, such as butterflies or trembling. Generally, research shows us that it is ok to have cognitive anxiety if somatic anxiety is low or vice versa. However, it is problematic when we have both. This was best explained by Hardy & Fazey (1987) and catastrophe theory.

Catastrophe theory is a multidimensional theory of anxiety and performance because it contains two dimensions of anxiety: cognitive and somatic. Arousal is a more simple, *uni*dimensional theory because there is somewhere between a little and a lot of it and that's it. With anxiety, though, there are levels of both cognitive and somatic anxiety, and the relationship between these influences performance. We can picture this as a three-dimensional diagram as shown in Figure 2.2.

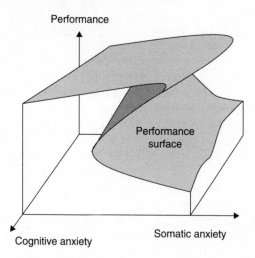

Figure 2.2 Catastrophe theory

The key to catastrophe theory is that it includes both cognitive and somatic dimensions. Also, you will see from Figure 2.2 that the drop in performance is not a gradual one, but a very dramatic cliff edge, hence the term 'catastrophe'. Hardy & Fazey (1987) explain that when moving beyond the point of optimal arousal, performance falls away in a catastrophic fashion. Examples of this may include making a reckless challenge in football, rugby or hockey and getting sent off, or capitulating in golf and rushing several shots on one hole that can ruin a round, or missing a corner and crashing a racing car.

You must be choking

Golf has seen many incidents of choking in its rich history of Majors. Recent years have seen Rory McIlroy leading the Masters by four strokes in 2011, only to make a host of errors on the back nine to shoot eight over, and Adam Scott card four consecutive birdies at the Open in 2012. A little earlier, in 1996, Greg Norman blew a six-stroke lead at the Masters to lose by five strokes. The most infamous choke though belongs to Jean van de Velde.

Van de Velde was an outsider for the 1999 Open Championship at Carnoustie, Scotland, but found himself three shots clear when teeing off at the final hole. He chose to use a driver and hit the ball just right of a burn. A six would have been enough to clinch the championship so you would expect a safe lay-up for his second shot. Van de Velde, however, went for the green but his shot ricocheted off the grandstand, on to a wall and ended up in knee-deep rough. On his next shot his club got tangled in the rough and the ball flew into the burn. Clearly not thinking straight at this point, Van de Velde took off his shoes and socks and climbed into the water, debating whether he could play the ball out of the shallow water. He eventually decided on taking a drop. His fifth shot found the greenside bunker before he eventually made the green and sunk his putt for a triple-bogey seven. He then went into a three-way playoff, losing to Paul Lawrie.

It is a great skill to be able to think clearly when under pressure and perform as one would if the pressure were not there. There are actually many more stories of golfers doing exactly that, as McIlroy did at the US Open just weeks after his failure in 2011. By understanding how people appraise stress and the subsequent impact on their performance, we can help to make choking very rare.

Trait and state anxiety

Anxiety is often referred to in terms of trait anxiety or state anxiety. As with our discussion in the first chapter, it should not be assumed that all experiences of anxiety can therefore be placed in either box A or box B, but the distinction between these does help us to understand things better. As a trait is relatively stable and enduring, trait anxiety is considered as a disposition. This means that an individual with trait anxiety is predisposed to perceive certain circumstances as threatening. Often, these circumstances are objectively non-dangerous and our disproportionate reaction is because of acquired trait anxiety, such as an irrational fear. This is common when people are scared of mice. A small mouse is of course non-dangerous. However, some people have learned to perceive this objectively non-dangerous circumstance of a small, furry and harmless creature as something to be fearful of. In these circumstances, it is highly likely that this learned response has come from a parent.

State anxiety is different. This represents situational changes in feelings of nervousness, worry and apprehension (Spielberger, 1966). It is transient. Typically, this is a more rational form of anxiety. An individual can be predisposed to be low in trait anxiety and appear, generally, as very relaxed. For example, they might be prepared to go on large rollercoasters without exhibiting fear. This is because they have complete belief in the safety and recognize this as a fun and non-dangerous situation. But sometimes there are genuine threats.

Genuine threats are situational and therefore the emotional response is specific to the situation, which is why this is understood to be state anxiety. It is associated with physiological arousal created by a surge of adrenaline. In these circumstances, state anxiety can be useful, as sometimes it is necessary to flee a situation. In sport, we each bring our natural level of trait anxiety. Some people will be more likely to be anxious regardless of the situation. State anxiety is dependent upon the situation. Even those low in trait anxiety will likely experience state anxiety before a major event.

Stress appraisal

Can nerves be a good thing? Many sports stars and musicians readily admit to having nerves but claim that it is helpful rather than a hindrance. The reasons for this range from it being a sign that you care, it helping you to focus, that it keeps you 'on your toes' or that it is all part of the adrenaline effect.

> 'If you're not nervous, it means you don't care.'
> Tiger Woods, US golfer and multiple Major winner

Indeed, many elite performers report that their anxiety is helpful, or facilitative when compared to non-elite performers. Graham Jones (1995) suggested that the amount of anxiety experienced by the individual was not the real issue. Rather, Jones and others (e.g., Jones, Hanton & Swain, 1994) claimed, it is the athlete's interpretation of the anxiety symptoms that they are experiencing that matters. Some performers perceive anxiety to be facilitative, whereas some see it as debilitative.

The idea of anxiety being perceived as facilitative or debilitative is sometimes called **directional perception**. This notion has received support from a string of studies. Specifically, Jones, Swain & Hardy (1993) reported that young female gymnasts performing better than others did not experience more or less anxiety. However, they perceived anxiety to be more facilitative than the poorer performers did. Jones & Swain (1995) replicated this result using elite and non-elite cricketers. Jones & Hanton (1996) found that swimmers who felt more positive about achieving their goals viewed anxiety as facilitative and Swain & Jones (1996) found more competitive athletes to do likewise.

So what is happening here? Are the elite performers genuinely believing that anxiety can be a good thing? At the start of this chapter I mentioned that stressors are non-directional and that the athlete's appraisal is vital for the impact on anxiety. Here, I am going to attempt to explain this process as simply as possible, which I do by explaining the theory of **cognitive appraisal** (Lazarus & Folkman, 1984).

The best way to think about stress is by seeing it as a two-way process: the environment presents stressors and we appraise them. According to Lazarus & Folkman (1984) this includes both a primary and secondary appraisal. To understand these, think about situations that you have been in that are potentially stressful and follow the flowchart in Figure 2.3.

Most significantly, there is a primary appraisal that will lead you to firstly determine how important the situation is to you and whether you focus on the potential positive outcomes or potential negative outcomes. The extent to which you consider

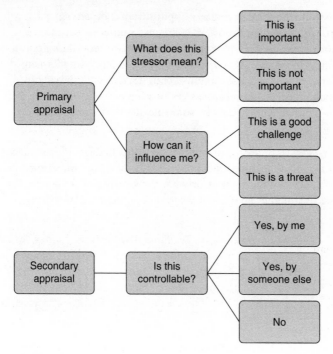

Figure 2.3 Primary and secondary stress appraisals

the stressor to be important is known as **centrality**. If you do not feel that it is personally important, the extent to which you feel stressed is likely to be much lower than if you consider it to be of great importance. Imagine our tennis player is now playing an exhibition match compared to a Grand Slam match and is a set point down (i.e., losing this point will lose the set). In the exhibition match, centrality is low so the level of stress will be lower.

Now consider contrasting appraisals. Our tennis player could view facing a set point as a threat, focusing on the negative possibility of falling behind in the match. However, they could also view this as an opportunity/challenge to play a great point. This might then impact the opponent, as they may feel that they missed their opportunity.

Despite the term, secondary appraisals do not necessary happen after primary appraisals, they are just a different set that may in turn alter our primary appraisals. The main secondary appraisal refers to control. When we feel that a situation is under control, we normally feel less anxious about it. At this point, we can make three appraisals: the stressor is either controllable by the individual, controllable by someone else or uncontrollable by anyone.

The key is to be able to 'control the controllables'. These include things like the athlete's decisions, body language and effort. What the opponent does or what the weather is like are largely uncontrollable, so it is not worth getting stressed by them.

> 'Ain't no use worryin' 'bout things within your control, 'cos if you've got them under control, ain't no use worryin'. Ain't no use worrying 'bout things beyond your control, 'cos if they're beyond your control, ain't no use worryin'.'
>
> Ed Moses, US athlete, double Olympic 400m hurdles gold medallist

Combined, the primary and secondary appraisals lead us to adopt a position of stressfulness. If we perceive that we have a positive challenge that is under our control, we experience more positive emotions and are more likely to perform to our potential. The role of the sport psychologist is to enable athletes to experience this positive appraisal of stress more than a negative one.

Emotion in anxiety

When appraisal occurs, the next logical step is to consider an emotional response. If we take a positive appraisal, such as a controllable challenge, for example, we are likely to experience positive emotions as a result. Conversely, if we perceive a threat, we are more likely to experience more negative emotions. In turn, this impacts on satisfaction with the sport (Nicholls, Polman & Levy, 2012).

We will not discuss emotion in detail here, as it is covered in Chapter 6. However, it is worth recognizing that this is clearly very important when examining anxiety. Following a conference presentation in 1996 where Lew Hardy put forward the idea of **facilitative anxiety,** Burton & Naylor (1997) submitted their response. Drawing on theories of stress, they argued that Hardy and others had mistakenly labelled other positive emotions, such as challenge and self-confidence, as facilitative anxiety.

There have been conflicting views on this topic since that time. Nicholls, Polman, Levy & Hulleman (2012) examined the role of emotion in sport performance, relative to anxiety. To do so, they got 636 athletes to complete questionnaires assessing stress and emotion before playing and then coping strategies and subjective performance (i.e., how happy they were with how they played) after playing. Their results found a strong relationship between stress and negative emotions, including anxiety, anger and dejection. These were not related to performance. However, happiness and excitement were positively associated with performance.

Perhaps then, rather than perceiving anxiety as facilitative for performance and this leading to improved play, athletes experience a range of positive and negative emotions at the same time and some are better at focusing on the positive ones. To illustrate this, consider the image of a graphic equalizer in Figure 2.4 on an old-fashioned hi-fi.

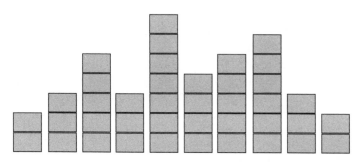

Figure 2.4 Representation of a graphic equalizer, which is similar to a range of emotions that we experience at any one point in time

In the 1980s and 1990s, hi-fi players presented a digital graphic – like the one above – when music played. Each line represents the impact of each frequency from different sound components, such as bass, treble, etc. You can consider human emotion in a similar way. We don't simply experience one emotion at a time. Rather, many emotions are occurring but some are more prominent than others. Those who interpret anxiety as facilitative are likely focusing on more positive emotions. As Kerr (1997) pointed out, it is difficult to distinguish between anxiety and other emotions. When performers refer to facilitative anxiety, it might be that their experienced anxiety is actually very low, but their excitement is very high. For example, if the higher bars represented excitement and pride, we are likely to perceive that the stressor has had a positive effect on our performance. Conversely, if the higher bars presented negative emotions, such as fear and frustration, we are likely to believe the stressor to have a negative effect. The key here is to focus more on the positive emotions that we are experiencing at any point in time.

Sources of stress and anxiety in sport

At the start of this chapter I explained that sport is a contrived and even cruel manipulator of stress and anxiety. It is beyond the scope of this chapter to systematically unpick all sources of stress and anxiety in sport, but we will discuss a few common ones here. Largely, these can be grouped into personal and situation factors.

PERSONAL FACTORS:

Here, I am referring to trait-like characteristics that individuals have that can lead to increased levels of stress and anxiety.

TRAIT ANXIETY

We have already discussed what trait anxiety is and explained that it predisposes someone to perceive a situation as threatening. This is elevated when social evaluation or personal importance are high. In many sport situations, both of these are very high and therefore trait anxiety becomes a key driver in performance.

SELF-ESTEEM

Self-esteem is covered in greater depth in Chapter 4. It reflects our overall emotional regard for ourselves and our worth. Athletes with high self-esteem are less likely to be anxious than those with low self-esteem. High levels of self-esteem are quite robust and cannot be broken easily by one or two defeats. The worrying combination here is those with high levels of trait anxiety and low levels of self-esteem. These people are likely to exhibit high levels of state anxiety.

FEAR OF FAILURE

This topic is discussed in greater depth in the chapter on motivation (Chapter 5). A fear of failure is quite a dispositional characteristic that some people possess. By focusing on potential negative outcomes and the subsequent negative emotions that come with that, anxiety is heightened.

PERFECTIONISM

To make it to an elite level in sport, athletes must strive to be the best they can be. There is a fine line between this and striving for flawlessness. Slaney, Rice & Ashby (2002) explain perfectionism as having two components: adaptive and maladaptive. Adaptive perfectionism is striving to reach high standards, which is necessary in competitive sport. Maladaptive perfectionism, however, concerns excessive worry about making mistakes (i.e., striving for flawlessness). The latter is problematic, as it is so unrealistic that failure is inevitable and inevitable failure creates more anxiety.

SITUATIONAL FACTORS:

Situational factors refer to things that occur specific to the context or environment and which can create heightened anxiety. These vary much more than the personal factors above.

CENTRALITY

Centrality is about how central, or important, the event is to the individual. If an upcoming match is deemed by the athlete to be the most important of their career, then it is likely to create higher levels of anxiety than if it does not mean much. This can be either a positive or negative thing. High centrality can induce many rewarding mindsets and behaviours, such as a will to win and increased effort. It depends on which emotions are most prevalent. If the performer experiences a lot of anxiety it can be a problem.

It is worth noting that centrality is not obvious from the outside. While an event may appear to be of greater or lesser importance, it is the individual importance and how much it means to them that is the key.

SELF-EFFICACY

As will be discussed in Chapter 4, confidence has several layers. The most specific version of confidence is self-efficacy. This is the extent to which an individual believes that they will be successful at a specific task at a specific point in time, such as a basketball player lining up a free throw. It makes sense, therefore, that self-efficacy is directly opposed to cognitive anxiety, as this is the extent to which we worry that we will not be successful. As self-efficacy increases, anxiety decreases and vice-versa.

Anxiety effects on decision making

The examples of choking referred to in this chapter often involve difficulties in consciously processing information and making rational decisions. While the effects of somatic anxiety could be a less steady technique, clearly one of the main effects of anxiety is reduced decision-making capability.

One of the reasons that anxiety has such an effect on our decision making is because of **attentional narrowing**. At any given time, we have an attentional field. This can be broad or narrow. Imagine that you are playing in central midfield in a football match. It is necessary to maintain optimal attentional focus. This means filtering out irrelevant information but focusing clearly on relevant information. If arousal levels are very low, you are likely to have a broad attentional field, which means that you will focus on both task-relevant cues, such as the runs of your teammates, and irrelevant cues, such as the opposition bench. Equally, if arousal is heightened, you begin to feel anxious and your focus becomes narrower. This means that you begin to filter out relevant cues as well as irrelevant ones. Your attentional focus can become so narrow that you become unaware of the play around you and feel rushed on the ball. Without all of the relevant information, it is very difficult to make good decisions.

Attentional narrowing is related to **attentional control theory** (Derakshan & Eysenck, 2009). The premise is that we have two main attentional systems (Corbetta & Shulman, 2002): a top-down system, which is driven by our identified goals, and a bottom-up system, which is driven by stimuli from the environment, such as a ball travelling towards us. Anxiety affects attentional control because when we are anxious we focus more on the bottom-up process and less on the top-down processes. Remember that top-down processes are often logical, rational and thought out. Bottom-up processes are responses to a changing environment. If you have ever been in a situation where you planned to do something, set out to do it, but ended up doing something completely different and you are not sure why, this is perhaps the explanation.

Case study: Playing safe under pressure

It has been well documented that the stress appraised as threat leads to changes in decision making. To explore this process in more depth, Clark et al (2012) examined the effects of stress on decisions made in a gambling task by using electric shocks to elicit a stress response.

In their study, 65 participants gambled on a wheel of fortune 112 times. This game provides an opportunity to bet on more likely results for a small return, or a less likely result for a greater return. While viewing the wheel on a screen, participants were told that if the screen background remained black, they were safe. When the background turned red, there was a chance that they would receive an electric shock.

The red background represented a stress to be appraised as threat. The researchers found that as well as changes in physiological factors, such as heart rate, participants became more risk-avoidant. That is, their approach to gambling was more to take the safe option when under pressure. This is extremely important in sport, as we regularly see performers choose safer options when stressed, but to win at an elite level it sometimes requires the performer to take a risk.

Another impact of anxiety on performance is through what is known as **conscious reinvestment hypothesis** (Masters, 1992). Masters explains that when we learn a skill, we move from a stage of conscious processing, where we need to think about specific movements, to an unconscious, automatic response. Take learning to drive a car, for example. Remembering each detail of required movements, rules of the road and anticipating the road ahead is effortful at first. After a few years, it just happens automatically. Learning sporting techniques is similar. A beginner at a golf driving range thinks about their stance, weight distribution, grip, backswing, forward swing, rotation, etc. When they become more expert, they just do it without thinking. That is, until anxiety becomes an issue.

When golfers start to hit bad shots, they regress back to this earlier version of themselves, whereby they think about the components of their technique in greater detail. This is what creates the commonly used **paralysis by analysis**. To overcome problems or anxiety, our golfer reinvests their knowledge into their technique by coaching themselves during performance in an attempt to start to play better again. Contrary to their desire though, it can actually have a detrimental effect on performance, as the once-fluent swing becomes jerkier and less proficient as a result of greater conscious processing.

Dig deeper

Lazarus, R. S. & Folkman, S. (1984), *Stress, Appraisal, and Coping.* New York, NY: Springer Publishing.

Nathan, P. E. (2010), *The Oxford Handbook of Stress, Health, and Coping.* Oxford: Oxford University Press.

Nicholls, A. R. & Jones, L. (2013), *Psychology in Sports Coaching: Theory and Practice.* London: Routledge.

Palmer, P. S. (2015), *Performing Under Pressure: All the secrets of sports psychology you'll ever need.* Midlothian, IL: Sports Motivation Clinic.

Weisinger, H. & Pawliw-Fry, J. P. (2015), *How to Perform Under Pressure: The Science of Doing Your Best When It Matters Most.* London: John Murray Learning.

Fact check

1 An event that leads to a response is a...?
- **a** stress
- **b** stressor
- **c** negative interpretation
- **d** appraisal

2 Inverted-U hypothesis states that...?
- **a** the relationship between anxiety and performance is curvilinear
- **b** what goes up must come down
- **c** arousal leads to improved performance
- **d** performers can be easily over-aroused

3 According to General Adaptation Syndrome, what follows alarm and resistance?
- **a** appraisal
- **b** adaptation
- **c** exhaustion
- **d** goal setting

4 IZOF suggests what?
- **a** performance deteriorates with heightened arousal
- **b** arousal leads to catastrophe
- **c** individual zones predict whether a performer appraises stress positively
- **d** optimal levels of arousal are specific to individuals

5 Catastrophe theory is multidimensional because...?
- **a** ...it says that performance changes drastically
- **b** ...it includes cognitive anxiety
- **c** ...it includes cognitive and somatic anxiety
- **d** ...it indicates that over-arousal leads to reduced performance

6 A situation-specific negative emotional state is:
- **a** trait anxiety
- **b** state anxiety
- **c** stress
- **d** somatic anxiety

7 The extent to which a stressor is important to us is known as...?

   a   centrality

   b   centricity

   c   appraisal

   d   emotional control

8 Key primary stress appraisals include...?

   a   stress and coping

   b   threat and control

   c   challenge and threat

   d   challenge and control

9 Stress caused by striving for flawlessness can be the result of...?

   a   poor emotional control

   b   self-efficacy

   c   perfectionism

   d   fear of failure

10 Attentional narrowing refers to...?

   a   losing concentration

   b   the reduced attention field as a result of anxiety

   c   the reduced attention field that helps us to focus

   d   being in the zone

3

Mental toughness

In this chapter you will learn:

▶ *what resilience is*
▶ *what attributes mentally tough performers have*
▶ *the 4Cs of mental toughness*
▶ *how mental toughness is assessed*
▶ *what the benefits of being tough are*
▶ *whether people are born tough*
▶ *how to improve mental toughness*

Bouncing back

Here's a hard truth that we must all accept: life is not fair. Sometimes things go wrong because we make bad decisions or mistakes. Sometimes things go wrong through no fault of our own. Whatever the reason, from time to time, we will all be faced with adversity. Some people are very good at bouncing back from adversity to succeed. In sport this could be a crushing defeat in a big tournament, a dramatic loss of form, or a career-threatening injury. The ability to bounce back is known as **resilience**.

Think about a time when you were faced with adversity and you overcame it. There are two main psychological processes to be able to achieve this.

1   First, you need to accept that something has gone wrong and take control of the situation. It is not up to anybody else to solve your problems for you. It is up to you to do something about it.

2   Whatever you decide to do, you need to stick at it and not give up. You need to show commitment.

'I've missed more than 9,000 shots in my career. I've lost almost 300 games. Twenty-six times I've been trusted to take the game-winning shot and missed, I've failed over and over and over again in my life – and that is why I succeed.'

Michael Jordan, US basketball legend

Attributes of mentally tough athletes

The main benefit that athletes and coaches are interested in is, of course, the positive impact on performance. This is reflected in a recent definition by Gucciardi, Hanton, Gordon, Mallett & Temby (2015, p. 28), who stated that mental toughness is 'a personal capacity to produce consistently high levels of subjective … or objective performance'. Practitioners as well as researchers typically acknowledge that mental toughness is a key component of athletic performance (Connaughton & Hanton, 2009).

Key idea: Resilience

Resilience is the quality of being able to recover quickly from adversity.

To that end, it is not surprising that several researchers have tried to measure the impact of mental toughness on sport performance. We will review some of these here.

Clough, Earle & Sewell (2002) conducted two studies. In the first study, 23 participants were grouped into a high mental toughness group or a low mental toughness group. Each participant undertook a VO_2 max fitness trial to determine their maximum capacity while cycling. They were then subjected to increasing workloads (30 per cent, 50 per cent and 70 per cent of maximum) on a stationary bicycle. At a low workload (30 per cent), both the high and low mental toughness groups perceived the physical demands equally. However, at the medium workload (50 per cent), the higher mental toughness group perceived the physical demands to be less than the lower mental toughness group. Finally, at the highest workload (70 per cent), the mentally tough group perceived the physical workload to be much less than the low mental toughness group did. As the authors explained, this illustrated the common cliché that when the going gets tough, the tough get going.

In their second study, Clough et al (2002) set a planning exercise as a cognitive task for 79 participants. Again, these were divided into high and low mental toughness groups. The experiment was designed to see how the participants would respond to positive and negative feedback. They found that while the low mental toughness group performed worse after receiving negative feedback, the high mental toughness group was unaffected by feedback. Mentally tough performers are less likely to be negatively affected by knockbacks. This is important in sport, as few elite performers make it to the top without dealing with failure and rejection at some point.

Bouncebackability

On the topic of bouncing back, there was a great popularization of the word 'bouncebackability' a few years ago. In fact, it wasn't a word but was used by then Crystal Palace manager Iain Dowie to explain the resilience shown by the team. After hearing this, *Soccer AM*, the popular Sky Sports football show, ran a campaign to get the word used frequently enough to become recognized by the dictionary authorities. It was subsequently used by commentators, players and pundits and eventually made it into the *Oxford English Dictionary*, where it is defined as 'the capacity to recover quickly from a setback'.

As we discussed in the previous chapter, sport creates great stress on performers. To gain the desired results, the athletes who cope best with this tend to be the most successful. Nicholls, Polman, Levy & Backhouse (2008) examined coping strategies used by athletes. They found that mentally tough performers used better coping strategies than more mentally sensitive performers. Specifically, they adopted more task-focused strategies, meaning that they sorted things out rather than burying their head in the sand. In a follow-up study, Kaiseler, Polman & Nicholls (2009) found that mentally tough performers were more likely to tackle a problem rather than focusing only on emotions. Generally, it appears that mentally tough sportsmen and sportswomen deal with stress much better.

The 4Cs of mental toughness

The 4Cs model of mental toughness was initially proposed by Peter Clough et al (2002). After interviewing professional athletes, they found that mental toughness was more than just resilience. It is not just about bouncing back from adversity, there is a proactive element too. Mentally tough athletes were more likely to seek out challenges and push themselves to get better. They were also very confident in their own abilities.

Their proposed model of mental toughness then was challenge, commitment, control and confidence, which became known as the 4Cs model:

- **Challenge:** to what extent you see challenges, change, adversity and variety as opportunities

- **Commitment:** to what extent you will make promises and the extent to which you will keep those promises

- **Control:** to what extent you believe you shape what happens to you and manage your emotions when doing it

- **Confidence:** to what extent you believe you have the ability to deal with what you will face and the inner strength to stand your ground when needed

Key idea: Mental toughness

A personality trait that determines in large part how people deal with challenge, stressors and pressure... irrespective of prevailing circumstances.

CHALLENGE

Imagine you are playing regularly for a team and you get on fairly well with the coach. The coach considers you a reliable player and you are consistently given reasonably important roles in the team without being the star. One day you hear that the coach is leaving and a new coach that you know nothing about is to be appointed. How do you feel?

One possibility could be to feel threatened because the new coach might not rate you as highly or might bring in a new player to take your position. You would perhaps lose your place or maybe even need to move to a new team. However, what if the new coach is even better than the old one? What if the new coach believes that you have the potential to be the star player? So rather than feeling threatened, this could be a great opportunity.

Essentially, this example is what the challenge component of mental toughness is all about – the extent to which we see opportunities or threats, and how we react to change. If we see opportunities, we are more likely to put in more effort and persist longer to reach our goals. If we perceive threats, we naturally want to shy away from them. Challenge is linked to the concept of optimism. Nicholls et al (2008) tested how mental toughness was related to optimism and pessimism on a sample of 677 sports performers. Their results showed that all aspects of mental toughness were positively related to optimism and negatively related to pessimism. That is to say, the more mentally tough someone was, the more optimistic they are likely to be and the less pessimistic they are likely to be.

People very high in challenge do not just react to a situation and see it as an opportunity or a threat though; they actually seek out new challenges. A really mentally tough individual is proactive in putting themselves in situations where success and failure are both possible. We call these **achievement situations** and we will discuss this further in Chapter 5 on motivation, but for now think of this as being proactive. To stand a chance of reaching your potential, you need to be prepared to push yourself outside of your comfort zone. This means looking for new challenges and perceiving them as opportunities.

COMMITMENT

Commitment is about sticking to promises. Highly committed people will not give up if they have promised someone (or themselves) that they will do something. For example, to train for an endurance event is incredibly physically and mentally demanding. Practice runs probably five times a week when the body is aching or the mind is exhausted can prove too much for many. Mentally tough people still do it though because they have said they will and they don't give up on anything. In a sense, commitment is your **stickability**.

Committed individuals are the people prepared to take on tasks, even though they may be assessed on them. Committed individuals are prepared to do what it takes to keep those promises. If something becomes harder that it first appeared, our committed athlete will stick at it. They might even enjoy it because, ultimately, the harder the journey the more satisfying the reward. After all, if you could win a football match 4-3, the best way to do it would be coming from 3-0 down wouldn't it?

Being able to stick at something is not simply a decision though. We can all think of examples when we want to stick at something but haven't. Most people make many New Year's resolutions over time, only to have written them off by February. Or decide to start a new exercise regime and 'this time I'm going to stick to it' and not done so. To stick at something requires great mental skill. This requires not only high levels of motivation but also focus.

> *'Winners never quit and quitters never win.'*
> Vince Lombardi, American football coach

Commitment is particularly important in situations where concentration is required. To investigate the neuropsychological basis of mental toughness, Clough, Newton, Bruen, Earle, Earle & Benuzzi et al (2010) examined MRI brain scans of 80 individuals and their relationship to mental toughness. Generally, higher levels of mental toughness were associated with more grey matter, which contains important cells, in several regions of the brain. Most notably, the authors found that highly committed individuals had more grey matter in the Precuneus part of the parietal lobe in the brain. This part of the brain helps us to focus and concentrate on things.

Blocking out thoughts is known as **cognitive inhibition**. This is an important mental skill that aids commitment. For example, imagine that you're training for an upcoming event and feeling tired. The motivational component of mental toughness might mean that you really want to get out and train harder, but blocking out that thought that keeps telling you to relax instead is a cognitive skill.

Key idea: Cognitive inhibition

The mind's ability to tune out stimuli that are irrelevant to the task/process at hand or to the mind's current state.

To explore the cognitive basis of mental toughness in greater detail, Dewhurst, Anderson, Cotter, Crust & Clough (2012) explored memory recall. They read two lists of unrelated words to a group of 60 participants and asked them to recall as many of the words as they could. After the first list was read, participants were told that this was just for practice and they were not required to remember it. However, after the second list of words had been read, participants were told to recall words from both lists.

When recalling words from list one, which they had been told to forget, mental toughness accounted for less than 1 per cent of variance. In effect, people who were mentally tough were no better or worse than those who were not. However, when recalling words from list two, mental toughness accounted for more than 20 per cent of the variance. This was largely explained by the commitment component. That means that the more mentally tough people were, the better they were at focusing on something when they believed it was important to.

CONTROL

The extent to which we maintain control is key towards being resilient. This component of mental toughness is divided into two sub-components. The first is life control, which indicates the extent to which we believe that we shape what happens to us. The second is emotional control, which is concerned with how we control our anxieties, frustrations, anger and other emotional states.

▶ **Life control**

There is a common phrase used by many that suggests a lack of life control: 'knowing my luck... ' The person beginning a statement with this phrase is typically implying that due to uncontrolled external forces, they will be unable to achieve their goal. Of course, it is frequently used without much consideration but it resonates with some of us every time we hear it because it is such a clear example of someone demonstrating a lack of perceived control over what happens to them in their life. This represents life control.

Case study: What's the point?

The control dimension of mental toughness is closely related to the concept of learned helplessness. Proposed by Seligman (1975), learned helplessness is a state whereby individuals perceive things that should be within their control as, in fact, outside of their control.

To demonstrate the concept, Seligman tested responses from dogs. He placed a group of dogs in a harness and subjected them to a mild electric shock. One group of dogs was able to press on a lever to prevent the pain. However, for another group, the lever did not stop the shocks. This group had learned that trying to stop the unpleasant experience was futile.

In the second part of the experiment, the dogs were placed in a box, which was separated into two halves by a small partition. The floor on the side that the dogs were on administered the mild shocks again, while the floor on the opposing side of the partition was normal. The dogs that had previously been able to stop the shocks by pressing the lever jumped the partition. However, the dogs that were previously unable to stop the shocks simply accepted the new shocks without attempting to jump free. This group has learned (falsely) that it was unable to avoid pain and so accepted it.

But there is hope! If we can learn helplessness, we can also learn optimism. By stopping negative thoughts and replacing them with more positive, optimistic thoughts, we learn to take control of our actions and therefore successes. In terms of life control, we can think of self-fulfilling prophecy. In psychology, Albert Bandura's work on self-efficacy (discussed in the next chapter) draws on self-fulfilling prophecy. Essentially, this means that we make our own future, we do not just predict it.

Key idea: Learned helplessness

A mental state whereby an individual becomes unable or unwilling to accept that they have control over a normally controllable situation.

▶ Emotional control

Controlling emotions is a huge part of sporting performance. These emotions can be anything: excitement, anger, frustration, elation, fear... The important thing is to make sure that we can keep these in check because emotions are often without logic, which is a function from a different part of the brain.

Controlling your emotions doesn't have to mean that you don't show any. Control means that if you do show an emotion, it is because you have chosen to show it. Equally, if you chose to hide an emotion, it is because you have chosen to hide it. Generally in competitive environments, we tend to show positive emotions and hide negative ones. So when an athlete feels excited and pumped up just before a performance, it is normally good to show this, as it lets the opponent know that they are ready and looking forward to the event. If the emotion the athlete is experiencing is fear, it is normally better not to show this, as it could boost the opponent's confidence.

Emotions are different in each individual. Some people experience much more intense emotions than others. That doesn't mean that they are more or less mentally tough, it just means that they need to sometimes work harder to control their emotions.

Emotional control is clearly linked to emotional intelligence, which is discussed in greater detail in Chapter 6. A recent study by Nicholls, Perry, Jones, Sanctuary, Carson & Clough (2015) examined this relationship in closer detail. Specifically, they asked 531 athletes to complete measures of mental toughness, resilience and emotional intelligence. They found that the concepts of mental toughness and emotional intelligence were very strongly linked. This means that mentally tough people also tend to be more in tune with not only their emotions, but perhaps the emotions of others as well.

Lucky socks?

Growing up, I used to go with my uncle to watch Grimsby Town play. At one stage, we were having a good season and I remember him saying it was because he wore his lucky socks to the game.

Not because of the skill of the players, the organization or the management, or the sheer hard work of the team... the positive outcomes on the pitch were all due to his socks. It's such a shame he must have lost them because we haven't had much luck in recent years!

It is interesting to consider superstition in sport. There exist many superstitions with varying strength of belief in playing their part in future success. There is little research in this area. A potential positive of adherence to superstition could be that it is a coping mechanism, which makes the performer feel relaxed. Overall, however, I would not recommend performers to adopt superstitions, as it misplaces control of events to external and uncontrollable factors. This is discussed again in the next chapter under attribution theory.

CONFIDENCE

Confidence is a key component of mental toughness. In my opinion, this underpins all of the other components because if you are confident, it is easier to see opportunities rather than threats; it is easier to stick at something if you are sure you will be successful in the end; and if you believe you are capable, you will want to be in control. The next chapter looks more specifically at confidence, so I won't go into great depth here, suffice to say that in terms of the 4Cs of mental toughness, confidence comes in two forms: confidence in abilities and interpersonal confidence.

> 'It's not who we are that holds us back, it's who we think we're not.'
> Michael Nolan

▶ **Confidence in abilities**

Do you believe that you have the ability to reach your goals? I want all of my athletes to answer this with a resounding 'Yes!'. This is so important because, for reasons discussed in the next chapter, when you are confident you think and act in a much more effective manner than when you are not confident. This aspect of confidence is all about the extent to which you can be sure in answering the question with a big 'Yes!'.

▶ Interpersonal confidence

Having confidence in your abilities is clearly very useful for sports performance. However, to maximize its effectiveness it is necessary to have interpersonal confidence. This refers to the extent to which you are confident in verbal challenges. For example, in a game of hockey, as much as you have belief in your ability to dribble and pass, you will receive more of the ball to demonstrate these abilities if you can assert yourself on the game and confidently call for, or demand, the ball.

There are many examples of the usefulness of interpersonal confidence in sport. Consider a team situation where you feel you have a point to make in a team meeting. You need interpersonal confidence to make that point and influence other people in the team. The people who are better at influencing others often become captain of a team or become better coaches.

Academic differences

As this is an introductory book, I do not wish to spend much time critically evaluating a range of arguments that have surfaced over recent years between academics presenting slightly different conceptualizations of mental toughness. However, it would be remiss of me not to acknowledge this, as it is prominent in recent sport psychology research.

The Clough et al (2002) 4Cs model described above is the dominant model, certainly in applied psychology. However, there are alternatives. Jones, Hanton & Connaughton (2002) defined mental toughness with reference to coping better than opponents in competition, training and lifestyle. The same authors elaborated on this in 2007 with a framework adding attitude/mindset to their earlier definition. Generally, this framework includes self-belief, focus, working towards goals and dealing with pressure.

Recently, Gucciardi and colleagues (2015), following a host of studies, presented seven indicators of mental toughness. These were: self-belief, attention regulation, emotion regulation, success mindset, context knowledge, buoyancy and optimism. The paper also engages in some discussion regarding whether mental toughness should be seen as multidimensional (i.e., having several components) or unidimensional. Personally, speaking from an applied perspective, a multidimensional concept is always of much greater developmental use.

I have acknowledged other approaches, and it is certainly worth expanding your reading to these papers cited. Overall, though, the result of the academic debate has been more of a cosmetic change than substantial theoretical understanding. All of the models presented here are theoretically sound and from a practitioner perspective they are more similar to each other than they are different. It is typically the name and amount of components that change. In terms of what we do to develop mental toughness, I think that remains similar whichever theoretical model you prefer.

Assessing mental toughness

There are a few methods of assessing mental toughness for both applied use and in research. By applied use, I am referring to measuring an individual's mental toughness to identify ways that they can improve. For research, I mean using a questionnaire in a large sample to help further understanding.

By far the most widely used measure of mental toughness is the Mental Toughness Questionnaire-48 (MTQ48; Clough et al, 2002). This measure is based on the 4Cs model and measures each of the components of mental toughness discussed above, plus an overall measure of mental toughness. The questionnaire contains 48 statements, which respondents identify a level of agreement on following a scale running from one to five. This measure was validated by Perry, Clough, Crust, Earle & Nicholls (2013) on a sample of over 8,000 people from around the world.

Psychometric measures usually go hand in hand with theoretical models so, just as there have been some disagreements with the theory, there have also been disagreements with measurements of mental toughness. Prior to the Perry et al (2013) study cited above, there was disagreement regarding the validity of the MTQ48 between Gucciardi, Hanton & Mallett (2012) and Clough, Earle, Perry & Crust (2012). Other measures that exist in this area include the Mental Toughness Inventory (Middleton, Marsh, Martin, Richards & Perry, 2004), which examines 12 factors of mental toughness. Gucciardi et al (2015) recently presented a short assessment of mental toughness, also called the mental toughness inventory. This contains just eight items that provide only an overall assessment of mental toughness. Sheard, Golby & van Wersch (2009) developed the Sport Mental Toughness Questionnaire, which is specific to sport and assesses confidence, constancy (determination) and control.

Key idea: Psychometric assessment

The objective measurement of skills and knowledge, abilities, attitudes or personality traits through questionnaire-based methods.

Physical toughness

A common association in mental toughness is its link with physical toughness. This is because toughness generally refers to withstanding some form of strain and this is often characterized physically. The extent to which someone or something can withstand strain without breaking is effectively how tough they are/it is. The first notable relation between physical and mental toughness came from Canadian psychologist Dienstbier (1989, 1991). Specifically, he examined physiological arousal when confronted with stress, and how within-person changes could be observed over time when repeatedly exposed to physical stressors. In essence, the premise is that exposure to challenges/ stressors results in a change in character. Dienstbier then predicted that exposure to mental challenges/stressors would cause mental toughening.

This link between mental and physical toughness was also examined by Crust & Clough (2005). Testing 41 male undergraduates, they held a weight (1.5 per cent of body weight) suspended with their dominant arm for as long as possible. Supporting Dienstbier's assertion that a tough mind and body are related, they found a significant positive relationship between mental toughness and endurance. In other words, the more mentally tough someone was, the longer they were able to hold the weight. Similarly, Levy, Polman, Clough, Marchant & Earle (2006) noted a relationship between mental toughness and pain tolerance during rehabilitation from injury.

Pain: a state of mind

Have you ever come across this idea that pain is a state of mind? Technically, it is not, but the intensity of the feeling of pain is. There are many studies that examine this. Typically, by offering inaccurate feedback, we can see that participants often report greater or lesser pain based on what they are led to believe rather than what is actually true. To ever see evidence of this, look at a toddler when they fall over. They take a moment to assess the reaction of people around them before deciding whether they should cry in immense pain or just carry on.

While we are discussing physical toughness, though, I'd like to address a common fallacy. The use of the word 'tough' can sometimes be misinterpreted as some sort of macho concept. As pointed out by Clough and Strycharczyk (2012), this is not the case. Indeed, after reviewing more than 50,000 cases of mental toughness assessments, I can gladly confirm that there are no substantive differences between males and females in mental toughness. The meaning of the word 'toughness' in the term 'mental toughness' is much more attuned to the notion of 'being comfortable in your own skin'. That is, a quality that can give an inner strength to people, which enables them to deal with all the things that life can throw at them.

Another common misconception about mental toughness is the notion that people who are mentally tough are less nice. This is not the case. As referred to in Chapter 1, Onley et al (2013) examined mental toughness in relation to the dark personality triad. They found that mental toughness was negatively associated with psychopathy and Machiavellianism. That is, the people who were mentally tough demonstrated low levels of these traits. Machiavellianism is the use of manipulation to reach desired outcomes. If you are genuinely mentally tough and comfortable in your own skin, you will be inwardly confident enough not to feel the need to manipulate others.

My only caveat to this is that being mentally tough requires an awareness that you are mentally tough and that is why you act in certain ways. For example, you may be very committed, which is likely to make you a competitive person. That is not necessarily a problem, but it is important to acknowledge that others might not be, and that is fine. If a highly committed person is prepared to do extra training, it does not mean that they should expect everyone else to do likewise. Their resolute commitment could also be related to perfectionism, which can be maladaptive. The best way to overcome such drawbacks of being very mentally tough is reflection and awareness. If someone knows that they have certain behavioural tendencies, they are more likely to recognize that it is individual to them and not expect everyone else to be like them.

Wellbeing

It is important to remember that just because someone earns a career by playing sport, they are still a person, and like all of us we work to live, not live to work. I would argue with anybody that wellbeing is more important than objective sporting success. There is not much point having success if you cannot enjoy it. Although it is not really within the scope of this book, it is worth acknowledging how some performers, regardless of objective success, enjoy much greater wellbeing than others.

Of late, there has been a host of studies that examines the effect of mental toughness on wellbeing. Specifically, researchers at the University of Basel, Switzerland, have been examining the role of mental toughness in adolescent health. They have found that adolescent exercise and physical activity are associated with mental toughness (Gerber et al, 2012), that mentally tough adolescents are more resilient in combating stress (Gerber et al, 2013a), that they adapt better to stress over time (Gerber et al, 2013b), and that they get better sleep (Brand et al, 2014).

Our existing understanding of mental toughness in sport actually developed significantly from studies in health psychology. Suzanne Kobasa (1979) noted that when encountering stressful life events, such as illness, some people seemed to cope with it better than others. She termed this as 'hardiness'. A hardy personality was someone who remained mentally strong despite significant stressful events. Kobasa argued that this was more than resilience, since some people saw a challenge in illness. This is now commonplace, as it is part of our everyday vocabulary. For example, almost everyone is familiar with what it means to fight a disease. The notion of fighting is a proactive one. Rather than sitting back and hoping it goes away, the approach is to see it as a challenge that must be overcome.

Key idea: Hardiness

The capacity to remain healthy under life's stresses.

Beyond a sport and health setting, research into mental toughness has explored performance in a number of settings. In business, Marchant, Polman, Clough, Jackson, Levy & Nicholls (2009) tested the mental toughness of 552 workers from different positions. They found that mental toughness increased from clerical positions to junior management, to middle management, and to senior management. What we don't know is whether people get jobs in senior management because they are mentally tough, or whether being in senior management makes them mentally tough. Knowing what we do know, I suspect that their mental toughness came first, but increased with experience.

Colbert, Scott, Dale & Brennan (2012) were also interested in how lessons from sporting performance could be related to lessons in other areas. Specifically, they examined mental toughness in Olympic rowers and surgeons. They found similarities in top performers in this regard.

It should be noted, though, that although mental toughness is clearly associated with positive performance, it is not the only determinant of success. Being mentally tough cannot guarantee success. I know that I am mentally tough, but being in my mid-30s with dodgy knees, no real sporting success and a lack of technical talent or physical prowess, I am just going to have to accept that I'm not going to make it as a professional athlete! As pointed out by Crust (2008), mentally tough performers are likely to make the most of their abilities, but this does not necessarily mean absolute success. A mentally tough tortoise will never be a hare.

Are people born tough or made tough?

This is a really interesting question. The answer seems to be that it is a bit of both. Mental toughness is considered as a personality trait, in that it is relatively stable over time. Studies show that gains in mental toughness over time through psychological intervention and training are around 20 to 30 per cent. This suggests that it is not easy to change mental toughness, but it can be developed. Moreover, because it is a personality trait, changes should stand the test of time.

The best way to answer any question like this one is by studying twins. This is exactly what Horsburgh, Schermer, Veselka & Vernon (2009) did. They collected data from 219 sets of North American twins and examined the extent to which their mental toughness was shared or unique. What they found was that part of the variance of all aspects of mental toughness was due to genetic factors, and part was due to environmental factors. So it seems that the answer to our question is 'a bit of both'.

Developing mental toughness

So we know that mental toughness has both genetic and environmental factors. We cannot change someone's genetic makeup so that leaves us with environmental factors to develop mental toughness. 'Environmental factors' is a very broad term though. It is not just one's surroundings, it is also the individual's perception of the world around them, how they affect it and how they are affected by it.

Clough & Strycharczyk (2012) categorized mental toughness interventions into five areas:

1 positive thinking

2 visualization

3 anxiety control

4 attentional control

5 goal setting.

I will not discuss each of these here, as most of them are picked up in the second part of this book. It is worth noting, though, that formal, structured development of mental toughness using these strategies can be effective. Development can also occur though coaching and mentoring. A test itself can raise awareness for the performer and motivate them to work on various aspects of their toughness. With an experienced practitioner working with them, they can progressively develop each component of mental toughness with regular meetings and tasks.

More generally, Crust & Clough (2011) proposed that effective ways to build mental toughness included providing challenging yet supportive environments, having effective social support and encouraging reflection. In terms of challenge and support, they stated that training sessions must stretch the physical capabilities of performers, also including some form of psychological pressure. Effectively, this means conditioning training to induce pressure. Sport is full of pressure. If you are training without pressure, you are not really practising the same skills that you need in competition. Setting challenging environments could also include the use of distraction. Crust &

Clough urged coaches to be innovative in creating environments that would require performers to problem-solve. The authors provide a clear example of how this can work in practice:

'To realistically prepare players for the demands of competition, one basketball coach we know has introduced pressure training at the end of training sessions when players are tired. Interspersed between short 5-minute games, the team (five players) who are behind at a given time, are forced to take two attempted free throws each as the opposing team lines up in their normal positions (i.e., observers). An appropriate target is set such as achieving six out of ten baskets. Thus the pressure on the team mounts as misses occur. Rewards or forfeits can be applied (on the basis of outcomes) to provide consequences for success or failure. The players are then encouraged to reflect on their experiences and examine different approaches/ ways of coping (i.e., such as gaining control of their breathing or blocking out distractions). The task can be made more difficult by adding additional distractions (noise, background movement). While this approach has not been scientifically tested, the basketball coach has reported better free-throw statistics, especially in tight games.'

Crust & Clough, 2011, p. 27

Social support is discussed later in this book when we review common coping strategies. It is often found to be the most effective way of coping with stress and anxiety. Establishing good social support networks can be a very effective way of developing mental toughness. This support can be emotional, problem-based or sometimes informational.

The use of reflection could easily appear in any self-development discussion. It is extremely effective though. I find a very effective way of initiating reflection is with assessment. If performers can learn something about themselves, which is largely through reflection, they can then consider appropriate actions to develop. We can encourage reflection by asking athletes to review performances on a regular basis and relate these to their goals. They can also reflect on the development of physical, technical, tactical and psychological skills.

It is also interesting to consider the effect of sport on mental toughness. I wrote a book chapter on this recently (Perry, 2014), suggesting that sport can intuitively develop mental toughness because it consistently presents achievement contexts in which success and failure are both inevitable. The success aspect is good for confidence, while there is much to be learned in failure. Failure should be cherished, as it enables us to grow and become more resilient. It encourages us to take on the next challenge with the determination greater than the last. Without failure, we can become fearful of it. Despite this, please do not be under any illusions that sporting performers are bound to be more mentally tough than people who do not perform sport. First, non-sporting performers may take on challenges in the arts (music, stage performances) or work challenges. Second, some sporting performers are successful because they are technically brilliant rather than mentally tough. This presents fantastic opportunities to work with them to enhance the probability of them maximizing their potential.

Dig deeper

Clough, P. J., & Strycharczyk, D. (2012), *Developing mental toughness: Improving performance, wellbeing and positive behaviour in others.* London: Kogan Page.

Dweck, C. S. (2012), *Mindset: How you can fulfil your potential.* London: Robinson.

Gucciardi, D. & Gordon, S. (Eds.) (2013), *Mental Toughness in Sport: Developments in Theory and Research.* Abingdon: Routledge.

Perry, J. L. (2014), Sport and its role in developing young people. In Strycharczyk, D. & Clough, P. J., *Developing mental toughness in young people: Approaches to achievement, well-being, employability and positive behaviour* (pp. 181–90). London: Karnac Books.

Sheard, M. (2012), *Mental Toughness: The Mindset Behind Sporting Achievement* (2nd ed.). Abingdon: Routledge.

Fact check

1 Resilience refers to...?
- **a** sticking at something
- **b** bouncing back from adversity
- **c** staying in control
- **d** seeking challenges

2 Making and keeping promises describes...?
- **a** challenge
- **b** commitment
- **c** control
- **d** confidence

3 Being able to tune out irrelevant stimuli is a description of...?
- **a** resilience
- **b** seeing opportunities
- **c** being confident
- **d** cognitive inhibition

4 Believing that we have control over our future outcomes is indicative of...?
- **a** learned optimism
- **b** learned helplessness
- **c** confidence
- **d** hardiness

5 Someone who believes in their capabilities but is shy demonstrates...?
- **a** high challenge but low control
- **b** high confidence in abilities but low challenge
- **c** high confidence in abilities but low interpersonal confidence
- **d** high interpersonal confidence but low control

6 Mentally tough people tend to be...?
- **a** manipulative
- **b** conscientious but manipulative
- **c** less manipulative
- **d** psychopaths

7 Mental toughness is...?
- **a** a trait that cannot be changed
- **b** a changeable state
- **c** a situation-specific feeling
- **d** a changeable trait

8 Someone who believes things just happen to them is...?
- **a** low in life control
- **b** low in emotional control
- **c** low in challenge
- **d** low in confidence

9 Concentration is most associated with which aspect of mental toughness?
- **a** challenge
- **b** confidence
- **c** commitment
- **d** control

10 People who see opportunities and challenges rather than threats are typically...?
- **a** optimistic
- **b** pessimistic
- **c** stressed
- **d** deluded

4

Confidence

In this chapter you will learn:

▶ *that confidence has many layers*
▶ *the importance of self-esteem*
▶ *what self-efficacy is*
▶ *how confidence affects performance*
▶ *how to build confidence*
▶ *that sport confidence can be robust*
▶ *the effects of overconfidence*

Self-belief

'Confidence' is a term used by sports performers, coaches, commentators, pundits, journalists and spectators as much as any other. To hear people speaking of confidence and the importance of it, you do not need to look much further than a post-match interview or a press conference regarding an upcoming event. Of all psychological terms that feature in this book, confidence is perhaps the most commonly used in all manner of contexts. We all have an idea about what it is and we all know that it is incredibly important. Ultimately, confidence is self-belief. It is the extent to which we believe that we will be successful in achieving whatever it is we want to achieve. It is the belief that we can successfully perform a desired behaviour.

Confidence is, of course, beneficial for performance. Collecting the experiences of sport performers, Jones & Hardy (1990) reported that athletes identify confidence as an important determinant of success. When we are more confident, we are more motivated to put in effort and continue to try our best (Bandura & Locke, 2003).

Confidence is often studied in combination with anxiety, as it is largely the opposite of it. If anxiety (particularly cognitive anxiety) is doubt about success, then confidence is directly opposed to it. To determine the relative effects of these two concepts, Woodman & Hardy (2003) conducted a meta-analysis. This means pooling together the results of many previous studies. First, they noted that 89 per cent of studies reported that confidence had a positive effect on performance. They found that the positive effects of confidence were more than twice as strong as the negative effects of anxiety. And that is before considering the knock-on effect of confidence leading to a better performance and further reduced anxiety next time. One thing is clear: that confidence is an excellent predictor of performance. So if we can understand it better, we can build confidence and therefore improve performance.

'You have to expect things of yourself before you can do them.'
Michael Jordan, US basketball legend

Layers of confidence

Would you describe yourself as a confident person? What about a confident golfer? What about confidence in putting? What about the last time you faced a difficult ten-foot putt, did you believe you were going to be successful in that instance? These questions are all related to confidence but are very different. This is because confidence has layers. At its most broad, confidence is a trait, something akin to what we refer to as self-esteem. At its most narrow, confidence is situation-specific and is about being able to successfully perform a certain action in a certain moment. Below, I discuss these layers working from broad to narrow.

SELF-ESTEEM

Self-esteem is how we see ourselves and whether we judge ourselves in a positive or negative way (Smith & Mackie, 2007). In effect, it is self-worth. It is the broadest confidence-based component in that it is an overall view of personal value. It is not specific to sport, a type of sport or a situation. It is a significant area of psychology, as it has been shown to predict so many things. For example, Herbert Marsh (1990) explored self-esteem/concept in high school students. He found that self-esteem was a clear predictor of grades in year 11 and year 12. Interestingly, grades themselves did not really change pupil self-esteem. More recently, Orth & Robins (2014) found that self-esteem was predictive of relationships, work and health.

Key idea: Layers of confidence

Confidence can be considered to have several layers from broad self-esteem to more situation-specific self-efficacy.

This sounds great. If we boost self-esteem we will see specific outcomes. Well, not quite. Baumeister, Campbell, Krueger & Vohs (2003) reviewed research in the area and suggested that although there is no doubt that self-esteem is a good thing – and we should encourage it – it is not quite as simple as raising self-esteem to guarantee some positive outcome. It varies greatly depending on the individual. Baumeister and his colleagues argued that people with high self-esteem tend to be likeable, and that this is lasting. They also found self-esteem to be positively related to talking in groups and to overall happiness. On the flipside, they found that there is no relationship between self-esteem and violence, children smoking, drinking, taking drugs, or engaging in early sex. If anything, they argue, high self-esteem encourages experimentation in children, which can be risky.

So how does this affect sport performance? Because of the broad nature of self-esteem, it is less researched in sport, as we are often more interested with very specific confidence beliefs. Clearly though, higher self-esteem is likely to be seen in mentally tough athletes and I would expect that they will demonstrate many of the benefits of a mentally strong performer.

Key idea: Self-esteem

The self-concept is what we think about the self; self-esteem is the positive or negative evaluations of the self, as in how we feel about it.

SELF-CONFIDENCE

Canadian sport psychologist Robin Vealey (1986, 2001) has written extensively on the layers of confidence specifically related to sport. She noticed that sports performers could appear very confident in some situations and unconfident in others. This was the conceptualization of sport confidence as multidimensional, since it was not just about confidence in executing physical skills. In addition to this, Vealey explained that confidence can be in someone's ability to use psychological skills, perceptual skills (like decision-making), physical fitness or ability to learn something new.

In 1986, Vealey first published the model of sport confidence and revised this in 2001 (Figure 4.1). The model begins with factors that influence sport confidence. Specifically, these are demographic and personality characteristics, and organizational culture. Demographic variables mean things like age, gender, background, type of sport participating in, level of participation, etc.

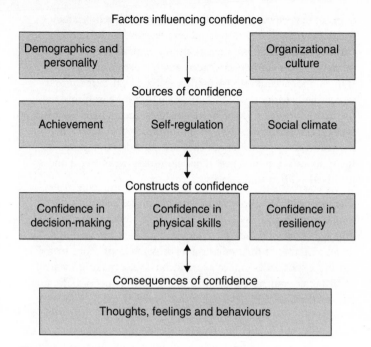

Factors influencing confidence

| Demographics and personality | | Organizational culture |

Sources of confidence

| Achievement | Self-regulation | Social climate |

Constructs of confidence

| Confidence in decision-making | Confidence in physical skills | Confidence in resiliency |

Consequences of confidence

| Thoughts, feelings and behaviours |

Figure 4.1 Robin Vealey's model of sport confidence

Personality characteristics as a factor acknowledges that everybody brings their own traits to sport confidence. For example, a naturally optimistic person is likely to judge situations more positively than a naturally pessimistic person. This means that they are more likely to believe that a successful outcome is probable and are therefore more confident. The organizational culture refers to the climate in which the performer operates. For example, some may be in a very intense environment, some very competitive, some relaxed, some where teamwork is emphasized more, some focused on personal development, etc. Combined, these factors influence sport confidence so they are important considerations for us when working with performers.

The next level of the model identifies sources of sport confidence. I will not discuss this here, as it is covered in more depth later in the chapter. Generally, though, we gain sport confidence from achievements (feel positive after success), self-regulation (managing emotional states and preparation) and social climate (the coach, support and the situation). Vealey's earlier (1986) model of sport confidence placed much more emphasis on state confidence and trait confidence. That is, the extent to which the broader types of confidence that remain stable are considered (trait), and the more situation-specific and changeable types are prominent (state). In the revised model shown here, the constructs of sport confidence are considered in terms of the individual's confidence in decision-making, physical and technical skills, and resiliency.

The key point to take from this model is that confidence is a much more complex concept than many first realize. It is affected by several factors, some of which are external and uncontrollable. It then relies on us drawing confidence from various experiences and interpretations, then making sense of this to make judgements on our likelihood of success. The final part of the model indicates that outcomes of sport confidence include the way we think (cognition), how we feel (affect) and, ultimately, our behaviour. This comprehensive model is a good starting point for understanding confidence in sport and informs much of the rest of this chapter.

SELF-EFFICACY

Self-efficacy is situation-specific self-confidence. It is the extent to which we believe we will be successful at executing a certain task at a certain point in time. The theory was developed by Albert Bandura in 1977 and refined in 1986. Bandura is famed for developing social learning theory (1963), which explains how children learn by copying the behaviours of adults. Most notably, Bandura, Ross & Ross (1961) found that children who observed adults attacking a bobo doll were more likely to copy this behaviour. In short, they claimed that children learn through observation and role models. He revised his self-efficacy theory slightly in 1997 to focus more on how it can explain people's ability to overcome challenges. At this time, Bandura referred to **self-regulatory efficacy**, since it acknowledged the importance of regulating emotions.

Key idea: Self-efficacy

Situation-specific confidence regarding the extent to which someone believes that they will successfully execute a particular performance.

Bandura also identified four key antecedents for self-efficacy. An antecedent is something that comes before a concept and is therefore causal, while a consequence occurs as a result of the concept. The four key antecedents identified by Bandura were:

▶ performance accomplishments

▶ vicarious experience

▶ verbal persuasion

▶ emotional arousal.

▶ Performance accomplishments

When you think about it, this one is quite obvious. If we have successfully executed a task previously, we believe that we are more likely to do so again. Conversely, if we have only ever failed at a task previously, we believe that we are less likely to succeed. Bandura stated that this is the most significant antecedent of self-efficacy.

Imagine that you are facing an opponent who you have played ten times and won all ten. Drawing on previous performance accomplishments, you would likely believe that your chances of success are very high. If you had won five of your ten meetings, you would be less sure, and if you had lost all ten, then it is likely that you would have very little self-efficacy.

In practice, most sport psychology consultants get performers to reflect on performance accomplishments. Often termed a **reflective interview**, asking a performer to describe previous good performances is a regular session. It is worth remembering that almost everything each one of us sets out to do, we do successfully. Think about your last performance in sport, at work or study. I bet that you did at least 95 per cent of things very well. The thing is, you probably expected to do those things well, so you tend to forget about them straight away and focus on the less good things. The purpose of a reflective interview is to do the opposite. By focusing on all of the good things, a client is able to recognize that they are very capable and should carry this thought forward next time.

▶ Vicarious experience

Now imagine that you are facing an opponent who you have never competed against before. How confident are you that you will be successful? This is, of course, a very difficult question because you do not have any information to base your response on. You may say that your self-efficacy is neutral at this point. Now what if you found out that this opponent recently lost to someone who you have regularly beaten in the past? Your self-efficacy would now likely be enhanced because you have gained experience of your opponent through others – vicariously.

To encourage vicarious experience, modelling is often used. This could be through video or watching the performance of someone admired by the performer. This is especially effective when working with children, as they do not have the necessary reflective skills to identify previous positive experiences, but they are likely to admire role models.

Case study: Anything you can do...

While studying learned helplessness, Brown & Inouye (1978) sought to test whether someone's expectations of inevitable failure could be induced by vicarious experience. The researchers had four groups of participants watch as people (models) performed an anagram task, repeatedly failing and showing frustration. One of the groups was told that they were of similar competency to the model group. A second group was told that they were of superior competency to the group they were observing, the third group did not receive any feedback about their competency, and the fourth group was the control group; they did not watch the modelling or receive feedback.

After the observation period, all participants took part in three anagram tests. The results showed that the group who believed they were of similar competency to the models they had witnessed repeatedly fail, put in less effort and persisted the least of all groups. Conversely, the group who had been told they were of superior ability demonstrated the greatest effort and persisted more than all of the other groups.

The influence of vicarious experience changed an individual's self-efficacy to the extent that it directly affected the effort and persistence exhibited. In sport, this is crucial in peak performance. Therefore, we know that if we can present positive vicarious experiences to an athlete, their efficacy expectations are likely to grow, increasing the chances of peak performance.

▶ **Verbal persuasion**

Remember that confidence is a subjective belief, not an objective truth. Therefore, we can be persuaded that we are more or less likely to be successful. Verbal persuasion can be a useful tool for building self-efficacy. Persuaders can be a coach, a parent, a teammate, a spectator, a teacher or even the athlete themselves.

The effectiveness of verbal persuasion relies on several factors. Most importantly, it depends who the persuaders are and how credible the performer perceives them to be. For example, if they respect their coach, they are more likely to take confidence from them offering support. It also depends how regularly and easily the coach offers the support. For *X Factor* viewers, it would be like getting up on stage and singing in front of the judges. Louis Walsh might say that he likes it, but he says that about everyone, even Jedward! Although the positive feedback will elicit positive feelings, leading to a potential increase in self-efficacy, it will be limited. Simon Cowell, of course, plays the almost pantomime-style bad guy and is much less forthcoming with praise. To receive this will likely have a greater effect on a performer's confidence than from a much more easily obtainable source.

The proximity of verbal persuasion is also a consideration. It is only a matter of time before our rational or irrational thought systems override the effects of the persuasion. As such, the closer to the event that it happens, the more of an emotional effect it can have. In effect, this is the quick pep talk before a performance to remind someone that they can do it.

One of the most effective verbal persuaders is often the performer themselves. This makes sense, really, since who better to impact on our belief in the probability of success than ourselves? Positive self-talk is covered in more depth later in this book so I will spend longer on it there but positive statements bring about a growth in efficacy expectations. Statements such as 'dominate the opponent', 'I can enjoy this' or 'I'm going to smash this' are very effective in making us feel confident. It triggers hormonal responses, which leads us on to the final antecedent of self-efficacy.

▶ Emotional arousal

Regulating emotional arousal helps a performer to stay focused on their task and implement various psychological strategies. Depending on the requirements for both the individual and the sport, the extent the performer needs to be aroused to perform at their optimum level can impact on self-efficacy. If the individual feels that they are over- or under-aroused, they are likely to perceive this as a negative, thereby lessening their efficacy expectation. By regulating arousal to be in the individualized zone of optimal functioning, we can present the performer with more positive emotions and appraisals, which in turn can increase self-efficacy.

Bandura noted that the impact of these four antecedents on efficacy expectations diminishes in the order of performance accomplishments > vicarious experience > verbal persuasion > emotional arousal. That is, that performance accomplishments as a factor has the greatest effect on predicting self-efficacy. Vicarious experience has the second most significant effect, then verbal persuasion and, finally, emotional arousal has the smallest notable effect.

Now you are aware of this, think about how things might be in a dressing room before a big game with the coach delivering a team talk. If you have watched *Any Given Sunday* with Al Pacino, or any other dramatization, you might think that it is always a stirring, passionate and emotion-filled speech to rally the team. I have sat in a few dressing rooms and in my experience it is not. For good reason, too. Emotional arousal is the least effective of the self-efficacy antecedents. For some performers, a logical identification of why they are likely to succeed if they do things right is better. That is not to say a passionate speech doesn't help, but it wears off. Imagine an international match. You could deliver the speech of your life, get the players riled up and then they go out and there is that small dead period while the TV adverts are on and the coin is tossed, then there's the national anthems, then shaking hands, then getting into position... and then the game begins, and any emotional response to your talk is superseded by an emotional response to events that occur in the game.

▶ Self-fulfilling prophecy

I often ask my students if confidence is a good thing. The straightforward response is always 'yes'. Then I ask why. This is actually a more difficult question than it first appears. While further examining self-efficacy, Bandura (1997) attempted to explain just why more efficacious performers were more successful. To do so, he described **self-fulfilling prophecy**.

Self-fulfilling prophecy is originally credited to sociologist Robert Merton (1948), who explained it like this:

'The self-fulfilling prophecy is, in the beginning, a false definition of the situation evoking a new behavior which makes the original false conception come true. This specious validity of the self-fulfilling prophecy perpetuates a reign of error. For the prophet will cite the actual course of events as proof that he (sic) was right from the very beginning.'

In other words, if you believe that you are going to be successful, you have made a prediction on a future event and will impart as much effort and persistence as it required to make this prediction come true. Equally, if your prediction is that you will fail, you begin to look for evidence of this in a bid to prove your prediction.

A prophecy is a prediction. Bandura's assertion was that because we are in control of our outcomes to a greater or lesser extent, if we make a prediction on the future, we are then able to shape it to meet with our original prediction.

As an example, imagine that you are about to walk along a tightrope. Before you begin, you tell yourself that you are going to fall off (don't worry, you can have a safety net). You have made a future prediction now – a prophecy. As you walk along the tightrope you experience imbalance. Because you have predicted failure, each lean, each tightening of the leg muscles serves as evidence to prove your prediction correct. As you wobble, you interpret this as failure and give up... then you fall. Had you made a positive prediction at the outset, you would have reacted to each lean and wobble purely with the focus being on staying up. Your attention, effort and persistence would have been better and, therefore, you would have stood a much greater chance of making it to the end.

Key idea: Self-fulfilling prophecy

Shaping outcomes via effort and persistence to meet a previous prediction of success or failure.

So self-fulfilling prophecy is a good way of explaining the relationship between confidence and performance. When we believe that we are going to be successful, we don't give up until we are. When we believe failure is inevitable, we are much likely to give up or reduce our efforts sooner. This is evident so often when sports commentators talk about a performer's head dropping when they are losing.

To summarize self-efficacy, our expectations are determined by performance accomplishments, vicarious experience, verbal persuasion and emotional arousal. At this point, we make a prediction on the outcome of the event and consequently invest a relative amount of effort and persistence (or even choice to do the activity). The outcome is determined by these behaviours hence confident people keep going and that is why they succeed more.

> 'Confidence is contagious... but so is a lack of confidence.'
> Vince Lombardi, American football coach

When we consider that previous performances are the key determinant on self-efficacy, and that self-efficacy leads to better performance, it is easy to see how confidence can spiral. This is great if you're winning but a bad performance could predict lower self-efficacy and therefore further poor performances. This is why performers and teams have form – good spells and bad spells. On any weekend you could pick out a sport and hear commentators talk about form, a particular run, or momentum.

Momentum

Momentum is a very interesting topic. There is little conceptual understanding of momentum. That is, there are no clear theories as to what it is, what causes it and how to change it. Although this topic receives little theoretical attention, perhaps because it is difficult to define and therefore test in research, there is some work in the area. I recommend *Momentum in Soccer* by Higham, Harwood & Cale (2005) for football fans. This considers the sway of momentum during a game.

In a discussion with the authors, we largely agreed that changes in momentum within a game are common but not necessarily brought about by things we might intentionally do. For example, in a football match, if one team were to miss a penalty, it might actually raise belief in the opposition and therefore swing the momentum in their favour. Perversely, if you could give away a penalty in a match knowing that it would be saved, you probably would. Your own team would feel like they have gotten away with something and receive a boost. It might sharpen their focus and resolve. The opposition might dwell on what might have been and feel like their big chance has gone.

On a streak

The history of sport is rich with famous winning and losing streaks. Some of the best winning runs include Nottingham Forest in 1978, who went unbeaten in all competitions for 40 matches. Arsenal managed 49 Premier League matches unbeaten in 2003-04. There are much longer runs though. In the 1970s, the UCLA Bruins men's basketball team won 88 matches in a row. These are small in comparison to the longest-ever recorded winning streak though, which is credited to Pakistani squash player, Jahangir Khan, who recorded a staggering 555 consecutive wins between 1981 and 1986.

Just as winning can become a habit though, losing can too. American football team Prairie View A&M Panthers lost 80 consecutive games between 1989 and 1998. The Schreiner Mountaineers women's basketball team have a record losing streak of 83. City College of New York men's lacrosse team managed a streak of 92. By far the longest recorded losing streak though is the Caltech Beavers men's basketball team who between 1996 and 2007 lost a staggering 207 games in a row.

It is difficult to say exactly what creates and destroys momentum, but it is certainly linked to a sway in confidence. I am a huge fan of Test match cricket. I love that it lasts for five days and I love that players take lunch and tea breaks. Most of all though, I love watching the changes in momentum, as a game can go for a day and a half with little change and then a bowler takes two wickets in consecutive balls and all of a sudden it looks like a different match altogether. Watching a fast bowler in a good spell is fantastic. When they take a wicket, watch out for the next ball, since I can almost guarantee it will be a few mph quicker. Why? Probably because of the self-efficacy gained from the previous ball and the fact that the new batter is not settled and is therefore more vulnerable. The bowler's belief that they are going to be successful with the next delivery soars, and the effort that goes into it does also.

Momentum doesn't just happen within a game though. The effect of momentum between games is a source of debate between commentators on sport even though it is not something really reviewed by academics. To see examples of this, simply tune in to interviews and press conferences between performances. Some talk of being confident going into a tournament because they have momentum, while others say that they do not consider this, as it does not really carry over. Typically, of course, this is selective since winning teams tend to believe that momentum flows to future performances, even if they are weeks apart, and teams on a bad run of form claim that it doesn't.

Sources of confidence

What makes you confident? Considering the sources of self-efficacy, it seems appropriate that some of those play a big part, especially performance accomplishments. Thinking about confidence in sport though, many researchers have sought to find out from athletes what makes them feel confident. Vealey & Chase (2008) reviewed the work of Bandura (1997) on self-efficacy and other researchers who had explored confidence. They focused on the social, cultural, demographic and organizational factors that are present within a sport setting. Bandura had not specifically considered sport when developing self-efficacy theory. Vealey & Chase recognized that athletes depend on a broader variety of sources of confidence than self-efficacy theory suggests.

The most substantial undertaking of establishing these further sources of confidence was by Vealey, Hayashi, Garner-Holman & Giacobbi (1998). They reviewed existing literature and came up with nine sources of sport confidence that they verified with athletes. The nine sources along with a brief description are presented in the table below.

This comprehensive consideration of sources of sport confidence appears to be fairly thorough. Newer research, however, has noted even more sources.

Table 4.1 Sources of sport confidence outlined by Vealey et al (1998)

	Source of sport confidence	Description
Achievement	Mastery	Performing well, improving, achieving personal goals
	Demonstration of ability	Gaining favourable social comparison by beating others
Self-regulation	Physical/mental preparation	Giving maximum physical effort and staying focused on goals
	Physical self-presentation	Perceived body presentation
Social climate	Social support	Getting positive feedback and encouragement from coaches, teammates and/or friends
	Coaches' leadership	Believing in the coach's skills in decision-making and leadership
	Vicarious experience	Seeing someone else perform successfully
	Environmental comfort	Feeling comfortable with the competitive environment
	Situational favourableness	Situations where athletes feel the breaks are going their way, like getting lucky

Specifically, Hays, Maynard, Thomas & Bawden (2007) interviewed 14 world-class athletes and identified 9 sources of confidence:

▶ preparation

▶ performance accomplishments

▶ coaching

▶ innate factors

▶ social support

▶ experience

▶ competitive advantage

▶ self-awareness

▶ trust.

While there is some overlap with previously identified sources, there are some novel ones also. In particular, innate factors were identified. This means that some believed that they were born with an innate ability such as being analytical, naturally confident, competitive, or naturally quick or agile. It is easy to see how confidence based on these beliefs is fairly unwavering. In addition to these sources, Hays et al identified six types of sport confidence:

- skill execution
- achievement
- physical factors
- psychological factors
- superiority to opposition
- tactical awareness.

As well as confidence having aspects that can be specific to sport, it also appears that each sport has different types of confidence. For example, the authors identified that physical factors and tactical awareness in their sources of sport confidence is dependent on the sport. You probably don't draw much confidence from physical factors if you are a darts player, but confidence is dependent upon physical factors if you are a marathon runner. Similarly, tactical awareness is much more important in some sports, particularly team sports. There is not much use for tactical awareness in long jump, as the performer will always adopt the tactic of jumping as far as they can!

In a final finding from their study, Hays et al (2007) found that there were some differences in how males and females derive confidence in sport. They found that females gained confidence from good personal performances, while male confidence was more determined by winning. In a follow-up study, Hays, Thomas, Maynard & Bawden (2009), again following interviews with 14 athletes, examined athlete perceptions on the effect of confidence on their performance. Generally, performers considered high sport confidence to be good for their performance because it has a positive effect on thoughts, feelings and behaviours. It was noted though that a lack of the things perceived to be a source of confidence was debilitating. This appears to be quite a common finding in studies examining sources of confidence. It is a fragile thing. As such, every source of confidence is also a source of a lack of confidence. For example, just as a good performance builds confidence, a bad performance reduces it. It is quite a plastic concept in this respect, in that it can change quickly.

Vealey & Chase (2008) built on Vealey's earlier work. One of the phrases they used was **robust sport confidence**. By this, they were referring to a resilient version of confidence that is enduring even in defeat. This was explored further by Thomas, Lane & Kingston (2011), who spoke with a group of four athletes and then held individual interviews with 16 elite individual sport performers. The researchers were interested in the idea of robust sport confidence and wanted to see what top performers believed this to represent. They ended up explaining it as a multidimensional set of enduring positive beliefs. It is multidimensional because it is made up of many facets. It is naturally positive but the enduring part comes from the strength of the beliefs. While state (i.e. situation dependent) sport confidence is great, it seems that it is fairly fragile and liable to change quickly. It can develop, protect or destroy momentum. Robust sport confidence, however, is what we should be aiming to develop in individuals. This is the sort of confidence that is most closely associated with mental toughness.

Attributions

Why is it always the referee's fault? How many times do we see the referee get the blame because 'if he'd given us a free kick on the halfway line then everything would have been so different and we wouldn't have gone on to lose 5-0'? It can't always be the referee's fault, at least sometimes it is that of the performer. Arsene Wenger is a great football manager and deserves enormous respect for his work, but some of his reasons provided in post-match interviews for his side's failures are very interesting. Like the time that the pitch at Wigan Athletic prevented his team from playing, or the bad start to the season caused by the new stadium, or disturbance due to the frequency of announcements made over the speaker system. While these seem like unlikely causes for failure, they all have something in common. Notably, they are not caused by his team and they are unlikely to happen in their next match.

Whenever something happens in an achievement context, which is normally success or failure, we search to attribute this to a reason. Often, these are sensible, logical reasons. Other times, people attribute the success of their team not to the meticulous tactical preparation, technical ability and hard work of the players, but because they wore their lucky pair of socks. Whatever the reason, and whether valid or not, we make these attributions all of the time.

Attribution theory was originally proposed by Fritz Heider in 1944 to make sense of how we determine the cause of a personal outcome. Weiner (1974) eventually produced a common 2 × 2 model of attributions that distinguished between the locus of causality and stability. Weiner (1979) then added a third dimension: controllability (Table 4.2).

Table 4.2 Weiner's (1979) model of attributions

| | Locus of causality | | | |
| | Internal | | External | |
	Stable	Unstable	Stable	Unstable
Controllable	Typical effort	Unusual effort	Typical help or hindrance by others	Unusual help or hindrance by others
Uncontrollable	Ability	Mood	Task difficulty	Luck

Locus of causality refers to whether we attribute the cause of something to internal or external factors. An internal attribution means that we believe that the outcome was caused by something we did. Conversely, an external attribution is down to factors that are not directly attributable to ourselves. Stability refers to how likely the cause is to remain in the future. A stable cause is likely to lead to a stable outcome. Therefore, if we believe that the cause of something is going to remain stable, we think that it will happen again next time. Controllability indicates the level of control that we have over the cause.

If an attribution is internal and stable, it is caused by yourself and likely to remain, especially if it is uncontrollable. Something like ability would be an internal, stable and uncontrollable attribution. So if a performer succeeds at something and they consider the cause of that success to be their ability, they feel that they produced the outcome and they will likely produce it again. This is a great attribution for success, but could be very damaging to confidence if failure is attributed to this. If the attribution is controllable, however, it could be something like effort. If a performer believes that they are responsible for a defeat, but they feel that it is because of something that can be changed, then there is no need to expect the outcome next time to be the same. Another example could be decision-making. Perhaps a poor decision was made but we have learned our lessons from this and next time we will be sure to make better decisions. So while it was caused internally, it is likely to change next time.

An unstable version of internal, controllable attributions are things that a performer can do but not consistently. This links with some of the things we will discuss about motivation in the next chapter. Sometimes, whether it is to prove a point or some other motive, we can find that something extra. That extra bit of desire that means we put in more effort than usual. This is less stable than typical effort though, since we don't produce this every time. More changeable than our effort, is mood. This is difficult to control, and in many ways it is regulated by parts of the endocrine system that we have very little control over. As such, our mood, while being internal, is an unstable and largely uncontrollable attribution.

Key idea: Attributions

The establishing of causes for personal outcomes that are experienced. This affects future predictions of success.

The difficulty of a task or the ability of an opponent are external, stable and uncontrollable attributions. These things are unlikely to change and we can't do much about that. For example, the outcome of a match against Serena Williams could be put down to her ability. She is very, very good at tennis. You don't generate that and it is unlikely to change any time soon. What we may be able to control is the help or hindrance we receive from other people. This is externally generated, because it requires others to provide the help and when it is typical help it is stable. By typical, I am thinking of the sort of help regularly provided by someone. As a result, it is expected. Unusual help is help requested in an atypical situation. For example, a person who gives you a lift to work in their car each morning is providing expected help. If you are stranded somewhere and ring to ask for a lift, it is specific to the situation, as they might be busy elsewhere. As such, it is unusual and therefore unstable. The attribution comes from your arrival at your destination on time. If you perceive that although it was helped by someone else, it was because you organized it that way and it was expected, it is a stable attribution. If you called that person without any prior notification, it worked out, but might not next time.

The final attribution is external, unstable and uncontrollable. This is where the individual rejects the internal cause and stability of the outcome. This is where we see Arsene Wenger place the blame for many results. Pitches, stadiums, referees, tannoy systems... all of these are external attributions. If the team loses, it is not because of what it did or didn't do. This protects the confidence of the individuals. I note here that this is simply based on public statements from Wenger. I have no idea if this changes when he is in the dressing room with no TV cameras or journalists.

Some of the attributions are external, unstable, and uncontrollable. The most common attribution of this kind is luck. Luck can be a lucky bounce of a ball, an opponent error or moment of brilliance, an officiating decision or sometimes a freak incident. I could enter a debate about luck and its existence versus simple probability based on the volume of people – but I won't. For what we are interested in, luck is an external, unstable attribution. It allows the attributor to dispense with responsibility for the event. They may even just want to forget about it and move on.

Shades of grey

During a Premier League match in 1996, Manchester United found themselves 3-nil down at Southampton at half time. Rather than attributing this to ability, effort or the skills of the opponents, they claimed that they could not see each other due to their new grey away shirts. They changed them at half-time and ended the match losing 3-1!

As stated briefly in the previous chapter, superstition is particularly interesting but largely under-researched. In terms of attributions, a superstition generally attributes the cause of an event to a completely external, unstable, uncontrollable and often irrelevant factor. Despite this, superstitions are incredibly common. Famous examples include Michael Jordan wearing university shorts under his uniform, Björn Borg growing a beard for Wimbledon, Paul Ince putting on his shirt after entering the pitch and Serena Williams bringing shower sandals on to court. There is no doubting that these athletes were all extremely successful and I am sure if they were asked, they don't really believe that success was down to these odd behaviours, but perhaps they just felt comfortable with them.

Typically then, advice offered is that success is attributed to internal factors, be they stable or unstable. This depends on whether we wish to congratulate someone on innate ability or their effort and decisions. Failure, however, is normally attributed to unstable factors. To forget about it and move on will be an external attribution. When appropriate, I like to see internal, controllable attributions for success and failure, even though it may be unstable. Because if it is external to ourselves, then why do we focus so much on trying to develop performance? We must take responsibility. Having tried and typically failed to predict the outcome of many sports by placing bets, I can assure you that a defining characteristic of sport is that it is unpredictable! That is why we love sporting events – because we can't be certain what the outcome will be. So by its very nature, sport is unstable and our attributions typically should be, especially in defeat. As the popular coach's saying goes: 'we've lost the match, let's not lose the lessons'.

As research in this area developed, Weiner (1985, 1992) began to focus more on the impact that attributions had on expectancies and the emotions they brought about. Referring to the expectancy principle, Weiner (1985) explained how the attributions of past events increased or decreased the amount of certainty with which we feel we can predict future events. Essentially, this refers to self-efficacy. In 1992 he focused more on the emotional impact of attributions. Specifically, he stated that when controllable, internal attributions led to pride in success and guilt in failure. Controllable external attributions, however, led to gratitude in success and anger in failure. We will address emotions more in Chapter 6.

Developing confidence

So, with a good idea of what confidence is, what causes it and what destroys it, we can now look at ways of building self-confidence. Retraining attributions is one way to do it. Reading the section above, it is clear to see how we can shape attributions to build confidence for future events. In practice, I find it useful for athletes to keep a reflective account of their performances. By noting down after each performance how they felt and what they believe were the reasons for what happened (positive and negative), we can gain an important insight into their attributions and consider the effect this has on their emotional response and future confidence.

My aim here is not to present an exhaustive list of things to do to build confidence. In truth, much of what makes people confident is a mixture of what is contained in all the chapters of this book. One thing that is clear from this chapter is that there is no single off-the-shelf way of building confidence. It seems that athletes have very different beliefs as to what makes them confident, so one size certainly does not fit all.

To review some of the strategies available, I refer to some recent research by Beaumont, Maynard & Butt (2015). Based on evidence from recent years and after interviewing ten practising sport psychology consultants, they presented ten strategies (*see* Table 4.3 *below*) for developing and maintaining robust sport confidence in athletes. The overriding message from their work was to build on athletes' strengths, increase pressure in training and identify a range of broad, stable sources of confidence for each performer.

Table 4.3 Strategies for building robust sport confidence from Beaumont et al (2015)

Building confidence	Developing understanding and awareness of confidence
	Logging evidence
	Manipulating the coaching environment
	Tailor for the individual
	Using psychological skills
	Developing an athlete's signature strengths
Maintaining confidence	A continuation of the development process
	Influence the athlete's environment
	Stable beliefs
	Reinforcing abilities

The results present some very sensible, commonsense and practical suggestions. The first thing acknowledged is the development of an understanding and awareness. Essentially, this means knowledge of what confidence is and understanding the theory. If you have stuck with this chapter throughout, hopefully you are well on the way with this now! Logging evidence refers to continuous reflection – the use of diaries and videos. This makes perfect sense, since we know that past experiences and their attributions create efficacy expectations for the future. Reflection enables performers to see the bigger picture, which includes identifying progress.

Reflection occurs after a performance or a series of performances and is very useful. Equally, training is a significant area for confidence development. Much sport psychology work occurs in training or after the event, which is perhaps a surprise to some. Manipulating the coaching environment refers to creating conditioned practice that re-creates some of the psychological aspects of performance and working closely with coaches. I have subtly referred to off-the-shelf psychological practices at times so far in this book (there will be more to come on this!). It is vital that all consultancy work is tailored to the individual. Ultimately, much of behaviour change is created by the relationship between practitioner and client. If interventions are not tailored for the individual, it is very unlikely to work. The use of psychological skills training is discussed in Chapter 11 and includes things like goal setting and imagery. Strengths-based approaches are discussed in Chapter 10.

So after this, we can help sport performers to become confident – great! But robust sport confidence is about maintaining confidence, even through more challenging circumstances. We want our performers to stay confident when times are difficult. It is easy to be confident when you are winning all of the time. The sport psychology consultants interviewed by Beaumont et al (2015) identified four strategies for maintaining robust sport confidence. The continuation of the development process reflects the ongoing nature of confidence. Building confidence is not a simple fix. No matter how robust it is, development should be constant. Let's draw an analogy to technical skills again. When Novak Djokovic became the world number one male tennis player and won multiple Grand Slam events, he didn't just decide he had now mastered tennis. He employed Boris Becker as his new coach in order to keep on developing to be the best he can be. It is important that we treat psychological skills with the same respect.

Key idea: Robust sport confidence

Resilient confidence that is enduring even through differing individual performance outcomes.

The athlete's environment again refers to time outside of competitive performance. Notably, training is key. Personally, I believe that to create a consistent and ongoing message, the work needs to come through others, such as the coaching and medical staff. Stable beliefs include attributions and reframing. This may include considering processes and not just outcomes, which are more changeable. Equally, by focusing on attributions, performers can increase the stability of their perceived cause and effect. Finally, Beaumont et al (2015) found that psychologists believe reinforcement to be one of the keys to maintaining robust confidence.

There are many ways to build confidence (and many ways to break it of course!). Here, I have focused on a very recent paper that identifies a host of ways, but there are others. Most sport psychology consultants love working with confidence because you can target it at so many levels. A quick approach is to look at self-efficacy, specific to a certain skill in a certain situation. With more time, perhaps more general, robust sport confidence can be targeted with an overall aim of raising self-esteem.

Overconfidence

Remember the meta-analysis study by Woodman & Hardy (2003) that said 89 per cent of studies report positive effects of confidence? So where does that leave us with the remaining 11 per cent? Are there occasions where confidence is a bad thing? The short answer is 'yes'. It is rare, but overconfidence can lead to complacency. Just as high levels of confidence are seen to predict effort, and therefore performance, *extremely* high levels of confidence may lead the performer to believe that they can win without trying.

Obviously confidence is not an exact predictor. There is no way that performers of a very small team can expect to overcome a huge team who might be existing champions. For every sporting upset, there is something to investigate. When a Premier League team loses to a League 2 team in the FA Cup, for example, surely the Premier League team must be more confident than the League 2 team? Perhaps the difference in levels of confidence is so extreme that the smaller team believes that it has to be at its very best to even stand a chance. The bigger team, on the other hand, is confident that it can win without maximum effort. The teams take to the pitch and the difference in effort creates an upset.

The belief that success can be obtained with reduced effort is a clear sign of complacency. Vancouver, Weinhardt &

Schmidt (2010) examined the effects of goal discrepancy on confidence; that is, the extent to which a performer believes that they are close to their goal. They suggested that when self-confidence is very high, the discrepancy between where the athlete considers themselves to be and where they want to be is reduced. This means that they can effectively 'let their foot off the gas', since they are near their target. This produces a negative effect of overconfidence.

Bandura & Locke (2003) argued that a little self-doubt could be a good thing in these cases. They suggested that doubt maintains an appropriate distance between the current and desired states. To link to goal setting: if you set a goal that you are fairly certain that you will obtain, there is little incentive to try really hard. By setting a challenging but realistic one though, the incentive is there. Bandura & Locke's argument is that without any self-doubt, the goal appears an easy one so the incentive to master it reduces and therefore we become complacent.

We can see an argument as to why overconfidence could be an issue in a physical game like football, but how does it affect smaller, more discrete skills? By discrete, I am referring to skills that have a distinct beginning and end, such as shooting, archery and a golf swing. Confidence in something like shooting is very important: if you were not confident, your action would become less smooth and you might start to second guess yourself.

The cost of complacency

At the 1983 Open Championship at Birkdale, golfer Hale Irwin approached his ball no more than two inches from the hole to knock it in. He never got into a proper position, since it was so simple, but proceeded to hit his putter into the ground. The putter bounced up and missed the ball completely. Irwin went on to lose by just one shot. Still, with every loss comes a lesson right? Not for Hale... he did it again at a different tournament 20 years later, though he managed to win on that occasion.

A further explanation for reduced performance as a result of overconfidence could be that confident people tend to take more risks. While this might be great and lead to them winning, it could also explain very bad performances. To explore this, Campbell, Goodie & Foster (2004) conducted three studies to identify the relationships between risk attitude, narcissism and confidence. In their first study, 104 students completed a general knowledge test, identifying their level of confidence for each question. They found that narcissism was a significant predictor of overconfidence. In the second study, they presented 97 of the participants with trivia questions, but this time they could choose to bet or not on them getting the next question correct. Again, confidence was measured and those who were confident but incorrect were classified as overconfident. As before, narcissists were more overconfident. They also took more risks with their betting. This led to more losses and, therefore, a worse performance on the task.

This shows us that overconfidence can become a problem because people back themselves to do better than they are likely to perform and take unnecessary risks. For example, when batting in cricket, it is important to know your capabilities on a pitch against a certain bowler. If you rate your ability too highly, you could choose to play overly risky shots and get out.

In the final study from Campbell et al, 607 participants conducted the same betting and trivia task as before but also stated how well they expected to do, how well they did and how well they expect to do in the future. These assessments took place before, during and after the task respectively. The results indicated that narcissists remained positive in their beliefs despite the results. Overall, the results of these studies indicated that a pre-occupation with oneself can result in an unwavering confidence about performance. So much so that the performer becomes blind to failure and is prepared to take uncalculated risks.

Key idea: Overconfidence

The mistaken belief that success is much more likely than it objectively is.

Woodman, Akehurst, Hardy & Beattie (2010) looked at self-doubt to see if it could have a beneficial effect on performance. To do so, they asked 28 experts in skipping to skip for one minute and counted the number of turns completed. For half of the group they then reduced self-confidence by making the task more difficult, such as changing the rope and the requirements. While the other half of the group carried on performing at the same rate, this half showed that, although their confidence had lowered, their performance actually increased. The researchers questioned whether the link between self-confidence and performance is quite as straightforward as we thought.

SUBJECTIVITY

Belief is subjective. This means that we can very strongly believe something but it does not make it objectively true. Much like the deluded, tone-death noise-pollutant who steps on to the *X-Factor* audition stage believing they are the world's next pop superstar, confidence can be misplaced. They are shocked to find that the judges do not share their view and proceed to tell the multimillionaire panel that they will be sorry that they turned this particular talent away.

By considering the negative impact of overconfidence, we are reminded that, while confidence positively predicts performance (i.e., it is generally better to be confident), this is not a perfect relationship. The confidence of the individual is simply their perception. Indeed, all that observe the individual will develop their own perception on the capabilities demonstrated. While some of these perceptions might be more credible than others, one of them is objectively true. So be warned, confidence comes with no guarantees. We might be confident, but that doesn't mean that we are right.

Dig deeper

Bandura, A. (1997), *Self-efficacy: The Exercise of Control*. New York: W H Freeman.

Harris, R. (2011), *The Confidence Gap; From Fear to Freedom*. London: Robinson.

Rotella, B. (2004), *Golf is a game of confidence.* New York: Pocket Books.

Vealey, R. S. (2005), *Coaching for the Inner Edge.* Morgantown, WV: Fitness Information Technology.

Vealey, R. S., Hayashi, S. W., Garner-Holman, M. & Giacobbi, P. (1998), 'Sources of sport-confidence: Conceptualization and instrument development', *Journal of Sport & Exercise Psychology*, Vol. 20 Issue 1 pp. 54–80.

Fact check

1 The broadest layer of confidence is...?
   a self-confidence
   b self-esteem
   c robust sport confidence
   d self-efficacy

2 The most common model of sport confidence was presented by which author?
   a Robin Vealey
   b Graham Jones
   c Albert Bandura
   d Andy Lane

3 What is self-efficacy?
   a global confidence
   b a sense of identity
   c situation-specific confidence
   d how we feel after winning

4 The most predictive antecedent of self-efficacy is...?
   a verbal persuasion
   b vicarious experience
   c performance accomplishments
   d emotional arousal

5 Why do confident people perform better?
   a they are luckier
   b because they play for better teams
   c they don't
   d self-fulfilling prophecy states that they will exert more effort and persistence

6 Which of the following are sources of sport confidence?
   a achievement
   b self-regulation
   c social climate
   d all of the above

7 An example of an internal, stable, uncontrollable attribution is...?

  a luck
  b ability
  c mood
  d task difficulty

8 An example of an internal, unstable, controllable attribution is...?

  a unusual effort
  b typical effort
  c unusual help or hindrance by others
  d mood

9 A resilient confidence is referred to as...?

  a tough confidence
  b robust sport confidence
  c bouncebackability
  d stable confidence

10 Overconfidence has been shown to have negative effects on performance because...?

  a people leave their teammates to do all the work
  b overly confident performers don't care
  c overly confident performers take too many risks
  d it hasn't

5

Motivation

In this chapter you will learn:

- ▶ *what motivates professional athletes*
- ▶ *how different people judge success*
- ▶ *what achievement goals are*
- ▶ *what different types of motivation exist*
- ▶ *what self-determination is*
- ▶ *how a coach can create a positive motivational climate*

Risk and a fear of failure

Motivation is one of the most studied areas in sport psychology. It is the thing that explains why people do what they do. Ultimately, everything we do has a reason, and therefore a motive behind it. So what motivates an Olympic athlete to get up at 5 a.m. to train? The possibility of becoming a legend? Potential financial gain through sponsorship? Enjoyment? There are many, many possible motives. As such, there exist more than 600 definitions of motivation in the psychology literature. For now, though, we will keep it simple and stick with 'why people do things'.

The key point about motivation is that we want people to reach their potential. To do so, it is necessary to take risks, to push them outside of their comfort zone, and to take on challenges where failure is a possibility. That is exactly what we mean by an **achievement context**. This is a situation where people may succeed or fail. As an example, imagine you are a footballer and an important match has gone to a penalty shoot-out. Do you volunteer to take a penalty? As a sport psychologist, we want people to be quick to raise their hand to take on this responsibility. This is an achievement situation where the individual may succeed, but they are also to take this knowing there is a risk of failure. The opposite is a fear of failure, where people avoid achievement situations.

Need achievement theory

Need achievement theory (McClelland, 1962) is an old but useful theory to help us to understand the processes people go through when deciding to adopt a certain behaviour. The theory includes personality, situation, resultant, emotional and behavioural factors (*see* Figure 5.1 *below*).

The personality factors identify that some people are naturally more likely to be geared towards a **need to approach achievement** (NACH) while others are more naturally predisposed to **need to avoid failure** (NAF). These personality factors interact with situation factors such as the probability

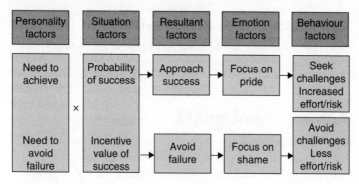

Figure 5.1 Illustration of McClelland's (1962) Need Achievement Theory

of success and the incentive value of success. Put differently, each individual will weigh up how likely they believe success to be (dependent on self-efficacy), and what they stand to gain from being successful. If we consider the rewards of success to be significant enough, the incentive is greater and we are more likely to approach success.

> 'You miss 100 per cent of the shots you don't take.'
> Wayne Gretzky, Canadian ice hockey legend

The resultant factors are to either approach success or avoid failure. If we approach success, we are focusing on positive emotions, such as pride or a sense of accomplishment should we be successful. Conversely, if we simply aim to avoid failure, we are focusing on negative emotions such as shame and fear. Ultimately, these factors lead to behaviour. When people have a failure avoidance approach, they are worried about making mistakes and will therefore choose safe options and are less likely to push themselves. The problem here is that our performers can only ever, at best, remain at the same level. What we want to see is performers prepared to take risks and push themselves, as this is what will lead to increased performance over time.

Key idea: Achievement motivation

The efforts of an athlete in achievement context where both success and failure are possible.

Achievement goals

How an individual judges success is an incredibly important factor in determining motivation. Do you judge success by beating your personal best or beating other people? Or both? Or neither? **Achievement goal theory** (Nicholls, 1984) attempts to explain people's approach towards achievement in terms of task and ego orientation. A task orientation explains how an individual is motivated towards mastery of skills and judges success from a self-referenced perspective. Ego goal orientation is when an individual is focused on social comparison and judges success from a norm-referenced perspective.

Key idea: Task orientation

A predisposition to judge success by self-referenced values.

To explain these concepts, imagine that you are a 100-metre sprinter who runs a personal best and finishes last. Have you been successful? From a task-oriented point of view, you have been very successful because you judge this by a self-referenced perspective. This means that you compare your performance to your past performances. Because you have run quicker than you have ever run before, you have demonstrated skill mastery and therefore you have been successful. From an ego-oriented point of view, you have been unsuccessful, because you judge success from a norm-referenced perspective. This means that you compare your performance to the performances of others. Since everybody else ran faster than you, you have been unsuccessful.

Key idea: Ego orientation

A pre-disposition to judge success by norm-referenced values.

People do not necessarily have a solely task orientation or a solely ego orientation, though. Rather, everybody has an element of both. It is possible to be high in task and ego orientation and it is possible to be low in both also. Being high in one concept does not mean that you are low in the other, as would be the case on a continuum (like introversion and extroversion). When the two concepts are unrelated to each other like this, they are known as **orthogonal**.

As well as considering goal orientation as task- and/or ego-oriented, more recent research also considers the extent to which individuals approach or avoid achievement contexts, which draws together aspects of need achievement theory and achievement goal theory. Elliot (1999) had noticed that there was a distinction in the way that task- and/or ego-oriented (which he refers to as 'mastery' and 'performance') people dealt with their goals. As such, he proposed that people can be mastery approach oriented, performance approach oriented or performance avoidance oriented. This is referred to as a 2 × 2 model by Conroy, Elliot & Hofer (2003). Elliot was unsure about mastery avoidance oriented. Mastery approach is about wanting to improve and setting out to do so. Performance approach is about wanting to beat others and setting out to do so. Performance avoidance is about focusing on not losing to others. There is a clear distinction between these last two, which sums up Elliot's main point completely. Although both are performance-related, in that they would be typical of an ego-oriented performer, the approach goal focuses on winning, while the avoidance goal focuses on losing. If the ego-oriented performer were less confident, they would likely phrase it as the avoidance target.

He who dares...

Golfer Doug Ford won the 1957 Masters at Augusta but not without a real dilemma on the par-5 15th hole on the final day. One ahead of Sam Snead at the time after a solid tee shot, Ford explained that his caddie was urging him to lay up with a 4-iron. Ford said that he wanted to go for it with the 3-wood. After a verbal exchange with his caddie, Ford explained:

Several researchers since Elliot (1999) have explored this idea and presented some support for mastery avoidance orientations. The reason why this is less clear is because if someone is task-oriented, they are concerned with self-improvement and it is unclear whether you can really strive to avoid this. Ciani & Sheldon (2010) stated that although these are rare, they exist as striving to avoid absolute incompetence – in effect, not wanting to feel that you have let yourself down by performing less well than you can.

Beware the ego?

It is very easy to form an opinion that an ego goal orientation is a bad thing. Research by Duda, Olson & Templin (1991) found that task orientation was positively associated with increased effort in training and lessened pre-competitive anxiety. This makes sense, since if a performer judges success from a mastery perspective, then the training ground can become the place where they strive to reach their goals. They know that practice and hard work will directly affect their likelihood of achieving their goal. The decreased pre-competitive anxiety also makes perfect sense. Imagine the 100-metre sprinter again. If they judge success purely from a task-orientation, they are not worried about the performance of others, as that is irrelevant. Instead, they are only focused on their own performance. This can reduce anxiety because one's own performance is controllable, while the performance of others is not.

In the same study by Duda et al (1991) ego orientation was positively associated with pre-competitive anxiety. There have also been reports of ego orientation leading to lower levels of sportspersonship (Dunn & Causgrove Dunn, 1999) and antisocial behaviour in sport (Sage & Kavussanu, 2007), which are discussed in Chapter 7 on character. It would be easy to think, therefore, that an ego orientation is something to be aware of. But isn't the goal of many sports to beat other people?

By its very nature, sport is designed to promote social comparison. Think about a podium at an Olympic Games where the person who finished first gets to stand higher and 'look down' on the person in second place. We then reward them with a more valuable metal and hoist the flag representing their nation – to the related national anthem – a little bit higher than the flags representing the nations of the people finishing in second and third place.

Many sports are professional and financial rewards through salaries, prize money and sponsorship are afforded to those who are comparatively more successful than others. So sport is egotistical by its very nature. With this in mind, I would never lambast a performer for demonstrating a high ego orientation. The important thing is that they also demonstrate a high task orientation.

'Some people say I have attitude – maybe I do... but I think you have to.'
Venus Williams, tennis player and winner of 22 Grand Slam titles

A performer who is low in task orientation, regardless of their ego orientation, is more likely to reduce their training levels. There is also a potential issue with perceived ability. If a performer is high in ego orientation but low in task, as long as they have high confidence in their abilities, they will likely try hard because they believe that they can be successful. However, if their perceived ability drops, then they are in a situation where they value success only comparatively to others, but don't believe they will be successful. In such circumstances it is common to see excuses, feigned injuries or withdrawal altogether. So in summary, an ego orientation is not necessarily a bad thing at all, as long as task orientation is high.

Self-determination

The essence of motivation is why people do things. Mainly, the reason why people do things is because they want to. You may be, have been, or will be a first-year degree student who has a 9 a.m. lecture to attend after a big night out. Some people will not even consider the possibility of not going and drag themselves into class. Others waver a little, while some just cannot get out of bed. But ask yourself, why are you in this situation? The likely answer is because you chose to be. You proactively decided to go to university, picked a course, applied and enrolled. Your behaviour is self-determined because you have made choices along the way.

Self-determination is key to explaining why people do things and therefore why some sport performers are better at getting up early to train, or able to make better decisions that affect the likelihood of them reaching their potential. Self-determination theory was devised and explained by Deci & Ryan (1985, 1991). The core element of this theory is that individuals strive to satisfy three basic needs: competence, autonomy and relatedness.

Key idea: Self-determination

To endorse one's actions at the highest level of reflection. Effectively, doing the things that you have chosen to and are happy to do.

We each have a need to demonstrate **competence** to improve our self-esteem and feelings of self-worth. The more we are able to feel competent, the more likely we are to feel that we are worth something. Demonstrations of competence can be to other people, such as teammates, coaches, spectators, teachers, parents, or to ourselves. The feeling of accomplishment is a very pleasant experience and one that all performers relish.

Autonomy refers to the amount of control you have in your life. If you have ever had a job with very little autonomy, you will know it. This means that you do not get to make any decisions over what you do. You must be somewhere at a certain time, perform a certain behaviour as instructed with no room to do it your own way. Conversely, some jobs have a great amount of autonomy where, as long as the target is met, you are free to do it however you wish. You may even have input on what your target is or what job you do. When we have a lot of autonomy, we get to choose what we do. Therefore, our behaviour is self-determined.

Relatedness refers to the extent to which we are happy and interact with our social world. In sport, this can be teammates, coaches, parents, agents, physiotherapists, sport scientists, etc. It is common that we seek to undertake behaviours that improve our relatedness.

'When self-determined, people experience a sense of freedom to do what is interesting, personally important, and vitalizing.'
Edward Deci and Richard Ryan, psychologists

INTRINSIC AND EXTRINSIC MOTIVATIONS

In terms of sport psychology, the most useful conceptualization from self-determination theory is the distinction between intrinsic and extrinsic motivations. Specifically, Deci & Ryan (1985, 1991) identified three types of intrinsic motivation, four regulations explaining decreasing self-determination that make up extrinsic motivation, and amotivation.

Intrinsic motivation describes motivation that is internally generated and is an end in itself. Examples provided by Deci & Ryan were intrinsic motivation towards knowledge, towards accomplishment, or towards experiencing stimulation. Intrinsic motivation is considered as the most self-determined type of motivation, as behaviours are chosen by the individual solely for engaging in them. Examples of this in everyday life are prominent. Since the invention of smartphones, I have noticed my intrinsic motivation towards knowledge can be quickly satisfied. Sometimes I might hear a song on the radio and wonder in what year it came out. My motivation here is purely an end in itself – it serves no purpose beyond satisfying my own need for this fairly insignificant knowledge. With the aid of a smartphone and a data signal, I can find the required information in just a few moments. In sport, a performer demonstrates intrinsic motivation towards knowledge by taking an interest in learning about their technique or tactical elements of the game.

Accomplishment is a key driver in understanding motivation. Achieving something is a good feeling and therefore we engage in activities for this as an end point. Often, the more effort expended on the path to accomplishment makes the feeling even greater. Imagine ascending a mountain and making it to the top. The reason for doing this is likely to be self-determined, in that it will have been a personal decision and it is likely to be largely undertaken for the feeling of accomplishment rather than any kind of external reward. The more challenging the mountain is, the greater the feeling of accomplishment that comes with making it to the top. In sport, we drive this desire for accomplishment by setting challenging goals for athletes to strive for.

The final example of intrinsic motivation is experiencing stimulation. This is simply the feeling the performer experiences during participation. This is the primary motivation behind many extreme sports. It is the buzz that you can experience just by taking part in something exhilarating. When people identify enjoyment as their reason for doing something, they are likely to mean experience stimulation.

So intrinsic motivation is the pinnacle of self-determination – when we strive to do things purely for their own sake. However, we regularly do things as a means to an end. I like my job, but if I wasn't going to be paid for it, I wouldn't do it. I would instead find a job that I would be paid for. Thus my motivation for work cannot be purely intrinsic, as my undertaking of tasks set out in my contract is contingent upon an external reward. Does an elite swimmer really enjoy getting up at 4 a.m. for training? They are motivated towards succeeding (accomplishing) in their sport, but it is a real stretch to believe that they would train so hard purely for intrinsic reasons. Extrinsic motivation is inevitable. It can though, be more or less self-determined.

The different forms of extrinsic motivation are known as **regulations**. Here, we will start with the least self-determined form, external regulation, and work towards more autonomous motivations.

Key idea: Extrinsic motivation

A drive to achieve something as a means to an alternative end.

External regulation is the least self-determined form of **extrinsic motivation**. A good way to think about this form is to consider a time when you have felt that you *must* do something. Technically, of course, this is not true: we don't have to do anything – everything is a choice to a greater or lesser extent. But despite this element of free will, the perception is that we must do something. Often, this type of motivation is governed by some sort of sanction if we do not. You do not have to turn up for that exam, but you will fail if you do not. Assuming that accepting the negative consequences of not doing something is not a realistic option, we perceive this controlling regulation that we must do it. When self-determination is very low, behaviour is largely governed by external forces. This is sometimes referred to as **controlled motivation**.

A slightly more self-determined regulation, but still very controlled, is **introjected regulation**. This is when we internalize the demand and perform a behaviour to appease potential feelings of guilt. This can be thought about in terms of 'I should'. Imagine here that you have just committed to your new year's resolution to get fit by joining the local gym and attending three times per week. Fast forward to about 7 January and you start to question whether you can be bothered to go to the gym. If you're anything like me, the answer is not 'it'll be great fun' or 'I can't wait to find out how I do today'. It'll more likely be: 'I've joined and I've said I'll go. I'm paying for my membership... I should go.' This is still lacking self-determination, as clearly the motivation here is not brought about by intrinsic reasons, but it has been internalized more than the 'I must' perspective of external regulation.

Identified regulation is perhaps the most common form of extrinsic motivation. This time, we want to do something, but it is contingent upon an external reward. It is a means to an end. Going to work to earn money is a good example, as is training hard in order to improve performance and reap the rewards. I sometimes ask my students if they go to the gym and of those that do, I ask why. The answers often range from 'to get fitter to play sport better', 'to improve my physique', 'to feel more confident', 'to recover from an injury' and 'to make new friends'. All of these have something in common; they are all identified regulations, as they are a means to an end. Should someone reply that they work out because they enjoy it, it is an end in itself and therefore an example of intrinsic motivation. This example brings about an important point that is often misunderstood when students of sport psychology discuss motivation. Extrinsic motivation is not necessarily externally generated. It is correct to say that intrinsic motivation comes from within, as it is always internally generated. But extrinsic motivation can either come from an outside influence (e.g. a coach, teacher, parent, teammate, etc.) or internally generated but cognitively processed as a means to an end.

The final extrinsic regulation is **integrated regulation**. This is somewhat of a grey area, as it is the most self-determined form of extrinsic motivation. In this form, behaviours are undertaken because the performer wants to do them and that motivation aligns with other goals, but there is still a requirement for an external influence. The best example of this, to continue the gym discussion, is the use of personal trainers. Although the performer has set goals and a genuine desire to achieve them for their own sake, they still believe that they require the influence and encouragement of another. Identified and integrated regulation can be considered more autonomous forms of motivation than external and introjected regulation because there is a wish on behalf of the individual to perform the behaviour.

Giving 110%

We've all heard people say that they are going to give 110% and we know it's not true. The problem arises when people assume that they can give 100% effort. In reality, you can only try to give 100%, that doesn't mean that you do. For an example, look at any performance where there is a rivalry based on historical matches or locality. Here, the team that aims to try its best every match finds that extra something, often supported by a crowd, and it enables them to achieve more. Another example can be seen in cricket, where a fast bowler bowling as fast as they can always seem to find an extra couple of mph after taking a wicket. People rarely try their hardest, they try to try their hardest and that is why when we do reach 100%, it feels like more.

There exists one final form of motivation: **amotivation**. In truth, this is not a form of motivation, as it represents an absence of motivation. A person with amotivation has no direction or desire to participate in a particular behaviour. This often happens when there exists no contingency between behaviour and outcome. Said differently, it is when you think that what you do makes no difference. Imagine that you are a substitute in your team and you want to make it into the starting line-up. You seek advice from the coach who tells you how to improve your game. You then work extremely hard on this and find yourself as substitute again. You continue to work hard and get compliments on your improvement but no matter how much you improve, you remain on the bench. At this point, it is very easy to begin to believe that no matter how hard you train, you'll get the same result. Consequently, if you believe that putting in a lot of effort or little effort yields the same result, your drive to train extra hard drops. This is an experience of amotivation.

Key idea: Amotivation

A complete absence of motivation, often when contingencies between effort and reward are no longer present

Cognitive evaluation theory

So what do you get if you add extrinsic motivation to intrinsic motivation? More motivation? No, not necessarily. By increasing extrinsic motivation, we can actually undermine intrinsic motivation. This is explained by **cognitive evaluation theory** (Deci & Ryan, 1985).

Cognitive evaluation theory is a sub-theory of self-determination theory. It was developed to explain the impact of external events on intrinsic motivation. The theory has three main propositions. The first is that events that impact positively on perceived competence will increase intrinsic motivation, while events that diminish perceived competence will reduce intrinsic motivation. The second proposition is that the locus of causality will affect intrinsic motivation. That is, if we believe that success was generated internally, our intrinsic motivation increases. If it was generated externally, our behaviour is controlled by other factors and intrinsic motivation is decreased. If we repeatedly fail at something, then we have heightened perceived incompetence, which increases amotivation and decreases intrinsic motivation. The final proposition is that informational rewards, such as constructive coaching, increase intrinsic motivation while controlling rewards, such as money, decrease intrinsic motivation.

Key idea: Cognitive evaluation

The process of changing intrinsic and extrinsic motivation based on external rewards.

The overwhelming impact of cognitive evaluation theory in sport is the awareness that many rewards that we offer actually serve to decrease intrinsic motivation, which is the type of motivation that we want to encourage. Consider a young golfer who loves playing golf. They go along to lessons and receive information rewards by means of increased technical knowledge. Their intrinsic motivation is very high. Now imagine that they begin to experience success on the amateur circuit and become professional. With it comes controlling rewards. Sponsorship money, prize money, fame... all of these undermine our golfer's intrinsic motivation as they become more driven towards achieving these. Now striving for self-improving by putting in extra training hours and listening to the coach is no longer the primary driver for playing. It is easy to see how performers can plateau, especially when they encounter extrinsic rewards at a young age. Rather than being the one taking ownership of their development by seeking informational rewards, our young golfer is now controlled by external rewards, like a dog being trained to roll over for a biscuit.

Case study: Play for fun, end up winning

To test achievement goal and self-determination theories in a physical sports setting, Spray, Wang, Biddle & Chatzisarantis (2006) manipulated PE sessions for 147 secondary schoolchildren. After measuring their goal orientations and perceived ability, the researchers randomly assigned the pupils to one of four conditions. They either received a task-involving induction, where they were told the purpose of the task was to master a skill, or an ego-involving induction, where they were told the purpose was to outperform the other pupils. In addition, half of each group received an autonomous communication style, whereby they were afforded choice and given a full rationale, while the other half were subjected to a controlling communication style, where there was no choice or rationale.

The physical task was to putt a golf ball into a hole on an artificial grass mat. Each participant was given ten practice trials and ten assessment trials two weeks after the inductions. Their results found that those who experienced an autonomous communication style reported greater enjoyment, persisted longer and performed better than those who experienced the controlling communication style. Further, those who were exposed to the task-involving condition significantly outperformed those exposed to the ego-involving condition. This study shows us that providing autonomy to support self-determination and promoting a task-involved climate will yield more enjoyment and better results.

Motivational climate

Throughout this book we take time to consider the extent to which we are predisposed to behave in a certain way compared to how we are shaped by our environment. Motivation is no different and there is certainly significant evidence to suggest that the extent to which we seek self-referenced mastery or norm-referenced comparative success is, at least in part, manipulated by our environment. This is known as **motivational climate**.

Ames & Archer (1988) and Ames (1992) originally made a distinction between two forms of motivational climate while studying student behaviour in classrooms. This distinction was between mastery and performance climates. Seifriz, Duda & Chi (1992) related this to a sport setting. Later, Newton, Duda & Yin (2000) elaborated on the original model, including two higher-level dimensions of task-involving mastery and ego-involving performance climates, which each contain three sub-dimensions. The task-involved dimensions are cooperative learning, effort/improvement and importance role, while the ego-involved dimensions are intra-team member rivalry, unequal recognition and punishment for mistakes. Typically, a task-involved climate will encourage performers to identify success by self-improvement. In contrast, an ego-involved climate uses social comparison as a measure of success.

Ruling by fear?

In footballer Theo Walcott's autobiography (which came out when he was 22!), he describes an occasion when the then England manager, Fabio Capello, led a training session before the 2010 World Cup for which Walcott was not selected. Walcott recalled:

'It was the second day, and I made a run inside from my position out wide on the right. Suddenly Mr Capello started screaming at me at the top of his voice. Training stopped and everyone stared at their feet and looked embarrassed. "Theo," he was yelling. "I will kill you if you come inside like that again." Despite Mr Capello's outburst, I never quite knew what was required of me. I was confused.'

The good thing about motivational climate is that it is something that can be taught to coaches and delivered in practice. Epstein (1988, 1989) promoted the use of the TARGET acronym as a practical way to develop a mastery climate. This identified six environmental characteristics:

▶ the nature of tasks

▶ locus of authority

▶ recognition

▶ grouping

▶ evaluation practices

▶ the use of time.

A representation of how these characteristics foster a motivational climate is detailed in Table 5.1 below. By following the guidelines in this table, coaches can develop a climate that encourages a more task/mastery goal orientation and intrinsic motivation among their performers.

Table 5.1 How to 'TARGET' a mastery climate

Mastery		Performance
Challenging and diverse	**T**asks	Absence of variety & challenge
Students given choices and leadership roles	**A**uthority	No participation by students in decision-making process
Private and based on individual progress	**R**ecognition	Public and based on social comparison
Cooperative learning and peer interaction promoted	**G**rouping	Groups formed on the basis of ability
Based on mastery of tasks and on individual improvement	**E**valuation	Based on winning or outperforming others
Time requirements adjusted to personal capabilities	**T**ime	Time allocated for learning uniform for all students

Dip deeper

Hagger, M. & Chatzisarantis, N. (2007), *Intrinsic motivation and self-determination in exercise and sport.* Leeds: Human Kinetics.

Hodge, K. (2005), *The complete guide to sport motivation.* London: A & C Black.

Ness, L. (2015), *The sports motivation master plan* (3rd ed.), Colorado Springs, CO: Create Space Independent Publishing Platform.

Roberts, G. & Treasure, D. (2012), *Advances in motivation in sport and exercise* (3rd ed.). Leeds: Human Kinetics.

Whyte, G. (2015), *Achieve the impossible.* Ealing: Bantam Press.

Fact check

1 The incentive value of success is which type of factor from need achievement theory?
- **a** personality factor
- **b** situation factor
- **c** resultant factor
- **d** emotion factor

2 Striving to achieve a personal best is an example of...?
- **a** a task orientation
- **b** an ego orientation
- **c** a need to avoid failure
- **d** an avoidance orientation

3 Judging success by social comparison describes...?
- **a** mastery approach
- **b** mastery avoidance
- **c** task goal orientation
- **d** ego goal orientation

4 Focusing on not wanting to lose to others is an example of...?
- **a** mastery approach orientation
- **b** mastery avoidance orientation
- **c** performance approach orientation
- **d** performance avoidance orientation

5 Doing something for a sense of accomplishment is an example of...?
- **a** external regulation
- **b** identified regulation
- **c** amotivation
- **d** intrinsic motivation

6 Introjected regulation refers to...?
- **a** feeling that there is no choice
- **b** participating in something to avoid feelings of guilt
- **c** wanting to do something as a means to an end
- **d** doing something for enjoyment

7 Which one of these refers to a lack of motivation?
   a amotivation
   b external regulation
   c extrinsic motivation
   d intrinsic motivation

8 How does using controlling rewards affect motivation?
   a They increase intrinsic motivation
   b They decrease intrinsic motivation
   c They decrease extrinsic motivation
   d They increase amotivation

9 A mastery-based climate encourages which type of goal orientation?
   a avoidance
   b approach
   c task
   d ego

10 Autonomous communication and choice are related to...?
   a task orientation and intrinsic motivation
   b task orientation and extrinsic motivation
   c ego orientation and intrinsic motivation
   d ego orientation and extrinsic motivation

6

Emotion in sport

In this chapter you will learn:

▶ *how emotion can affect sport*
▶ *what emotional intelligence is*
▶ *different approaches to understanding emotional intelligence*
▶ *how mood affects performance*
▶ *if music can impact training performance*
▶ *how to manage emotions*

Emotion

Emotions have many definitions but for the purposes of this chapter we will take emotion to mean how a person feels. We all experience a raft of cognitive and physiological changes concurrently and emotions are ways that we can make sense of them. We understand some emotions to be positive, such as excitement, joy and happiness. Other emotions are negative, such as fear, anger and sadness. The purpose of this chapter is to understand how these manifest themselves in sport and, importantly, how we can manage them.

Emotional intelligence

In 1983, Howard Gardner published the book *Frames of Mind: The Theory of Multiple Intelligences*. Here, Gardner proposed the idea of eight multiple intelligences from musical-rhythmic and harmonic, to logical-mathematical and bodily-kinaesthetic. There followed some debate regarding types of intelligence. One particular type of intelligence that gained notoriety and is now a very fashionable term is emotional intelligence. It is worth noting straightaway that some leading psychologists (e.g. Eysenck, 2000) argue that emotional intelligence is not a form of intelligence at all. That said, it has received much attention and, whether or not it is technically a form of intelligence, understanding and managing emotions is certainly of benefit to sport psychologists. In a seminal article, Salovey & Mayer (1990) defined emotional intelligence and in 2004 Salovey, Brackett & Mayer (p. 1961) revised the concept as:

'the subset of social intelligence that involves the ability to monitor one's own and others' feelings and emotions, to discriminate among them and to use this information to guide one's thinking and actions'.

Key idea: Multiple intelligences

Rather than seeing intelligence as a single general ability, it is comprised of several modalities.

We know that being able to recognize and control our emotions is important, but this definition goes beyond that. Salovey & Mayer (1990) suggested that emotional intelligence includes four branches:

- the perception of emotion
- the ability to use emotion to facilitate thought
- the ability to understand emotion, and
- the ability to manage emotions.

This view of emotional intelligence is seen as an **ability model**. In a sense, this approach views emotion as a rich source of information to help us to understand our social environment. Salovey & Mayer claim that these are abilities. The ramifications of this, of course, are that we can utilize them and further develop them. Here, I will look a little further at each branch.

'If your emotional abilities aren't in hand, if you don't have self-awareness, if you are not able to manage your distressing emotions, if you can't have empathy and have effective relationships, then no matter how smart you are, you are not going to get very far.'

Daniel Goleman, US author and psychologist

PERCEPTION

If we are to understand the emotional environment around us, it is vital to be able to perceive the emotions of others. Perception refers to nonverbal signals like body language and facial expressions. Assessment of this often occurs by looking at pictures, particularly of faces, and identifying the emotions being experienced by the person. This is a very useful skill for performers, coaches and support staff, including sport psychologists.

Imagine that you are coaching a team. If you have good abilities in perceiving emotion experienced by your players, you can tailor your words and actions to elicit the most positive response. Without this, you have a one-size-fits-all policy, which, unless you have a team of identical personalities, can only ever be effective for some of the team.

FACILITATION

Emotions drive and prioritize our thoughts. In most situations, we experience an emotion first, which could be positive or negative and that determines our subsequent thought processes. Facilitating thought as an ability refers to the extent to which we are able to use emotion to prioritize positive and helpful thoughts. This may also have an impact on creativity, which requires us to use a range of emotions positively. In sport, many times people refer to channelling an emotion or using previous negative emotions to spur on an upcoming performance. Such uses of emotion refer to the ability to use it in a facilitating way.

Perception and facilitation together make up what Salovey & Mayer (1990) call **experiential emotional intelligence**. This means the identification of emotion and productive use of it in thought. It is not just about recognizing the emotion, but using it productively. The branches of understanding and managing emotion are referred to as strategic emotional intelligence. This requires a higher-level conscious processing of emotions, as it is about planning and organizing emotions to chart a personal course for success.

UNDERSTANDING

As we become more attuned to recognizing emotions, we develop a kind of emotional literacy. Our vocabulary expands so that we are able to label a wider range of emotions and distinguish between them. This demonstrates the extent to which someone understands emotion. With this, we also understand more about what causes an emotion and acknowledge the wide range of possible or probably causes. For example, if a teammate were angry at you, it may be because of something you have done, or it may be the result of something completely external to you, such as frustration at their own performance or annoyance from perceived poor officiating. With greater understanding of emotion, you are able to better empathize with others to interpret where it may have come from. Similarly, you are able to understand how emotion changes with new information and circumstances.

The blends of emotion are a very important component of understanding emotion. Emotions can progress in terms of severity very subtly. For example, someone can feel irritated, but if this intensifies, it can progress to annoyance, then to anger, and eventually to rage. Each of these emotions elicits a different action. We do not respond as drastically to something that irritates us as we might do if it enrages us.

MANAGING

The idea of managing emotions is most closely linked to the emotional control that we discussed in Chapter 3 on mental toughness. As stated then, it is not about suppressing emotions, it is about the extent to which the display of emotions is voluntary. At a more strategic level, we can plan intended emotions by undertaking behaviours to stimulate them. For example, by listening to a certain type of music, a performer can trigger emotions that they believe will help them perform closer to their maximum. This is a strategic form of planning and managing emotion. We also use learned behaviours to regulate emotion. For example, if we feel fearful of something, we can use relaxation techniques to manage that emotion.

Managing one's own emotions is such a vital part of sport psychology. Whichever theoretical model of emotional intelligence you may prefer, there is no doubt that the regulation of emotion and being able to consciously plan emotions is of enormous benefit to a performer. As well as being able to manage our own emotions, being able to manage the emotions of others is also extremely valuable. Imagine a coach or team captain trying to reduce fear and create excitement in their performers. This works best if techniques have been considered beforehand. An official may want to reduce excitement in favour of relaxation. The competitive element of me also thinks about how we also try to manage the emotions of our opponents. Rafael Nadal often sprints from his chair after a change of ends during a long tennis match. This is to suggest he is full of energy but could also serve to manage the emotions of the opponent. Imagine having played for four hours, feeling drained, and seeing him sprint towards the baseline with a spring in his step – it would be easy to feel dejected.

Abilities *versus* trait models

This abilities-based model of emotional intelligence (described above) comes from the idea that we have multiple intelligences. It is rooted in the idea of emotional-related cognitive abilities; in a similar way to how an IQ test works, the abilities model of emotional intelligence examines maximum performance. An alternative approach is to consider emotional intelligence as an aspect of personality, which is how it is treated in the trait model. Here, it is measured via self-report responses to questionnaires, much like other personality measures. The trait model focuses more on people's perception of their emotional abilities. It is sometimes called **trait emotional self-efficacy**.

Key idea: Trait emotional self-efficacy

An alternative term for the trait emotional intelligence model

The abilities model is a practical method of understanding emotional intelligence because by viewing it as an ability the applied implication is that we can then work on that ability to improve. This is very popular with applied practitioners, because we like to feel as if we can help people to improve. However, critics of the approach, such as Petrides (2011), list several problems with the model.

First, Petrides claims that it is simply not a form of intelligence that can be measured in a test with correct and incorrect answers. He has a point, because in IQ tests we can determine that there was an error in someone's reasoning if the answer provided is objectively wrong. In emotional intelligence, though, our perception of emotion is subjective. What one person considers to be a strong emotion may differ from another. What one person considers joy could be a different level from another. How can we therefore grade such subjective, individualized feelings in an objective test?

I am not advocating one approach and condemning another. I think the abilities model has some excellent applied benefits but the trait model is a more scientifically rigorous and testable theory. We've covered the abilities model above, so now we will look a little more at the trait model.

Trait emotional intelligence

Trait emotional intelligence is a personality-like approach to understanding people's perceptions of their emotional ability. Petrides, Pita & Kokkinaki (2007) refer to a 'constellation of human perceptions'. This provides an image of the many facets that we try to understand about ourselves. Indeed, in our constellation of emotional intelligence, the trait model identifies 15 facets, which are listed in the table below.

Table 6.1   Facets of the trait emotional intelligence model

Facets	High scorers perceive themselves as...
Adaptability	...flexible and willing to adapt to new conditions.
Assertiveness	...forthright, frank and willing to stand up for their rights.
Emotion expression	...capable of communicating their feelings to others.
Emotion management (others)	...capable of influencing other people's feelings.
Emotion perception (self and others)	...clear about their own and other people's feelings.
Emotion regulation	...capable of controlling their emotions.
Impulsiveness (low)	...reflective and less likely to give in to their urges.
Relationships	...capable of having fulfilling personal relationships.
Self-esteem	...successful and self-confident.
Self-motivation	...driven and unlikely to give up in the face of adversity.
Social awareness	...accomplished networkers with excellent social skills.
Stress management	...capable of withstanding pressure and regulating stress.
Trait empathy	...capable of taking someone else's perspective.
Trait happiness	...cheerful and satisfied with their lives.
Trait optimism	...confident and likely to 'look on the bright side' of life.

Having looked at the table, it makes sense why Petrides et al (2007) use the term **constellation**. The model suggests that we perceive an ability in each of these areas. For example, for adaptability, we each have a belief as to how well we can adapt to new conditions. To provide an example from sport, imagine that a new coach is employed. Each performer who is to work under that coach will have a trait for how much they embrace new methods or feel fearful of them.

There is certainly significant overlap between trait emotional intelligence and the content of Chapters 2–5 of this book. There is reference to stress, confidence and motivation. Perhaps the largest overlap is with mental toughness. In Chapter 3 I explained the 4Cs model of mental toughness as well as some others. Largely, they cover similar ground. The 4Cs model identified challenges, which include adapting to new conditions, commitment, which is about not giving up, control, including emotional control, and confidence, referring to self-esteem and assertiveness.

> 'Learn to control your emotions or they will control you.'
> Edgar Martínez, US baseball player

Moving away slightly from talking about different models of emotional intelligence to consider it more broadly, there is a burgeoning area of research in the notion of **superior performance intelligence**. This was introduced by Jones (2012) and focuses on using emotional intelligence for performance, which is of interest to sport psychology consultants. After interviewing elite performers in sport, military, business and performing arts, Jones identified three common themes that make up superior performance intelligence: knowing how to maximize your potential, knowing how to work with your environment and knowing how to deliver high performance. Although there is a requirement for more conceptual understanding in this area through sustained research, there is the potential for some use of the practical implications for those working in sport psychology.

Key idea: Superior performance intelligence

Reaching superior performance through knowing how to maximize potential, work with the environment and deliver high quality.

Knowing how to maximize your potential refers to understanding yourself, who you are, what you are capable of, and being able to stretch yourself in the sustained effort of self-improvement. Knowing your environment is about an awareness of – but particularly importantly being able to shape – the environment and being attuned with it. High performance refers to planning, delivering and evaluating performance. This is achieved through a structured approach to maximizing the potential to perform well. Some writers on this subject are now beginning to introduce the term **intelligent emotions** as opposed to emotional intelligence, as it more about the holder of those emotions and how they can use them to shape the world around them.

Case study: Learning self-control

We seem to acknowledge that having high emotional intelligence is a good thing, so the next logical step is to address whether it can be taught and developed. The abilities model is very much based around the notion of skill and lends itself towards being developed, but what about trait emotional intelligence? Nelis, Quoidbach, Mikolajczak & Hansenne (2009) sought to test this by developing a four-week training course.

They tested the emotional intelligence of 37 participants before splitting them into an experimental group, who received four sessions of two and a half hours over four weeks, and a control group, who received no training. The sessions looked at understanding, identifying, expressing and managing emotions. When the researchers tested emotional intelligence at the end of the intervention, they found that the taught group significantly improved their trait emotional intelligence, emotion regulation, emotional management, openness to emotional experiences and emotional understanding. The control group showed no improvement. Overall, trait emotional intelligence only improved by around 5 per cent, but emotional regulation increased by almost 57 per cent. Considering this was achieved in just four sessions, it does support the idea that emotional intelligence can indeed be taught.

Measuring emotional intelligence

The measurement of emotional intelligence is another area of academic debate. It has been said before that if you put two academics in a room, you come out with three opinions! There are a few common ways of assessing emotional intelligence. Based on an abilities model, the most widely used is the Mayer-Salovey-Caruso Emotional Intelligence Test (MSCEIT). The main assessment using a trait model is the Trait Emotional Intelligence Questionnaire (TEIQue). I will briefly introduce these here but more information can be found on these by following the references.

The MSCEIT (Mayer, Salovey & Caruso; 2000, 2002) is the most widely used assessment of emotional intelligence, certainly by those adopting an abilities-based model. It measures four components of emotional intelligence, all of which were discussed earlier: perceiving emotions, facilitating thought, understanding emotions and managing emotions. The MSCEIT does this through 141 questions, styled like an intelligence test. The applications of this test are useful, though the conceptualization of the branches used to identify areas of emotional intelligence has been questioned (Palmer, Gignac, Manocha & Stough, 2005).

The TEIQue (Petrides, 2009) comes in the form of a personality-style questionnaire with 153 items that form the facets shown in Table 6.1. There is also a short version (Cooper & Petrides, 2010). The psychometric properties of the TEIQue are certainly more robust than the MSCEIT. That is, from a scientific validity point of view, it is stronger. Proponents of an abilities model claim that because it uses traits, it is less coachable. I would argue that as long as it is accurate, which it appears to be, this is not an issue.

Kids don't care

Obviously emotional intelligence develops over time. You only need to look at children to know this. They are completely egocentric and rarely demonstrate empathy towards others. If you don't believe me, ask a child if they had a good day – they seldom respond by saying 'yes thanks, how about you?'.

Mood

Being in a good mood can be incredibly advantageous in many ways. Things seem easier, people respond to you better, and you have a real 'can do' approach to things. Conversely, the opposite could be said for when you are in a bad mood. You just don't feel like doing anything and cannot be bothered with daily hassles and often, people. So mood is clearly linked to emotion, but how does it affect sport performers?

Much of the literature on mood is from a mental health perspective and is born out of the development of the Profile of Mood States (POMS; McNair, Lorr & Droppleman, 1971). The POMS contains 65 emotions that participants respond to by identifying their level of agreement. These emotions are then categorized into six profile scores: tension, depression, anger, vigour, fatigue and confusion. When studying these scores, Morgan (1979, 1980) noticed that mentally healthier people displayed what he called an 'iceberg profile'. By an iceberg profile, Morgan meant that healthy people would score lower than most on tension, depression, anger, fatigue and confusion, but higher than most on vigour. This is illustrated in Figure 6.1.

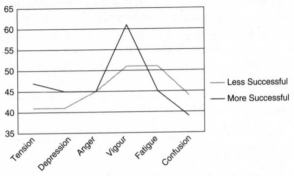

Figure 6.1 Example of iceberg profile in more successful performers

The key premise of Morgan's work was that positive mental health would predict successful sport performance, which can be seen in the iceberg profile figure above. However, there is not much evidence to support this. For example, Morgan (1979) used the POMS iceberg profile to predict the finalists of the 1974 US heavyweight rowing team. He got 10 of the 16 correct. This is just better than half, which is not exactly strong support for his theory. The idea that mood state could be used to predict athletic success was effectively quashed by Rowley, Landers, Kyllo & Etnier (1995), who conducted a meta-analysis of all previous studies on the subject and found that variation in mood accounted for less than 1 per cent of variation in performance.

Key idea: Iceberg profile

Preferred profile obtained from the Profile of Mood States (POMS) questionnaire, indicating low tension, depression, anger, fatigue and confusion, but high vigour.

If mood doesn't predict athletic performance, then why am I telling you all this? Well, it does tell us about mental health and it does tell us about the extent to which a performer is enjoying their time. Mental health is extremely important and very difficult to manage in elite level sport, and there is so much pressure and risk for everything to go wrong very quickly. We also know that performers who are happier will look forward to training, put in more effort and, ultimately, stand a better chance of reaching their goals in the long run.

The wrong side of the bed

You likely know the saying – getting out of the wrong side of the bed means being in a bad mood all day. There's no such thing as a bad day really though, they are just days. Bad things happen but it is only our interpretation that the day is bad. The day itself is just a day. This ties in closely with self-fulfilling prophecy, so if you catch yourself having a 'bad day', stop it from being a bad one and focus on it being a good, or even great one.

Runner's high?

The runner's high is a feeling of euphoria, which is a short-term neurobiological effect of exercise that makes an individual experience strong feelings of contentment, elation and wellbeing. In this state, people report feeling invincible or not experiencing pain. It is widely reported and many have pointed to endorphin-based explanations. There is no scientific reason to see how this could change our outlook though. Perhaps it is more a sense of achievement for having hit a challenging goal. I regularly come across people undertaking enormously difficult physical challenges like walking, running and cycling across countries and even continents. This is often for great charitable causes but the enjoyment must also come from the sense of achievement.

Key idea: Euphoria

Mental and emotional condition in which a person experiences intense feelings of wellbeing.

Music

Music is a very common way of maintaining enjoyment and/or motivation during exercise, but does it really make a difference? And if it does, is there a particular type of music that is more beneficial? The selection of music for such things is normally based on intuition and mood, but could there be a more scientific approach to improve training performance? If so, then we can regulate our emotions during training, which will ultimately have an impact on competitive performance.

In the past 20–30 years these questions have been of interest to many, but the findings have been very inconsistent. Terry & Karageorghis (2011) presented previous research that suggested, overall, there was a trend to suggest that selecting an appropriate form of music to exercise to has beneficial effects. Specifically, they identified how it diverts attentional focus, triggers and regulates certain emotions, changes mood, controls arousal, evokes memories and encourages rhythmic movements. It makes sense, then, that if we select the right music for the right occasion, we can improve training performance.

A host of research has found there to be nuances in preference, including males preferring greater bass frequencies than females (McCown, Keiser, Mulhearn & Williamson, 1997) and extroverts being more likely to favour lively music than introverts (Crust & Clough, 2006). Generally, performers report that this can have an effect on strength, endurance and speed. There is no one-size-fits-all type of music though. No rules to say 'if you listen to music with a certain amount of beats per minute, you will run for longer'. Just as emotions are very individual things, so are musical preferences and memories evoked by listening to music. That means that, 'yes', music can have a positive effect on training, but which type of music needs to be calibrated for each individual.

What's this chimp thing?

Many readers will have heard of Steve Peters in recent years. He gained acclaim working with the British cycling team as they became dominant in track cycling. He has also famously worked with Liverpool FC, snooker player Ronnie O'Sullivan, and travelled to Brazil and the 2014 World Cup with England. Peters is actually a psychiatrist though, not a psychologist. He is a very good one, who has become involved with sport almost by accident. His model, made famous in his 2012 book *The Chimp Paradox: The Mind Management Programme for Confidence, Success and Happiness*, introduces basic brain anatomy to explain why humans often underperform under pressure.

So if you come across people talking about controlling their chimp, they are referring to the work of Steve Peters. It is worth a read. I won't attempt to explain it fully here but the general idea is that if you look at the anatomy of the human brain, it contains eight main regions. At the very centre of the brain is the limbic system, which contains the amygdala. This region is fast-acting and is the emotional centre of the brain. When faced with a stressor, this system engages in the 'fight or flight' response. It is responsible for the feel and expression of core emotion. Peters refers to this as the inner chimp. Chimpanzees are very driven by their emotional responses and these are often irrational.

'Bottling emotions... is probably the worst thing that you can do because it will come back to attack you and others. It isn't clever, it is foolish. When you have got things off your chest it will ease the stress and you will start to unwind. Remind yourself of the first "Truth of life" and live by it – "Life is unfair". Don't just say it, live by it.'

Steve Peters, British psychiatrist

One of the major evolutionary changes between humans and the rest of the great apes has been the development of the frontal lobe. This is located at the front of the brain and the part of this known as the pre-frontal lobe is why humans have a more pronounced forehead than other apes. This area controls logical thought, reasoning and analysis. It is entirely logical and rational. Peters calls this section the human, as it is the key distinction between humans and chimpanzees.

The area towards the top of the brain in the centre is the parietal lobe. Here, most memory function takes place. For that reason, Peters calls this the computer. The idea of managing the chimp is that when we are placed in stressful situations, the chimp (amygdala) will try to take control of the computer (parietal lobe) and we will behave in a fearful, excitable or irrational way. This is not fundamentally a bad thing, it is an evolutionary advantage that enables us to act quickly. In some cases, this can save our lives. If, however, we stop and think logically, we train ourselves to use the frontal lobe more, which results in rational decisions. After years of trying to help first-year undergraduate students understand brain function, Peters has developed a useful way of describing why we sometimes do irrational or stupid things that is easy to understand. It is because of this simplicity that it has been so successful. The book and his talks include some more complex topics also – I have presented the most basic version for now.

Dig deeper

Goleman, D. (2004), *Emotional Intelligence and Working with Emotional Intelligence*. London: Bloomsbury.

Kerr, J. H. (1999), *Motivation and Emotion in Sport: Reversal Theory*. Abingdon: Psychology Press.

Peters, S. (2012), *The Chimp Paradox: The Mind Management Programme to Help you Achieve Confidence, Success and Happiness*, London: Vermilion.

Petrides, K. V. (2011), 'Ability and trait emotional intelligence'. In Chamorro-Premuzic, T., Furnham, A. & von Stumm, S. (Eds.), *The Blackwell-Wiley Handbook of Individual Differences*. New York: Wiley.

Thatcher, J., Jones, M. & Lavallee, D. (Eds.) (2011), *Coping and Emotion in Sport* (2nd ed.). London: Routledge.

Fact check

1 Who presented the four branches of emotional intelligence?
- **a** Goleman
- **b** Salovey & Mayer
- **c** Petrides
- **d** Peters

2 The four branches are perception, facilitation, understanding, and what?
- **a** promoting
- **b** evaluating
- **c** persuading
- **d** managing

3 Which of the following are trait emotional intelligence facets?
- **a** assertiveness
- **b** relationships
- **c** stress management
- **d** all of the above

4 '...capable of taking someone else's perspective' describes which facet?
- **a** social awareness
- **b** self-esteem
- **c** trait empathy
- **d** trait happiness

5 Using emotional intelligence for performance refers to...?
- **a** superior performance intelligence
- **b** superior intelligence quotient
- **c** performance intelligence
- **d** environmental intelligence

6 The MSCEIT measures emotional intelligence. Which model is it based on?
- **a** an abilities model
- **b** a trait model
- **c** both
- **d** neither

7 The iceberg mood profile has high...?

   a   tension

   b   anger

   c   confusion

   d   vigour

8 The feeling of euphoria experienced after exercise is known as...?

   a   jumper's knee

   b   runner's high

   c   cyclist's buzz

   d   swimmer's high

9 The best type of music to listen to when exercising is...?

   a   65–80 bpm

   b   > 80 bpm

   c   rock music

   d   all depends on personal preference

10 Steve Peters uses the chimp analogy for which part of the brain?

   a   frontal lobe

   b   parietal lobe

   c   amygdala

   d   occipital lobe

7

Character

In this chapter you will learn:

▶ *whether sport builds characters*
▶ *what we mean by character*
▶ *what are the types of moral behaviour*
▶ *why good people do bad things*
▶ *what it means to be a good sport*
▶ *how to develop character*

Sport: good for character?

Many make this claim: sport is good for character. And why not? It provides us with competition, encourages teamwork, leadership, and regularly places us in positions of success and failure. From such experiences, we have the chance to grow as individuals into better characters. This logic seems to make sense. So where is the evidence?

It seems that little evidence really exists to support our claim that sport is good for character. However, this does not mean that it is not – perhaps we have just not yet found the evidence. Maybe it is neutral. Perhaps sport is not necessarily good for character, but not bad either? Continued research will help us to find out more about this. But this is a book on sport psychology, so what we are really interested in is why people demonstrate positive or negative characteristics and behaviours.

Footballers dive, rugby players deliberately injure opponents, cyclists take performance-enhancing drugs, and cricketers disrespect umpires... instances like this are unfortunately common. While studying the frequency of good and poor sporting behaviours, Shields, Bredemeier, LaVoi & Power (2005) found 27 per cent of youth sports performers reported acting like 'bad sports' and 31 per cent indicated that they had argued with an official.

'Morality is not just any old topic in psychology but close to our conception of the meaning of life. Moral goodness is what gives each of us the sense that we are worthy human beings.'
Steven Pinker, psychologist

What is character?

Think about this question for a moment... difficult to answer isn't it? The truth is that very little research in sport psychology actually uses the term *character*. There must be an element of resolve, resilience and mental toughness. Characters are mentally strong and do not wilt under pressure. But more than that, character requires a significant morality component. Before we can really answer this question then, we need to think about morality.

Moral behaviour

Morality is a very complicated area. Moral theorists have for many years attempted to understand why people do good and bad things. In sport, this can range from a football player diving to win a penalty, to helping an opponent up off the pitch. It could be a golfer calling their own fouls or a sprinter taking performance-enhancing drugs. To understand more about behaviours, Bandura (1999) identified **inhibitive** and **proactive behaviours**.

Inhibitive behaviours refer to refraining from doing something bad. Conversely, proactive behaviours mean doing something good. For example, if a football player dives to win a penalty it is clearly against the rules and ethos of the sport. Such behaviour is widely condemned as cheating. By not diving, they are demonstrating inhibitive moral behaviour. Well done for not cheating! But now imagine that our footballer falls over in the penalty area and is incorrectly awarded a penalty by the referee. Would you say something? Would you say 'Hey ref, I just fell; that should not be a penalty'? To not do so is not necessarily an act of poor morality – it isn't an act at all. However, if you were to say this to the referee, that would be an act of proactive morality. You would be intentionally doing something positive.

Key idea: Dual nature of morality

Inhibitive morality is manifested in the power to refrain from behaving inhumanely whereas proactive morality is expressed in the power to behave humanely.

Bandura was not thinking specifically of sporting situations when he distinguished between inhibitive and proactive morality. Kavussanu & Boardley (2009) did however. They explained that behaviour in sport generally falls into one of four categories:

- prosocial teammate
- prosocial opponent
- antisocial teammate
- antisocial opponent.

Although this ignores behaviours towards officials, the vast majority of behaviours in sport can be explained this way. Behaviours can be positive for the situation (prosocial) or negative for the situation (antisocial). They can also be towards teammates and towards opponents. This is useful for categorizing behaviours, but it still doesn't explain why. For that, and to really establish what character is, we need to look at the reasons behind the behaviours.

Moral reasoning

Much of the literature on morality is indebted to US psychologist Lawrence Kohlberg. Kohlberg (1958) first proposed a set of moral dilemmas to investigate people's reasoning behind moral decisions. His most famous dilemma was that of Heinz:

'In Europe, a woman was near death from a special kind of cancer. There was one drug that the doctors thought might save her. It was a form of radium that a druggist in the same town had recently discovered. The drug was expensive to make, but the druggist was charging ten times what the drug cost him to make. He paid $400 for the radium and charged $4,000 for a small dose of the drug. The sick woman's husband, Heinz, went to everyone he knew to borrow the money and tried every legal means, but he could only get together about $2,000, which is half of what it cost. He told the druggist that his wife was dying, and asked him to sell it cheaper or let him pay later. But the druggist said, "No, I discovered the drug and I'm going to make money from it." So, having tried every legal means, Heinz gets desperate and considers breaking into the man's store to steal the drug for his wife.'

The participant is then asked 10 questions from 'Should Heinz steal the drug?' to 'Suppose it's a pet animal he loves. Should Heinz steal to save the pet animal?' and 'It is against the law for Heinz to steal. Does that make it morally wrong?'. At each question, the participant is asked to explain their reasoning. For example: 'Heinz should not steal the medicine because he will consequently be put in prison which will mean he is a bad person' is an example of very simplistic reasoning, as it demonstrates obedience as the primary method of moral reasoning. However, 'Heinz should steal the medicine because saving a human life is a more fundamental value than the property rights of another person' highlights an understanding of greater principle.

To differentiate between levels of moral reasoning, Kohlberg (1976) proposed a model of moralization (Table 7.1). This model contained three levels of morality: pre-conventional, conventional and post-conventional. Within each level, there were two stages. An important consideration here is that although there are stages, progression through these is not automatic. Indeed, Kohlberg noted that many never make it past stages four and five.

Table 7.1 Kohlberg's (1976) model of moralization

Level and stage	What is right	Reasons for doing right	Social perspective of stage
LEVEL I – PRE-CONVENTIONAL			
Stage 1 – Heteronomous morality	Avoid breaking rules backed by punishment	Avoidance of punishment	*Egocentric.* Doesn't consider the interests of others
Stage 2 – Individualism, instrumental purpose and exchange	Following rules only when it is in someone's immediate interest to do so	To serve one's own needs or interests	*Concrete individualistic.* Aware that everybody has their own interest to pursue and these conflict

(Continued)

Level and stage	What is right	Reasons for doing right	Social perspective of stage
LEVEL II – CONVENTIONAL			
Stage 3 – Mutual interpersonal expectations, relationships and interpersonal conformity	Living up to what is expected by people close to you	The need to be a good person in your own eyes and those of others	*Individual in relationships.* Aware of shared feelings, agreements and expectations
Stage 4 – Social system and conscience	Fulfilling the actual duties to which you have agreed	To keep the institution going as a whole	*Differentiates societal point of view.* System defines roles and rules
LEVEL III – POST-CONVENTIONAL or PRINCIPLED			
Stage 5 – Social contract or utility and individual rights	Being aware that people hold a variety of opinions, that most values and rules are relative to your group	A sense of obligation to law because of one's social contract	*Prior-to-society.* Aware of values and rights prior to social attachments and contracts
Stage 6 – Universal ethical principles	Following self-chosen ethical principles	The belief as a rational person in the validity of universal moral principles	*Moral point of view.* Recognize the nature of morality or the fact that persons are ends in themselves

Pre-conventional morality is all about following or breaking rules. As stage one identifies, rules are right and the reason for doing something considered right is simply to avoid punishment. This is common in young children, as they are unable to reason at a sophisticated level. That they do not consider others in their moral decision-making, meaning that they are at a very early level of moralization. In sport, a child knows it is right not to hit an opponent because it is a rule. The primary reason that they do not hit an opponent is because of the punishment that they would receive if they did.

As people develop their moral maturity they become more aware of relationships. The right thing now is not simply dictated by whether there is a rule or not, it is influenced by expectations. At the conventional level of morality, the individual wants to believe that they are a good person and wants other people to consider them a good person. This is a motivating factor behind why we observe many of the examples of good sporting behaviour. For example, shaking hands after a game is not part of any rules, but it is a social expectation. To not do so would be considered unsporting. To help an injured opponent is an act that promotes a positive society. If everybody does this, it is preferable to nobody or only some people doing it.

Post-conventional morality is beyond society and expectation. Here, the individual acknowledges that even if someone has a minority opinion, it is still worthy. This includes if others are of a different moral view. Someone at the post-conventional level of morality will follow their carefully selected ethical principles rather than go along with the crowd. During the 1990s and early 2000s, there were many instances of doping in the Tour de France. Some of the competitors who have since admitted to doping have blamed coercion. That is, because others were doing it and they would suffer if they did not, they took performance-enhancing drugs also. Someone at the post-conventional level would not do this, as they would have a more resilient approach to their ethical principles.

Key idea: Principled morality

The highest level of morality where individuals follow self-chosen ethical principles.

So moral reasoning is not about people being good or bad, or even whether it is right or wrong for Heinz to steal the drug. It is about why. How we reason that an action is right or wrong is a sign of our moral competence... regardless of whether people agree.

Why do good people do bad things?

Now we are getting to the really difficult questions! Have you ever told a lie? If you answered 'yes', then you have previously lied, if you answered 'no', then I would guess that you are lying now. We all do things below our normal moral standing. In sport, very few children dream of growing up and winning an Olympic gold medal by cheating. Imagine that conversation: 'When I grow up, I want to be a drugs cheat and win lots of medals!' No, the vast majority of those who enter sport and, indeed, even those who cheat, never intended to earlier in life.

So how does it happen? We all seem capable of doing things that we believe to be immoral. Bandura (1991, 1999) explains this through a process called **moral disengagement**. He suggested that undesirable social behaviours are committed due to an individual's disengagement with their own morals through a series of eight psychological manoeuvres. These range from changing the meaning of something, to passing the responsibility, to reducing the expected consequences. Related to changing the meaning, moral justification (cognitively restructuring harmful behaviours into honourable ones), euphemistic labelling (labelling culpable activities as less harmful) and advantageous comparison (comparing transgressive behaviours to more reprehensible ones) refer to harmful acts.

To make this clearer, consider some sport examples. Euphemistic labelling is very common in sport. Do you ever break the rules? That would be bad. How about bending the rules? That doesn't sound as bad does it? But what is the difference? In reality, I suspect that these two things are two and the same. If we want to break the rules, though, we don't want to feel guilty about it. One way of doing this is to change the language we use from 'break' to 'bend' and because it doesn't sound as bad we don't feel as guilty. We have disengaged with our morals through this psychological manoeuvre.

Key idea: Moral disengagement

A series of psychological manoeuvres a person goes through to convince themselves that normal ethical standards do not apply to a situation.

In terms of responsibility and accountability, we can use displacement of responsibility (viewing personal actions as a directive of others) and diffusion of responsibility (dividing responsibility for decisions among a group). So in sport, if your coach tells you to do something, you are simply carrying out orders. What is so wrong about that? Equally, if everyone is doing it, responsibility is diffused among many. To combine diffusion of responsibility and euphemistic labelling, many commentators refer to poor moral behaviour as 'part of the game'. That sounds ok. I do not feel guilty about taking part in a game that many others are. I might feel guilty if I were called a cheat.

Regarding consequences, distortion of consequences minimizes harmful consequences of detrimental actions and dehumanization (cognitively depriving the victim of human qualities) and attribution of blame (viewing oneself as the victim) moves the victim role to the perpetrator (Bandura, Barbaranelli, Caprara & Pastorelli; 1996). These manoeuvres often lead to physically aggressive behaviours. It is the sort of moral reality bending that the tabloid press thrives on, referring to opponents in non-human terms.

It's not all bad

Despite the widespread attention that bad sporting behaviour receives, there are many incidents of positive behaviour. Notable examples include Robbie Fowler playing for Liverpool against Arsenal in 1997, who tumbled over England teammate David Seaman and was awarded a penalty. Fowler got up and told the referee that the decision was wrong and that he simply fell. The referee still awarded the penalty though and, although Fowler's spot-kick was saved, his teammate, Jason McAteer followed up to score on the rebound.

A further example from football came when West Ham forward Paolo Di Canio elected to catch the ball and stop play at Everton in 2000 when the opposition's goalkeeper lay injured. Many would have attempted to score instead. In golf, Brian Davis, despite being close to a first-ever PGA tour win, called a foul on himself when he accidently moved a loose reed with his club. Equally as impressive was when Australian cricketer Adam Gilchrist was given not out against Sri Lanka in the semi-final of the 2003 World Cup. Gilchrist though 'walked', giving himself out.

There are many more great acts of sportspersonship, so even when there is controversy it is worth remembering that it is not all bad.

Recent literature in the sporting domain has provided reasonable support for the use of a slightly adapted understanding of moral disengagement. In particular, the work of Boardley & Kavussanu (2007, 2008, 2009, 2010, 2011) has effectively applied moral disengagement to sport. One particularly interesting study by Long, Pantaléon, Bruant & d'Arripe-Longueville (2006) sought to explain the moral reasoning of young (aged 15–18) male athletes when transgressing rules. Their results demonstrated frequent use of displacing responsibility, moral justification and diffusion of responsibility. Corrion, Long, Smith & d'Arripe-Longueville (2009) supported this when they found that sports performers often use displacement and diffusion of responsibility and minimization of transgressions and their consequences. Put differently, sports performers use reasoning pertaining to 'It's not my fault' and 'It's not serious'.

Case study: Winning at all costs

Sage & Kavussanu (2007) were interested in examining the effects of task and ego goal orientation on moral behaviour. To do so, they recruited 96 participants who each played two 10-minute games of table football that were secretly filmed. To explore goal orientation effects, three groups were created: a task-involved group, an ego-involved group and a control group.

The task-involved group was given a presentation stating that the purpose was to focus on skill improvement. The group was told that the purpose was to improve between the first and second game, was provided with some skill-based tips and told that skill improvement would be rewarded with a ticket into a raffle prize draw for £50. The ego-involved group was told that results would be presented on a website, was provided with tips for beating the opponent and told that for achieving a greater goal tally than the opponent they would get a ticket for a £50 prize draw. The control group was simply told about table football but offered no tips.

Instances of verbal and physical prosocial and antisocial behaviour were examined. The results revealed that the task-involved group demonstrated more prosocial behaviour than the other groups. The ego-involved group demonstrated significantly more antisocial behaviours than the other two groups. Indeed, the task-involved group presented more prosocial and antisocial behaviour, while the ego-involved group presented more antisocial than prosocial behaviour.

The implication of this study is that it not only confirms the relationship between goal orientation and moral behaviour, but demonstrates that this can be manipulated by encouraging a task-involved climate.

Bracketed morality

Do people who cheat in sport cheat in life and vice versa? Generally, psychological characteristics, such as personality, mental toughness and emotional intelligence, remain fairly stable in everyday life and in sport. Moral behaviour might be different though.

Bredemeier (1994, 1997) suggests that games and sport are conceptually and emotionally distinct from everyday life. Further,

Bredemeier & Shields (1984, 1985, 1986, p. 348) support the divergence between a sporting context and everyday life, referring to Huizinga's (1955) quote that 'sport is a world within a world in which the normal restraints of everyday life are temporarily set aside in favour of a conventionalized structure which allows typical moral norms to be transgressed'. Bredemeier & Shields (2001, p. 7) also claim that 'sport is a unique context' and emphasize that sport morality differs from morality in everyday life. This forms what Bredemeier & Shields (1986) describe as 'game reasoning' and 'bracketed morality'. Since sport may be seen as spatially and temporally separate from everyday life, this desire to win is also a more temporary state than one's drive to be successful in life.

Bredemeier & Shields (1984) presented moral dilemmas to high school and college basketball players, swimmers and non-athletes. Some of the dilemmas were related to sport while others were not. The results suggested that the moral reasoning used in sport was significantly less morally developed (mature) than outside of sport.

The notion of bracketed morality has recently been revisited by Kavussanu, Boardley, Sagar & Ring (2013). They examined reported moral behaviour in sport and while studying in university. In contrast to Bredemeier & Shields' contention, there were significant relationships evident, in that those who reported more (or less) prosocial behaviour in sport also reported more (or less) prosocial behaviour in university. However, there were significant differences between the sport and university contexts in both studies. Primarily, prosocial behaviour was lower in sport than in university, while antisocial behaviour was higher. The authors suggested that a high ego orientation may be the cause for lower moral behaviour in sport. The findings that people behave worse in sport than in education is interesting, given that sport is so commonly referred to as being good for character development.

 Key idea: Bracketed morality

The idea that games and sport are emotionally and morally distinct from everyday life, meaning that moral behaviour in everyday life cannot predict moral behaviour in sport.

Sportspersonship

You are forgiven if you had to read that twice; it is a rather awkward phrase but at least it does not hold the gender-specific assumptions of the more common 'sportsmanship'. In sport psychology research, 'sportspersonship' has become a standard term and is used in this book.

A discussion of sportspersonship may sound easier than it actually is though. We immediately think of examples of sportspersonship but would have difficulty defining it. 'It's when a football team kicks the ball out of play because someone is injured and the opponents throw it back to them upon the restart' comes up a lot, as does 'shaking hands with an opponent after a game'. While it is true that these are indeed examples of sportspersonship, they do not describe what it actually is.

The first noteworthy conceptualization of sportspersonship was presented by Crawford (1957), who classified 1,115 unethical incidents into nine categories, specifying the frequency of which they were reported. The nine categories were:

▶ officiating (463 incidents)

▶ opponent relationships (156)

▶ rules of the game (152)

▶ player relationships (121)

▶ professional relationships (69)

▶ recruiting (66)

▶ public relations (47)

▶ eligibility rules (31)

▶ scouting (10).

Crawford's incidents were obtained from surveying 300 colleges and universities. This included a range of athletic directors, officials, coaches and trainers. The makeup of this group explains the inclusion of some more organizational issues, such as recruiting and public relations.

Part of the game?

There are many examples of what would be classed as unethical incidents by Crawford (1957) being referred to instead as 'professional' or 'part of the game'. Indeed, in basketball players can commit a 'good foul'. The normalization of unethical behaviours makes it difficult to objectively identify incidents as right or wrong, as it is subjective. Take as an example the 2010 FIFA World Cup, when England played Germany in the second round.

Famously, Frank Lampard's long-range shot hit the crossbar and bounced over the line but the officials continued on rather than awarding a goal. Interesting, though, was Germany goalkeeper Manuel Neuer's later response:

'I tried not to react to the referee and just concentrate on what was happening. I realized it was over the line and I think the way I carried on so quickly fooled the referee into thinking it was not over.'

Essentially here, Neuer states that he cheated, and almost brags about it, yet this is seen as very normal. Imagine if he had alerted the officials to the truth. Would that make sport better?

The first useable definition of sportspersonship came from Vallerand, Deshaies, Cuerrier, Brière & Pelletier (1996). They suggested that sportspersonship has five components:

▶ one's full commitment towards participation

▶ respect for social conventions

▶ respect for rules and officials

▶ respect for the opponent

▶ the lack of a negative approach.

This was further supported with the development of a psychometric tool, published a year later (Vallerand, Brière, Blanchard & Provencher, 1997). This provided researchers with a sound basis of what sportspersonship was. Although most of the content was very good, McCutcheon (1999) was quick to point out that full commitment was not necessarily a sign of sportspersonship, as legendary tennis player and on-court angry man John McEnroe would be a great example of someone associated with full commitment, but certainly not with sportspersonship.

Earlier in this chapter I wrote about proactive moral behaviour and principled morals when discussing Heinz's dilemma. I was interested in introducing more of this positive approach to sportspersonship. I felt that existing understandings were all about obedience and not enough about principles. As such, I set about developing a new understanding of sportspersonship in my own research. Recently, Perry, Clough, Crust, Nabb & Nicholls (2015) presented a compliant and principled model of sportspersonship. This included some of the components from Vallerand et al's (1996) understanding. Specifically, we identified (a) compliance towards rules, (b) compliance towards officials, (c) legitimacy of injurious acts, (d) approach towards opponent, and (e) principled game perspective. The idea of perspective is unrelated to obedience. It is the extent to which the performer recognizes that the game that they are presently involved in is just that, a game. It might seem important, but it is only a game really. The more someone is able to maintain this perspective, the more likely they are to demonstrate good sportspersonship.

Play hard, play fair

For cricket fans, the 2005 Ashes was a standout series for quality and sportspersonship. After Australia thrashed England in the First Test, the two teams went to Edgbaston, Birmingham, for the Second Test. A fairly even game left Australia requiring 282 runs in the final innings to win. After being untroubled reaching 47 for 0, Andrew Flintoff came on to bowl for England and dismissed two Australian batsmen in his first over. By the end of the third day, England needed just two more wickets and Australia an unlikely 107 runs. However, they got incredibly close thanks to Brett Lee's dogged 43 not out. England finally won by just two runs before going on to win the series 2-1.

The game is best remembered for Flintoff's reaction upon England winning though, as he knelt to console Lee after his efforts. Ten years later when Lee retired, he recalled this moment as his favourite, saying:

'Even though we lost that series the spirit in which it was played, the sportsmanship, the toughness... I've never played in a series that tough where I've got Andrew Flintoff bowling 95mph trying to kill me... I'm in there trying to survive and then two minutes later after they finally win that game at Edgbaston we're in having a cold beer together, having a chat and a laugh... To me, that's what sport is about.'

Enhancing fair play

If we were to listen to every journalist, commentator or sports sceptic it would be easy to imagine that sport is this enormous stage of debauchery and greed with little hope. The reality is different though. For all of the significant incidents of unfair play that make the headlines, there are thousands of acts of sporting behaviour that do not – perhaps it just doesn't make as good a headline to say 'athletes train together in mutually beneficial way that helps everyone's performance level, thus resulting in a higher standard of entertainment for spectators'. But there is a lot of fair play in sport. It is also possible to enhance fair play through psychological approaches. With colleagues, I identified several ways that this could be done (Perry, Clough & Crust, 2013).

Psychological approaches to enhancing fair play can include developing a mastery climate, developing a moral community, role taking, reflection and power transfer. We came across **mastery climate** in Chapter 5. By fostering this, coaches can provide a climate more conducive to fair play and sportspersonship. A **moral community** is one that recognizes that each person's development and enjoyment is in some way contingent upon the acts of others. By including rewards for good teamwork, we encourage groups of performers to establish a mini society that benefits all. **Role taking** is designed to develop empathy for others. Here, performers undertake the roles of others to gain a greater understanding of what it is like. A particularly useful idea here is to include the roles of officials. If you have a greater understanding of what someone else's experience is like, you are likely to be more empathetic towards them. **Reflection** is something that all coaches and psychologists should be encouraging performers to do more of. By reflecting on your moral performance as well as your athletic one, you may be more driven towards improving both. Finally, **power transfer** requires greater responsibility to be passed to performers. We tend to stick to the rules we make more than the rules of others. As such, providing greater influence in not just rules, but the direction and running of the team heightens responsibility and accountability. This reduces the likelihood of moral disengagement.

> 'One man practicing sportsmanship is far better than 50 preaching it.'
> Knute Rockne, American football player

So can we develop characters? If we accept the moral obligations in doing so, we can improve the sportspersonship of individuals. If this is combined with the resilience or mental toughness we spoke about in Chapter 3, I believe that sport can be used to develop character, but this requires effort, it does not happen just by playing sport.

Key idea: Power transfer

Transferring greater responsibility to participants through enabling choice and influence to foster increases in accountability.

Character development

Although I have not quite defined what character is, it is clear that it is a broad term that encapsulates several smaller concepts. Shields & Bredemeier (1995) viewed it as an overarching term that integrates fair play, good sporting behaviour, compassion and integrity.

Compassion is closely related to empathy, as it refers to the ability of an individual to appreciate the feelings of others – in effect, putting yourself in their shoes. When we can do this, we are more likely to behave towards them in a way that is going to make them feel better. For example, having just beaten an opponent, we know that gloating would not elicit good emotional responses in them, because we can put ourselves in that position.

Integrity is about maintaining fairness while making sure that moral intentions are fulfilled. For example, a performer will have an idea of right and wrong. They will have beliefs about what is fair to do and what they would dislike in others. Integrity is similar to principled sportspersonship in that it requires the performers to know what is right, believe that they can do what is right and then to carry it out. This is in spite of all other temptations. This requires the mental toughness and/ or emotional intelligence to be able to regulate emotion to the point that we can be confident in our ability to behave with integrity.

Attempts have been made to introduce greater moral development into school sport. One of the few reported research studies in this area came from Gibbons, Ebbeck & Weiss (1995), who examined the impact of an educational activities programme called Fair Play for Kids. This included activities around problem-solving for moral conflicts, identifying how to solve fair play dilemmas and acting them out, and taking part in relay games to learn how to resolve team conflicts. In this study, 452 elementary school children were divided into three groups and monitored for seven months. The first group had Fair Play for Kids embedded in all parts of their curriculum. A second group had it embedded into its physical education sessions only, and a third was the control group, who did not take part in the programme but moral development was still measured. After the seven months, the two groups who took part in the programme both displayed significantly more moral development in terms of moral judgement, reason and intention. This shows us that, although it requires effort, character can be developed in young performers.

To enhance understanding of the processes that children go through in developing their moral identity in sport, Miller, Bredemeier & Shields (1997) considered an earlier moral reason and action framework proposed by James Rest (1984). This meant that a moral action is a consequence of: first, a perception, second, a decision on the best course of moral action, third, making a choice as to whether to choose to act in a certain way, and fourth, implementing the action (*see* Table *below*).

Table 7.2 Moral action processes, programme goals and interventions

	Stage 1	Stage 2	Stage 3	Stage 4
Moral action process	Perception and interpretation	Judgement and deciding	Choice	Implementation
Programme goal	Empathy	Moral reasoning	Task orientation	Self-responsibility
Intervention	Cooperative learning	Moral community	Mastery climate	Power transfer

These processes are fairly complex and best explained with an example. Imagine that Frankie is playing cricket for his school. While fielding, the ball loops up towards him and he dives forward to catch it. It bounces an inch before his hands but nobody has seen this and his teammates cheer while the batter walks off. Frankie must first interpret the situation, identify what options he has, make a choice and act on it. The programme goals are to get Frankie in this situation to first consider how others would feel. How would he feel if he were batting? This encourages empathy. He is then faced with three options: to claim the catch, to say that the ball bounced and that it is not out, or to say he is not sure, which would likely be given not out but weigh a little lighter on his conscience. His choice can be affected by promoting task goal orientation, as we know that this is positively related to sportspersonship

Dig deeper

Clifford, C. & Feezell, R. M. (2009), *Sport and Character: Reclaiming the Principles of Sportsmanship.* Champaign, IL: Human Kinetics.

McNamee, M. (2008), *Sports, Virtues and Vices: Morality Plays.* London: Routledge.

Perry, J. L., Clough, P. J. & Crust, L. (2013), 'Psychological Approaches to Enhancing Fair Play', *Athletic Insight*, Vol. 5 Issue 2.

Rest, J. R., Narvaez, D., Thoma, S. J. & Bebeau, M. J. (1999), *Postconventional Moral Thinking: A Neo-Kohlbergian Approach.* Abingdon: Psychology Press.

Shields, D. L. & Bredemeier, B. L. (2009), *True Competition: A Guide to Pursuing Excellence in Sport and Society.* Champaign, IL: Human Kinetics.

Fact check

1 According to research, does sport develop character?
   a yes
   b no
   c some sports do
   d we don't know

2 Refraining from antisocial behaviour is an example of...?
   a post-conventional morality
   b proactive morality
   c inhibitive morality
   d laziness

3 Doing the right thing to avoid punishment is an example of...?
   a conventional morality
   b pre-conventional morality
   c post-conventional morality
   d proactive morality

4 Doing something because it aligns with one's own principles is...?
   a conventional morality
   b pre-conventional morality
   c post-conventional morality
   d inhibitive morality

5 Labelling culpable activities as less harmful is...?
   a euphemistic labelling
   b moral justification
   c displacement of responsibility
   d diffusion of responsibility

6 Psychologically manoeuvring to avoid feelings of guilt is known as...?
   a sportspersonship
   b bracketed morality
   c power transfer
   d moral disengagement

7 Displaying different moral values in sport is known as...?
- **a** sportspersonship
- **b** power transfer
- **c** bracketed morality
- **d** moral disengagement

8 Sportspersonship includes...?
- **a** compliance towards rules
- **b** not legitimizing injurious acts
- **c** game perspective
- **d** all of the above

9 Power transfer is a way of...?
- **a** getting people to do what you want
- **b** promoting morality by increasing accountability
- **c** promoting morality by decreasing accountability
- **d** promoting a method of moral disengagement

10 Taking the blame as a large group is which form of moral disengagement?
- **a** diffusion of responsibility
- **b** advantageous comparison
- **c** moral justification
- **d** displacement of responsibility

8

Measurement

In this chapter you will learn:

▶ *about questionnaires*
▶ *how questionnaires are developed*
▶ *what questionnaires are commonly used in sport psychology*
▶ *what response scales are used*
▶ *about qualitative approaches to measurement*
▶ *about observational and biofeedback measurements*

In this book there are two very different chapters relating to the measurement of sport. We have this chapter, which forms an element of Part One on understanding psychology, and we have Chapter 10 on assessment, which is integral to Part Two on applying sport psychology. On the face of it, these two chapters may sound quite similar but actually, they are much less alike than most chapters in the book. Chapter 10 on assessment relates to practical assessments of mental skills performance, such as the type that a sport psychologist may undertake with their clients when trying to set or evaluate personal goals. Here, the focus is on the theoretical measurement of psychological constructs. In short, Chapter 10 is about practice, this chapter is about research.

'I have been struck again and again by how important measurement is to improving the human condition.'

Bill Gates, US businessman and philanthropist

Chances are that you have completed psychometric assessments in the past. Often, these are measured on scales from 1 *'Strongly disagree'* to 5 *'Strongly agree'* or something similar. You may have done this to a greater or lesser extent. This could range from taking part in a psychological study to simply filling out a test on Facebook entitled something like 'What kind of fruit is your personality?'. Obviously the latter normally has less credibility, but the general principle is the same; by responding to a set of probing questions, a measurement of a particular psychological construct takes place.

Key idea: Likert-type scales

A psychometric response scale anchored by numbered statements that can be summed to create a subscale score.

Questionnaires

Questionnaires are a staple diet of thousands of psychology research papers. Essentially, the aim is to develop an understanding of an underlying construct by identifying responses to questions that, when combined, reveal individual traits, tendencies, typical behaviours or orientations. But why do we need to do this? Well, because people are very complicated and, as such, theories become very complicated. Imagine a measure of neuroticism: this personality trait that refers to the extent to which we remain stable or are changeable is too broad and complex to simply ask someone to identify 'How neurotic are you?'. We could not rely on responses to this question. How would you know? If you were genuinely neurotic, you might respond in different ways depending on your mood anyway! To answer such a question would require the person filling out the questionnaire to have a good working knowledge of complex personality theory. Rather, it is the researcher who should have this. Therefore, we instead identify several questions that are easier to respond to and do not require a working understanding of personality theory. Items that require a level of agreement such as being anxious, easily upset, calm or emotionally stable are much easier to respond to because we can all identify with what these terms mean. By summing up the responses to these items or calculating mean responses, we can make a judgement on the individual's level of neuroticism.

Key idea: Reliability

The consistency of a measurement.

In psychology, we actually talk about things that do not exist. A theoretical construct, such as extroversion, is not a real, observable thing. It is unobserved. A response to questions about the extent to which an individual likes being in groups and being centre of attention, however, can be observable. They are likely to be represented by a circle around a number or a tick in a box to indicate a level of agreement with a preceding statement. In questionnaires, we use a collection of these observed variables (ticks in boxes) to make a judgement about the unobserved (theoretical) variable. That is why when you complete questionnaires, you might feel as if some questions are asking the same thing – they are – because having several questions all referring to the same unobserved variable means that the consistency of the response increases.

To illustrate, imagine that you have three questions about extroversion. You indicate a 3 on the first, a 3 on the second and a 1 on the third. The score of one is inconsistent with the first two scores of 3 but how do we know that it is not the scores of 3 that are wrong? Well, if we had five or six questions for the same unobserved variable, we would have a better chance of detecting consistency and error, which are sometimes called **outliers**.

Key idea: Outliers

An outlier is an unusual observation in collected data that can lend bias to statistical analysis.

Questionnaire development

You may be surprised to learn the extent of work required in developing the questionnaires that are regularly used in psychology research. Typically, researchers spend time gaining information on the subject matter by interviewing people, getting responses from focus groups and reviewing the work of other researchers. From here, an expert panel made up of psychologists and practitioners develops a host of potential questions for the scale. This will probably be very long at this point, based on all the information provided by the interviews. Then the questionnaire is drawn up and completed by several hundred people. Statistical analysis examines which questionnaires provoke similar responses and therefore can be grouped together and the questionnaire is refined. The refined questionnaire is then completed by a different sample of people (again, this will be several hundred) and more analysis is completed to see if the results confirm the earlier findings. If they do, the questionnaire can move onto the next phases of validation, which includes testing if it provides expected results compared to other questionnaires, whether it remains stable over a period of time and whether it can predict actual behaviour. And I haven't even included pilot studies or inevitable problems here. Most questionnaires, therefore, take between 2 and 5 years to develop... and even then they often get refined further.

Key idea: Validity

The extent that a measurement instrument actually assesses the unobserved variable it is intended to.

It is a lot of work, isn't it? Some questionnaires are very short (e.g., 8–10 questions), which makes the process a little less cumbersome, but some are very long. For example, the Trait Emotional Intelligence Questionnaire (TEIQue; Petrides et al, 2007) has 153 questions and the NEO Personality Inventory – Revised (Costa & McCrae, 1992) has 243 questions. It all depends on the complexity of the theory that is being measured.

'Science cannot progress without reliable and accurate measurement of what it is you are trying to study. The key is measurement, simple as that.'

Robert D. Hare, Canadian psychologist

Response scales

A key consideration when taking a measure is the scale on which it is collected. Simple 'yes/no' scales are very limited in terms of their use. All this enables us to do is to place people into one category or another. The preferred method is to collect measurements on an interval scale. This means that the intervals between each measurement point are equal. For example, if I were to measure height in metres, the difference between each centimetre is equal. The gap between 5cm and 6cm is the same as the gap between 93cm and 94cm. Twenty centimetres is double the measurement of 10cm. When we use Likert-type scales, be they on a 1–4, 1–5, 1–7, 1–10 scale or any other, we normally assume that these are intervals. There are some that prefer to treat these as ordinal scales, which suggests that the difference between each point is not the same, but there is no really strong evidence to support this claim.

Another common contention with little evidence to support it is the belief that when faced with a 1–5 scale, people gravitate towards the centre and, therefore, scales should not include a neutral value. Although some researchers have found small differences when examining results on 4-point, 5-point and 6-point scales, generally, there is found to be no substantive difference.

Example questionnaires in sport psychology

It is useful to be aware of common measures in sport psychology. Those considered in this chapter are all used for research purposes. Some of them are used in practice, also, but that is discussed in Chapter 10. This is not designed to be an exhaustive list of measures used, nor is it to make recommendation of any measures, but hopefully it is a useful guide should you wish to examine any of the concepts later.

ANXIETY

The most common assessment of anxiety in sport psychology research is the Competitive State Anxiety Inventory-2(CSAI-2; Martens, Vealey, & Burton, 1990). The CSAI-2 recognizes the multidimensionality of anxiety, as discussed in Chapter 2. It comprises 27 statements to which the respondent identifies the extent to which they feel each one on a scale from 1 = *Not at all* to 4 = *very much so*. Because it is a measure of state, it is intended to get a picture of the person's level of anxiety at the time of completing the inventory. It includes three subscales: cognitive anxiety, somatic anxiety and self-confidence, with nine questions in each of these. The CSAI-2 is sometimes referred to as the Illinois Competition Test and is freely available from many sources.

You will recall that in Chapter 2 we discussed the notions of facilitative and debilitative anxiety. To accommodate this, a modified version of the scale was developed by Swain & Jones (1993) that adds a second response section to each question. This second section means that after indicating how they feel, athletes then identify between −3 to +3 how it affects their performance. This is often a little confusing, as a third of the questionnaire measures self-confidence (and it is unlikely that people will identify that they feel confident) and that it will negatively affect their performance.

If you are interested in measuring trait anxiety, the most frequently used assessment is the Sport Competition Anxiety Test (SCAT; Martens, 1977). This is a fairly simple, unidimensional measure. This means that it only provides a score of overall anxiety, not subcomponents of cognitive and somatic anxiety. It contains only 15 questions and the respondent has three options for each: *rarely*, *sometimes* and *often*. Five of the questions are not scored, meaning that a score of 1–3 is obtained from each question, totalling somewhere between 10 and 30. Scores below 17 are considered as low anxiety, 17–24 is average, and scores greater than 24 present high levels of anxiety.

An alternative measure of anxiety in sport is the Sport Anxiety Scale (SAS; Smith, Smoll & Schutz, 1990). This is trait based, since it asks respondents to identify how they *usually* feel before or while competing in sports. After it was found that some of the questions were challenging for younger participants, Smith, Smoll, Cumming & Grossbard (2006) developed the SAS-2, which refined the content. The SAS-2 contains three subscales: somatic anxiety, worry and concentration disruption. Each subscale has five questions, which are rated from 1 = *not at all* to 4 = *very much*. It was validated on a range of participants, including 9- and 10-year-olds.

Men from Mars, women from Venus?

I am often asked about differences between large groups. This can be social, national, but most often they are gender-based. People are often surprised to learn that there is no difference between men and women in personality, mental toughness, concentration, etc. This is because the differences within the groups are larger than the differences between the groups.

For there to be a significant difference between men and women, the average man would have to be different to the average women. For this to be significant, this would likely have to be a greater difference than the highest or lowest scoring man and woman to the average man and women, which is almost never the case.

Think about it, who is more different – the average man compared to the average woman, or the average man compared to the freakish man?

CONFIDENCE

I have mentioned above that confidence is measured as part of the CSAI-2. It is also measured in some of the mental toughness assessments described below. Specific measures of sport confidence are largely on account of Robin Vealey, whose model of sport confidence was described in Chapter 4. Vealey (1986) developed the Trait Sport Confidence Inventory (TSCI) and the State Sport Confidence Inventory (SSCI). Both of these are simple unidimensional measures with 13 questions that identify how confident an athlete is generally (trait) and at that specific moment in time (state). Vealey is also behind the Sources of Sport Confidence Questionnaire (SSCQ) that was originally developed by Vealey, Hayashi, Garner-Holman & Giacobbi (1998). It has nine subscales, which are the nine sources of sport confidence explained in Chapter 4. These are measured using 43 questions led by the statement: 'I usually gain self-confidence in sport when I…' Responses are collected by identifying a score from 1 = *not at all important* to 7 = *of highest importance*.

The Sport Confidence Inventory (SCI; Vealey & Knight, 2002) is multidimensional, in that it has subscales for the athlete's confidence in physical skills and training, cognitive efficiency, and resilience. Considering this, the SCI is a very short measure, as it only contains 14 questions. Another short assessment of confidence is the Carolina Sport Confidence Inventory (CSCI; Manzo, Silva & Mink, 2001). This contains just 13 questions and includes three subscales: dispositional optimism, perceived competence and perceived control.

The final confidence-related measure I will mention is the Collective Efficacy Questionnaire for Sports (CEQS; Short, Sullivan & Feltz, 2005). This is different from many psychometric scales as it is used to determine group or team collective profiles. Specifically, each team member completes the 20-question scale, stating their confidence between 0 = *not at all* and 9 = *extremely confident* and scores are added to produce an overall team profile. This includes subscales for ability, effort, persistence, preparation and unity.

MENTAL TOUGHNESS

As identified in Chapter 3, the Mental Toughness Questionnaire-48 (MTQ48; Clough, Earle & Sewell, 2002) is the most widely used measure of mental toughness. This uses the 4Cs model of mental toughness previously described and provides feedback on each of the subscales. Mental toughness appears to be pretty robust across disciplines, so mentally tough individuals are normally mentally tough in several aspects of their life. There are, however, some sport-specific measures of mental toughness. Most common of these is the Sport Mental Toughness Questionnaire (SMTQ; Sheard, Golby & van Wersch, 2009). This is just 14 questions long and assesses confidence, constancy and control on three subscales. Largely, there is no enormous difference between these and the 4Cs model, since they correlate quite highly, but, as Crust and Swann (2011) found, there are some differences in the theoretical understanding.

Some researchers have developed even more specific versions of mental toughness measurements. Gucciardi, Gordon & Dimmock (2008) developed a mental toughness inventory for Australian rules football and in 2009(b), Gucciardi & Gordon did the same for cricket. Since this time, Gucciardi has recently developed a more general approach to mental toughness.

MOTIVATION

If I were to really discuss all of the psychometric assessments of motivation, even those specific to sport, this book would be twice as long. As such, I have just highlighted a couple of very common ones here.

The most common assessment of sport motivation is the Sport Motivation Scale (SMS; Pelletier, Fortier, Vallerand, Tuson, Brière & Blais, 1995). This is rooted in self-determination theory and therefore examines the extent to which individuals are intrinsically motivated, extrinsically motivated or amotivated. It contains 28 questions and seven subscales, as it distinguishes between three types of intrinsic motivation and three types of extrinsic motivation. However, since this time, Mallett, Kawabata, Newcombe, Otero-Forero & Jackson (2007) have developed a similar measure, grouping together the types of intrinsic motivation. This was presented as the SMS-6. Pelletier, Rocchi, Vallerand, Deci & Ryan (2013) revisited the original SMS and developed the SMS-II, which also had just one subscale for intrinsic motivation. This new questionnaire contains just 18 items and has started to be used in a lot of research.

'It is the mark of a truly intelligent person to be moved by statistics.'

George Bernard Shaw, Irish playwright

For those interested in investigating exercise motivation rather than sport, the Behavioural Regulation in Exercise Questionnaire (BREQ; Mullan, Markland & Ingledew, 1997) and its newer versions, the BREQ-2 (Markland & Tobin, 2004) and BREQ-3 (Wilson, Rodgers, Loitz & Scime, 2006) are useful. Like the SMS, these questionnaires are rooted in self-determination theory, examining intrinsic motivation, extrinsic motivation and amotivation.

Moving away from self-determination, the other most commonly assessed area of motivation is achievement goals. The Task and Ego Orientation in Sport Questionnaire (TEOSQ; Duda, 1989; Duda & Nicholls, 1992) is a short measure of task and ego goal orientation. It contains just 13 questions and requires participants to respond to the lead question: 'I feel most successful in sport and physical activity when…' This is followed by statements relating to task orientation, such as learning new skills, or ego orientation, such as being the best. It has been used in countless research papers and continues to be popular, since it provides a quick, reliable indication of an athlete's orientation. Very similar to the TEOSQ is the Perception of Success Questionnaire (POSQ; Roberts, Treasure & Balague, 1998), which also measures task and ego goal orientation but on 12 questions.

In Chapter 5, I explained that goal orientation is often now considered as a 2 × 2 model with mastery approach and avoidance and performance approach and avoidance. In line with this, Conroy et al (2003) developed a psychometric measure to test the theory. The Achievement Goals Questionnaire for Sport (AGQ-S) has demonstrated good validity and provided strong support for the 2 × 2 theory.

Motivational climate was a topic discussed in Chapter 5. Like all theories, a measurement was developed to be able to test this: the Perceived Motivational Climate in Sport Questionnaire-2 (PMCSQ-2; Newton, Duda & Yin, 2000). This questionnaire contains two overarching scales: task/mastery climate and ego/performance climate. Within each of these there are a further three subscales. In the task/mastery factor, the PMCSQ-2 provides a measurement of cooperative learning, importance role and reward for effort. The ego/performance factors contains subscales for punishment for mistakes, unequal recognition from the coach and intra-team rivalry. It is a very useful measure if you are interested in researching the effects of coach behaviour on athlete motivation.

MORALITY

Morality is particularly difficult to measure. My measure of sportspersonship is the Compliant and Principled Sportspersonship Scale (CAPSS, Perry et al, 2015). This contains 24 questions that participants respond to on a 1–4 scale to note their level of agreement with each statement. The CAPSS contains five subscales: respect for rules, respect for opponent, the legitimacy of injurious acts, respect for the opponent and game perspective. Sportspersonship in this context is a personal orientation.

A measure of moral behaviour is the Prosocial and Antisocial Behavior in Sport Scale (PABSS; Kavussanu & Boardley, 2009). This scale contains 20 questions and four subscales: prosocial behaviour towards teammates, antisocial behaviour towards teammates, prosocial behaviour towards opponents and antisocial behaviour towards opponents. On the PABSS, respondents identify how frequently they adopt the behaviours listed from 1 = *never* to 5 = *very often*.

If you are looking for a measure referring to moral reasoning in sport, the Moral Disengagement in Sport Scale (MDSS; Boardley & Kavussanu, 2007) has been used in research to show how it predicts moral behaviour. This is a measure of eight moral disengagement manoeuvres (e.g., moral justification, euphemistic labelling, etc.), and contains 32 questions. For researchers interested in measuring overall moral disengagement only, Boardley & Kavussanu (2008) developed a short version of the scale with only eight questions.

As discussed in Chapter 7, the climate and the role of the coach is important in shaping attitudes towards sportspersonship. To that end, Bolter and Weiss (2012, 2013) developed the Sportsmanship Coaching Behaviors Scale (SCBS). This contains 40 questions and measures the athletes' perception of their coach with regards to eight sportspersonship-related behaviours: (1) sets expectations for good sportsmanship, (2) reinforces good sportsmanship, (3) punishes poor sportsmanship, (4) discusses good sportsmanship, (5) teaches good sportsmanship, (6) models good sportsmanship, (7) models poor sportsmanship, and (8) prioritizes winning over good sportsmanship.

....

Many of these questionnaires are freely available either because they have been published, or if you contact the authors they are often happy to provide copies to people wishing to conduct research. Some of these, however, are copyrighted and a fee is payable if they are to be used. This is because they are used in an applied sense and people are licensed users who aid the development of characteristics as a form of consultancy.

Questionnaires are not only helpful instruments for gathering data to test theory, they can also be instrumental in developing theory. Most theories are developed with a bit of a mixture of a feeling and evidence. When the researcher has a hunch, a good way to gather evidence is to write questions that would measure something. At this stage, the researcher often doesn't really know *what that thing is*, but by conducting sophisticated statistical analyses on data collected we can start to see how responses to items can be grouped together. This is what forms the basis of a lot of theory. I have given a very simplified version of it here, but it gives an insight into the development and testing of psychological theory.

There are of course limitations to questionnaires, also. Most, though not all, of the questionnaires identified here are primarily for research purposes. That means that they are not intended to be used on just one person, as their reliability is obtained by being used on groups of people. We know that each questionnaire has error contained within it. That is why questionnaire-based research studies tend to use hundreds, or even thousands, of participants. Small errors can make a big difference in a handful of people, but in large groups those errors become negligible.

Informed opinions?

People's grasp of the world around them can be better informed with statistics. For example, in a 2013 survey from the Royal Statistical Society and King's College London, the following public misconceptions were found:

▶ The public thought that £24 out of every £100 of benefits is fraudulently claimed. The actual amount is 70p.
▶ The public thought that 31 per cent of the population were recent immigrants. The actual percentage is 13 per cent.

> ▶ More than half (58 per cent) of the public did not believe that crime was falling. Actually, it is less than half of what it was 20 years ago.
>
> Perhaps a society better informed by statistics would hold more reasonable views.

Qualitative methods

The questionnaires discussed are quantitative methods of measuring something. That is, they quantify what it is we are researching by putting a number on it. Qualitative methods are about the quality of information gained and do not try to quantify it. In the simplest terms they are about words (or pictures, observations, etc.), not numbers. Most commonly, this is achieved through interviewing.

Interviews are great for understanding an individual in much greater depth than responses to a questionnaire ever could. There is more about this in Chapter 10 on assessment in Part 2 of this book. Interviews can have a range of approaches, from being very structured in terms of questioning to assure parity across participants, or being unstructured so as to very much let the conversation flow to where the participant would like it to. Often, they are somewhere in between.

In developing theory, interviews are often used early on in the process. For example, even when researchers intend to develop a questionnaire, they will often first use interviews to gain an understanding of what it is like for performers or coaches, etc. This can inform the future questions to be asked. By allowing performers to explain their experiences freely, rather than asking them direct questions, we open ourselves up to areas that perhaps we had not even thought of before. We can also understand sport psychology more by interviewing sport psychology consultants about their experiences. This helps us to understand more about practice and how it can be improved. Sometimes, interviews are conducted in groups, which are known as **focus groups**. These can be effective in terms of efficiency and sometimes participants' thoughts trigger those for others and so more information can be achieved. It depends upon what the researcher is trying to find out as to which method is most appropriate.

Other measurements

Ultimately, it is the enactment of thoughts, beliefs and attitudes that has the greatest impact on a person. As such, studying behaviour is an enormous area of psychology. Some variables that we wish to measure are outcome related (i.e., they are the result of other things). Common psychology experiments include those things that cannot be observed, such as attitudes, personality, etc. and an observable outcome (i.e., a behaviour). For example, if I developed a hypothesis that extroverts dance more at weddings, I would first measure the unobservable quantity, which is extroversion, and then the observable, which in this example is time spent dancing at weddings. Extroversion would be measured through a questionnaire but I don't need to give someone a questionnaire to ask them how much they dance. I could do, but there are limitations with this. The most significant one is they could lie or, likely after a wedding, not remember! Instead, it is more accurate for me to go and observe them, timing them as they dance. I can then determine if my hypothesis was correct.

Other observations rather than just behaviour take place in studies though. For example, when we encounter stress, we produce increased amounts of cortisol. There is a period, which is normally around 20–30 minutes after waking in the morning, when we produce a peak cortisol level. This is known as the cortisol awakening response. It is affected by stress and studies have shown how stressful situations mean that the cortisol awakening response is greater. In terms of measurement, it can be taken by salivary analysis, taken from a simple mouth swab. This is an example of biofeedback, which is the process of gaining greater awareness of physiological responses. Other common measures of biofeedback include heart rate, blood pressure, brain activity, muscle activity, sweat response and various hormonal responses.

Case study: A recipe of measurements

Díaz, Bocanegra, Teixeira, Tavares, Soares & Espindola (2013) examined cortisol awakening response in a study that demonstrates varying types of measurement well. Using 11 athletes on two successive days of competition, the researchers tested cortisol levels via a saliva swab upon awakening 7 a.m. on each day, 30 and 60 minutes later, immediately before competition in the afternoon, and 5 minutes, 20 minutes and 40 minutes after competition. During these times, they also assessed mood using the Profile of Mood States (POMS), which is a psychometric measure discussed in Chapter 6. Finally, the researchers asked athletes to complete self-reports on their performance.

To test the stability of these responses, the authors then repeated this procedure two weeks later on the same athletes. Overall, the study found that higher levels of cortisol were noticeable before competition and that this was associated with feelings of tension, anxiety and hostility. The research team also noted that the effects were less in well-trained performers, probably due to more effective coping strategies. Although this is an interesting study in its own right, particularly useful for this chapter is the way in which the researchers recognized the value that different types of measurement had.

Dig deeper

Ekkekakis, P. (2013), *The Measurement of Affect, Mood, and Emotion: A Guide for Health-Behavioral Research.* Cambridge: Cambridge University Press.

Morrow, J. R., Jackson, A. W., Disch, J. G. & Mood, D. P. (2011), *Measurement and Evaluation in Human Performance* (4th ed.). Champaign, IL: Human Kinetics.

Tenenbaum, G., Eklund, R. & Kamata, A. (Eds.) (2012), *Measurement in Sport and Exercise Psychology.* Champaign, IL: Human Kinetics.

Thomas, J. R., Nelson, J. K. & Silverman, S. J. (2015), *Research Methods in Physical Activity* (7th ed.). Champaign, IL: Human Kinetics.

Vernon, P. E. (2015), *Personality Tests and Assessments.* London: Routledge.

Fact check

1 Circling a number to indicate a level of agreement is an example of...?
- **a** boredom
- **b** a Likert-type scale
- **c** a qualitative scale
- **d** a Lombart-type scale

2 An unusual observation, often the result of measurement error, is...?
- **a** an outlier
- **b** a hypothesis
- **c** a Likert scaling
- **d** a correlation

3 The CSAI-2 is a common measure of...?
- **a** motivation
- **b** work-related stress
- **c** multidimensional anxiety
- **d** unidimensional anxiety

4 The TEOSQ measures...?
- **a** intrinsic motivation
- **b** achievement goal orientation
- **c** extrinsic motivation
- **d** morality

5 SCAT measures...?
- **a** unidimensional trait anxiety
- **b** unidimensional state anxiety
- **c** multidimensional state anxiety
- **d** multidimensional trait anxiety

6 A scale whereby the difference between each measurement point is equal is known as...?
- **a** a categorical measurement
- **b** an interval scale
- **c** an ordinal scale
- **d** an equality scale

7 Improving awareness of physiological responses is known as...?
  a biofeedback
  b bodyfeedback
  c heart measurement
  d cardiology

8 Which of the following is *not* an example of biofeedback?
  a cortisol testing
  b observing behaviour
  c heart rate
  d muscle activity

9 The SCBS measures...?
  a moral disengagement
  b motivation
  c sportspersonship from coaches
  d confidence in athletes

10 Reliability is a measure of...?
  a validity
  b consistency
  c the extent to which something measures what is intended
  d the extent to which something measures several things

Part Two

Applying sport psychology

Hopefully you have found Part One interesting. There is so much knowledge accrued about sport psychology and an enormous amount of research taking place to further enhance this knowledge. But what good is knowledge if you can't do anything with it? So far, the focus of this book has been primarily on understanding sport psychology. This has included understanding what it is about, some of the key theories in the subject, and how research continues to help us in our understanding of the subject. For Part Two, though, I will turn to applying sport psychology.

The proceeding chapters discuss how to become a sport psychologist, how to identify areas to work on with performers and some of the actual practices employed in order to enhance performance. This includes using some well-known, evidence-based interventions, some simple interventions and some commonsense solutions. By reading this, it is not going to qualify you as a sport psychologist, but hopefully it will give you some insight into what can be done to boost mental performance in sport and perhaps whet your appetite to learn more about it.

9

Becoming a sport psychologist

In this chapter you will learn:

▶ *what a sport psychologist does*

▶ *what skills are required by a sport psychologist*

▶ *how to become a sport psychologist in the UK*

▶ *how to become a sport psychologist abroad*

▶ *about ethics in consultancy*

Late one evening in 2013 after leaving a friend's wedding, I found myself trying to justify the role of sport psychology to a sceptical and argumentative taxi driver. He began the journey not by asking about the wedding, which I thought would have been a fairly typical conversation giving the circumstances, but by asking what I did for a living. After mentioning sport psychology, I was met with a host of questions – 'Does that stuff work then?', 'Why can't anyone get England to win the World Cup?', 'What does a sport psychologist actually do?'. I had encountered these before so I had answers, despite being caught a little off guard. We got into some debate (it was quite a long journey) and I spent much of it trying to explain to him that it is not just about standing on the sidelines shouting 'come on'. Needless to say, he didn't get a tip.

What does a sport psychologist do?

There are a couple of answers to this question: one is a functional response that provides examples of work undertaken by a sport psychologist when working with a client; the other is more of an exploration of people who work in sport psychology in different ways.

The functional response is the one I tell people who ask when I want to explain briefly. This is the response that the taxi driver received and one received by anyone who is asking as a pleasantly in-passing conversation. It goes like this:

Mainly, a sport psychologist helps performers improve their performance by developing their mental skills. In the same way that a coach helps their technical skills, and a fitness coach helps their physical skills, a sport psychologist is interested in helping someone to reach their potential by improving the mental side of their performance.

Often I have to follow this up with some examples, such as getting them to work on different areas of their game. This might be things like helping them to cope with stress, or train better, or concentrate better. That is normally enough for the polite enquirer. If you are asking this question though, I assume that you are interested in more detail. A good way of accessing this detail is further reading. I highly recommend *Applied Sport Psychology: A Case-Based Approach*, edited by Brian Hemmings and Tim Holder (2009). This book includes a series of case studies from sport psychology consultants, which provides tremendous insight into how they work. For now, I will explain the different roles that those working in sport psychology adopt. These include those working as employed sport psychologists, self-employed sport psychologists and academics.

EMPLOYED SPORT PSYCHOLOGISTS

Some sport psychologists are employed on a contract by professional sports clubs, organizations, governing bodies or centres of excellence. This group are actually in the minority, as the two groups mentioned below have more numbers. People are often surprised by the small numbers of sport psychologists employed by professional sports clubs. Indeed, very few Premier League football clubs have a sport psychologist, though most use external consultants. In individual sports, such as golf and tennis, it would be incredibly inefficient for a performer to employ a sport psychologist on a full-time basis. As such, they are more likely to use a self-employed consultant or someone working at a university.

Those who are employed are normally employed by performance centres. For example, the English Institute of Sport is a large employer of a range of sport and exercise scientists. Other centres of excellence include sport-specific centres. Employed sport psychologists can also be found here.

SELF-EMPLOYED SPORT PSYCHOLOGISTS

Many people decide to work for themselves. This career is appealing because it can be more flexible and varied. It requires excellent professional networks to establish a large enough client base to earn a living. It can be very rewarding though. Working for yourself provides excellent flexibility and travel opportunities. Highly successful self-employed sport psychologists can work in sports that they have a real passion for and gain tremendous satisfaction. While there are benefits to this, it is also important to be aware of some important caveats. First, it is imperative that the appropriate indemnity insurance is in place and that you are registered with a professional body. If you are not, then you must be careful about what you claim to be, your title and what you claim to do. It is also a much less stable position to be in, since if the work dries up you won't get paid.

ACADEMICS

I remember deciding that I wanted to be an academic and then I noticed that one definition of the term in the *Oxford English Dictionary* is 'Not of any practical relevance'. By this time I had a job in a university so it was too late for me!

Sport psychology practitioners working in universities are likely to be involved in research, consultancy and teaching. Each of these elements can be focused on to a greater or lesser extent. Research refers to the carrying out and publication of studies designed to extend our knowledge of sport psychology. These studies take a variety of forms such as experimental studies, questionnaire-based, longitudinal (over time), reflective (case studies) or interview-based. Whatever the method, the role is to further enhance what we know about how sportspeople function and how we can improve their performance.

The research conducted informs consultancy work. Some academics also work as consultants with teams and individuals, offering psychological support. This is akin to what employed and self-employed sport psychologists do, but typically on a short-term agreement. The other component of working as a sport psychology practitioner in a university is teaching. This means delivering lectures and seminars to students taking the subject. The extent to which these three roles are apportioned varies greatly in academic posts.

IKEA psychology

It is important to recognize the skills required to be an effective sport psychology practitioner and I do so in this chapter. There are many books on sport psychology that perhaps overlook the skills element in favour of providing more information on psychological skills like imagery and goal-setting. While these are very useful (indeed, Chapter 11 is dedicated to discussing these and other interventions), they are tools that can be employed by a skilled practitioner. The practitioners themselves are the ones who really effect the change though.

So what do I mean by 'IKEA psychology'? Well, I am referring to how IKEA works (a quick note – this is not a criticism of IKEA. This approach works superbly for great value furniture, just not as a method of practising psychology). First, everything is flat-packed and off the shelf. When shopping in IKEA you see something that looks good and go and pick it up at the end. Everything is already packaged. The components are already cut to size, the holes are pre-drilled, and oftentimes the required tools are already included. The end product is perfectly consistent every time and anyone (!) can put it together. By referring to 'IKEA psychology', I am thinking of occasions when people pick up a psychological intervention as if it were a flat-packed piece of furniture off the shelf and administer it.

The problem is, people are bespoke. We cannot apply the same interventions in the same way and expect the same results because each individual is different. Equally, while you can pick up worksheets and assessments online, to be effective these require important practitioner skills, such as developing rapport, having a sound theoretical knowledge and being highly reflective.

What skills are required?

Generally, a sport psychologist requires the same skills as most other psychologists, such as being analytical and being able to develop good relationships, but there are some skills that I think are particularly strongly required to work in sport. The first one, of course, is an interest in sport. I don't believe that this means that it is necessary to have played to a high level, or even played the sport in question, but an interest and enthusiasm to learn about different sports is essential.

AN INTEREST AND ENTHUSIASM FOR SPORT

I would have loved to have been good enough (or work hard enough) to make it professionally in several sports. That, however, never worked out. So when working with sports performers, a common question is asked of me 'have you played?' and if so 'what level?' I can see here that the issue is my credibility to be able to advise someone how to be a better footballer, cricketer, hockey player, shooter, golfer, tennis player, etc. when I myself have not got experience at that level. I was once asked: 'so what can you tell me about what it's like to perform in front of a large crowd and TV cameras?' I don't consider this relevant. The person asking the question had done this, but only ever as themselves. They brought to this situation their own personality, confidence, mental toughness, coping techniques, etc. I could just as easily ask 'what can you tell other people about it?', because they only have their own experiences. Indeed, their experience as a confident individual in this environment might mean that they find it particularly difficult to understand someone who is less confident in the same environment. You need to understand people, but you do not need to have been there and done that.

A good idea when encountering a new sport is to go along and have a go at it. This helps to understand the time, the energy required, the feel of equipment, etc., all of which can help you to understand the performer, the sport, and inform things like relaxation techniques and imagery.

BUILDING RELATIONSHIPS

Building a good rapport with clients is perhaps the most important skill that a sport psychology consultant can have. Essentially, rapport is about how well people understand each other. I think of it as being in tune with one another in a harmonious way. At the centre of rapport is trust. If the performer knows that you care about them and that you will do what is best to help them, you are well on your way towards building a very effective relationship. There are several ways of building rapport. Perhaps, most importantly, it is to listen carefully and remain non-judgemental throughout. Each performer is learning all of the time and they will, like everybody, make mistakes or do things differently to how others might. By continuing to understand their perspective rather than making external judgements, it is easier to build a relationship.

Key idea: Rapport

A close and harmonious relationship with good understanding of each other's feelings or ideas.

The decision on where meetings take place can have an impact on rapport. Many think of psychology being a very therapy-based, lying-on-a-couch-type setting. These myths can be dispelled by meeting the performer in their own environment. In some sports, if you have at least some ability, it might be worth engaging in practice. For example, a round of golf, a shooting round, some hitting in tennis. Of course, this also depends on what the sport psychology consultant finds comfortable. A significant impact on establishing rapport is being able to come across as existing on a level playing field. Regardless of who has the higher achievement in sport, and who has academic qualifications, you are simply individuals with your own personalities trying to help each other out. Some performers are extremely interested in the theory behind what you discuss but others are not – they just want to play better. It is really important that conversations happen in the performer's language. If an athlete is struggling to push themselves in training, they do not need a lecture on self-determination theory. An excellent sport psychologist once told me to 'make it not feel like psychology'.

> 'Trust is the glue of life. It's the most essential ingredient in effective communication. It's the foundational principle that holds all relationships.'
>
> Stephen Covey, US author

BEING LOGICAL AND ANALYTICAL

Much of what we try to do in sport psychology is to get performers to act in a rational, rather than irrational way. For example, fear often derives from irrational and unhelpful thoughts. Logical analysis is a coping strategy to identify that when things are considered objectively, fear is not a possible, logical emotion. Actually, much more positive emotions are far more logical. As such, the sport psychology consultant must maintain a logical mindset themselves.

Being analytical is important because it simply would not be possible to identify the requirements of performance, areas of strength and weakness, and changes in performance without this. The next chapter discusses in much greater detail how analysis in sport psychology assessment is essential for guiding support.

BEING MOTIVATIONAL

It is ok to know what to do and why, but you need to be persuasive enough to enable the performer to understand this. Most performers have something that they would dearly love to achieve at some point in their career. The sport psychologist has a unique opportunity to support them in achieving this and the rewards for all concerned will be great. Meetings, talks and text messages to performers have the potential to act as motivating and inspiring moments that can provide the athlete with the encouragement needed to reach that next level.

SOLVING PROBLEMS AND MAKING DECISIONS

Often, performers have pre-identified an area that they would like to improve before meeting with a sport psychologist. As such, the first meeting can be the confrontation of a problem. If it is not, it may be about identifying an area of their performance that could be more effective. As such, the ability to come up with solutions is key in these situations. Some solutions work and some don't, but a good consultant can identify a potential solution, decide how to implement it and try it. Moreover, they will carefully monitor this and make decisions regarding continuing an intervention, modifying it or scrapping it altogether. Time is often tight when working with performers so it is important to be able to make decisions in a timely fashion.

BEING FLEXIBLE

Because time is tight, it is necessary to remain flexible. Technological enhancements have made this much easier, since the use of video-calling and instant messaging means that formal and informal meetings/catch-ups are much easier to undertake. It is also worth remembering that sport is a very changeable environment. A win, a loss, a transfer or an injury can all change the best-laid plans in an instant. Flexibility will also provide greater opportunities to strengthen the relationship between the psychologist and performer.

Case study: A perfect partnership

An effective way to understand the usefulness of sport psychology consultancy is to examine it from the athlete's perspective. That is exactly what Sharp & Hodge (2014) did. They interviewed nine elite athletes who had experience of working with sport psychologists.

Their findings suggested that there was general agreement on what made an effective sport psychology consultant. The first finding was that consultants should be friendly, but not a friend, while maintaining professional boundaries. The athletes said that an athlete-centred style was vital. This means developing individualized programmes. They also identified flexibility, openness, honesty and respect as key factors in an effective partnership.

Routes to practice

To become a sport psychologist typically requires at least an undergraduate degree, a postgraduate degree and supervised experience. In recent times, this section has become more confusing to write than most would want it to be. However, I will try my best to explain this in a clear, concise way.

IN THE UNITED KINGDOM

To explain the process in the UK, it is necessary to introduce some professional and regulatory bodies. To start, it should be made clear that **Sport and Exercise Psychologist** and **Sport and Exercise Scientist** are protected titles. This means that it is unlawful to advertise oneself as one of these if the appropriate accreditation/registration is not held.

The first professional body I will introduce is the British Association of Sport and Exercise Sciences (BASES). Sport and exercise sciences essentially pulls together the sciences of psychology, physiology and biomechanics to understand and improve sport performance. Until 2008 it was this professional body that you would apply to in order to become a sport psychologist. BASES has a division of psychology, which I recommend that you join if you are interested in becoming part of a professional network. You don't have to be qualified – you can register as an affiliate. To become an accredited sport and exercise scientist, who may have a domain of expertise in psychology, you require an undergraduate degree, a BASES-accredited master's degree and at least two years' supervised experience.

The British Psychological Society (BPS) is the professional body for all forms of psychology (clinical, educational, forensic, etc.) and now includes sport and exercise. To become a chartered psychologist, it is necessary to gain Graduate Basis for Chartered membership (GBC), which is usually obtained by completing a BPS-accredited undergraduate degree. If you have studied a different subject, such as sport science, sociology, etc., you can undertake a conversion course to obtain GBC status in around one year. From here, a BPS-accredited master's degree is required, followed by at least two years of supervised experience. In very recent developments, it is now possible to combine a conversion course with a master's degree, which makes the process a little more efficient. BPS has a division of sport and exercise psychology, which works to enhance the quality of sport psychology consultancy and research in the UK.

It's all the same isn't it?

People in professional sport settings are sometimes unaware of what sport psychology can offer. I once met someone who worked in sport science at a club who told me that they had already 'done' psychology. They had actually used a hypnotherapist and the sport scientist said 'it's all the same isn't it?'

This actually highlights an important point for all sport psychology consultants, which is not to assume that others really understand what services are available. They may also be unsure of professional accreditations.

Since 2009, the title of **Sport and Exercise Psychologist** has been protected by the regulatory body, the Health and Care Professions Council (HCPC). This was to regulate the profession in the same way that other medical and therapy professions are regulated. Throughout this book, I regularly refer to **Sport Psychology Consultants.** This is intentional, as not everyone who works within sport psychology as a consultant is necessarily a **Sport and Exercise Psychologist,** as registered with the appropriate professional and regulatory bodies. It becomes a little bit of a minefield when there are many other titles out there that are not protected, such as **mental skills coach** and **performance coach.** There are also some out there who use the protected titles when they should not; so if you employ a sport psychology consultant, do check their qualifications!

OUTSIDE THE UK

The methods to become a recognized sport psychologist are different in each country. Obviously, I cannot go through every requirement but I will briefly consider some of the largest associations here.

▶ Australia

The Australian system is fairly similar to the British system. In Australia, all psychologists are registered on the Psychology Board of Australia (PBA), which endorses protected psychologist titles, including in sport and exercise. Following a degree, applicants must complete accredited postgraduate study (master's or doctoral) and undertake a minimum of two years' supervised experience. This is most commonly done through the Australian Psychological Society (APS).

▶ United States

In the United States, the path is typically to become a certified consultant with the Association for Applied Sport Psychology (AASP). To achieve this, applicants are expected to be a member of the association, have a doctoral qualification in sport science or psychology, have completed set coursework for certification, and undertaken at least 400 hours of mentored experience in sport psychology. They then register with the American Psychological Association (APA), Division 47.

► Canada

In Canada, professional membership is sought from the Canadian Sport Psychology Association (CSPA). This requires a master's degree in sport psychology or a related field, successful completion of a variety of accredited courses, and at least 400 hours of supervised practice with favourable supervisor and client evaluations.

More information is readily available on these and career routes in other countries on the web.

Ethics in consultancy

Guides for practitioners are available through their relevant professional bodies. BASES, BPS, HCPC, APS, AASP and CSPA, for example, all have some variation on a code of practice. This includes guidelines to ensure that people are treated fairly, that they are appropriately informed, charged and confidentiality is respected as appropriate. Because practice guidelines are available and trainee sport psychologists will receive support on this, I will not focus on this. Rather, I thought it worthwhile to reflect on some of the practicalities.

One of the most common aspects of ethics is confidentiality. To what extent should practitioners keep and break confidentiality? The most basic practical advice I can offer is to be as transparent as possible with performers and coaches or parents as to what information will be considered as confidential. Often, performers are happy to have much of the information divulged in a consultancy to other people. The key is to ask them. This becomes a little more complicated in some settings. For example, in team sports or individual sports with squads the very causes of stress can be teammates. Sometimes, coaches are also parents and the extra hat means that they may find it difficult to take information in the way it is intended.

Key idea: Confidentiality

A set of rules or a promise that limits access or places restrictions on information shared with external parties

The other point I would make on confidentiality is that it is an agreement that should work both ways. The whole consultancy process is a partnership and by engaging the performer in this way it will help to develop rapport. A difficulty some encounter in working with elite performers is that it can be tempting to treat some clients better than others. I'm sure this is never intentional, but imagine you were working with a teenage performer signed at a local club and an international athlete at the same time. The international athlete could be more exciting to work with, higher paying and good for your reputation. If you have a missed call from both, whose call do you return first? The professional answer is to call whichever is probably the most pressing for the performer. It is vitally important in professional ethics to ensure that all clients are treated equally.

Dig deeper

Andersen, M. B. (Ed.) (2005), *Sport Psychology in Practice*. Champaign, IL: Human Kinetics.

Hemmings, B. & Holder, T. (Eds.) (2009), *Applied Sport Psychology: A Case-Based Approach*. Oxford: Wiley-Blackwell.

Knowles, Z., Gilbourne, D., Cropley, B. & Dugdill, L. (Eds.) (2014), *Reflective Practice in the Sport and Exercise Sciences: Contemporary Issues*. London: Routledge.

McCarthy, P. & Jones, M. (Eds.) (2013), *Becoming a Sport Psychologist*. London: Routledge.

Williams, J. M. & Krane, V. (2014), *Applied Sport Psychology: Personal Growth to Peak Performance*. New York: McGraw-Hill.

Fact check

1 Which skills are required to be an effective sport psychology consultant?
  a analytical skills
  b flexibility
  c problem solving
  d all of the above

2 Which of these is not a protected title in the UK?
  a Sport and Exercise Psychologist
  b Sport and Exercise Scientist
  c Mental Skills Coach
  d Counsellor

3 Psychology in the UK is regulated by...?
  a HCPC
  b HPC
  c BPS
  d d APA

4 How many years of supervised experience is required to become a Sport and Exercise Psychologist in the UK?
  a 1–2
  b 2–3
  c 3–4
  d 4–5

5 What is the minimum amount of mentoring experience required to be a certified consultant in the US?
  a 200 hours
  b 300 hours
  c 400 hours
  d 500 hours

10

Assessment

In this chapter you will learn:

▶ *what sport psychology assessments look like*

▶ *about personal construct psychology*

▶ *what performance profiling is*

▶ *the importance of monitoring and evaluation*

▶ *psychometric approaches to psychological skills*

▶ *that we don't always need to consider weaknesses*

In Chapter 8 we looked at measurement using psychometric assessments for research. We acknowledged the rigour and importance of validity. That is because (in a research context) we try to make inferences from our measurements and conclusions that can be generalized to larger groups of people. Assessment in an applied sense is very different. The key difference here is that we are not intending to generalize our results to anyone else. Quite the opposite, in fact. When working with a client, all we are interested in is that the assessment is accurate for that person or team. It does not matter if it is relevant to anybody else.

The aim of assessment in applied sport psychology is to fully understand the client, their strengths and areas for development, and any goals they have. The key to this is detail. It is not enough to know if someone gets nervous, which negatively affects their performance. We need to know how this feels? What do they think about? Does it change during performance? What about when winning or losing? Or when fatigued? The more information we can garner from our assessment, the more we can target areas to develop. The most common approach to assessment, particularly when learning sport psychology, is **performance profiling**.

> 'Inches make a champion.'
> Vince Lombardi, American football coach

Performance profiling

Performance profiling is a client-centred assessment of performance strategies. The aims are to identify the attributes required to be successful for a particular sports performer, their relative strengths in these areas and their areas for development. The performance profiling technique taught frequently to trainee sport psychologists is that described by Butler & Hardy (1992). Performance profiling is a direct application of George Kelly's Personal Construct Theory (PCT; Kelly, 1955). PCT is often also discussed in terms of a more general approach:

Personal Construct Psychology (PCP). These terms are used interchangeably and they are, to all intents and purposes, the same thing.

Key idea: Performance profiling

A client-centred assessment of performance strategies.

Kelly's personal construct approach was to get clients to uncover their own personal constructs; that is, the way in which they see the world. This should be achievable with little input from the psychologist. Kelly developed a repertory grid, which comprised a topic, elements, constructs and ratings of elements and constructs. The topic is a part of an individual's experience, such as feeling pressured in a certain situation. Elements refer to components of this topic, such as the people involved or the perceived requirement. Constructs refer to how we make sense of the elements, which are then rated. A key premise of PCT is that the individual then uses their own constructs to anticipate future outcomes (Kelly uses the rather dated expression 'corollaries', which means a natural consequence). Some of these corollaries are common in that the perceived inevitable consequence of feeling a certain way is similar to others, and some corollaries are individual, in that they are different from others. To use personal constructs as a form of psychotherapy we test the accuracy of a client's constructed knowledge. This helps us to understand how they see the world.

Butler & Hardy (1992) identified that this approach could be very useful in sport. We do not want to impose our beliefs on performers since this could potentially limit our effectiveness. For example, a sport psychologist could begin working with a high board diver and assume that anxiety derived from fear could be an important issue. In doing so, we are imparting our view of the sport on to the performer. From the performer's perspective, this may be minor or not even a consideration. Indeed, they are likely to present a very different perspective of what it is to be a diver than someone without such experience. This is an important point, since a sport psychology consultant may not have experience of the sport (this is discussed a little later in this chapter).

In practice, then, there are two main stages to creating a performance profile: the identification of the personal constructs and scoring against them. To identify personal constructs, the sport psychology practitioner may ask the athlete what it takes to be successful in their sport. Remembering that this is a client-led conversation, it is important not to give too many hints that lead a performer into saying certain things. Some of the constructs will likely be technical, some tactical, some physical and some psychological. The key at this stage is to use the client's words and understand what they mean by them. For example, if a performer says that 'intensity' is important, they should be asked what they mean by that. They might be examining this from a motivational perspective and be referring to high levels of determination, they could be referring to tension caused by anxiety or they might be referring to concentration and the intensity that is lost by switching off. A thorough discussion is required about what really creates a top performer. In young performers, it is sometimes easier to get them to describe the characteristics displayed by performers they look up to.

Key idea: Personal constructs

An individual's perspective of what contributes to their view of the world.

Eventually, a set of personal constructs, identified by the client and of importance in their sport, is noted and understood. The next stage is to ask athletes to rate themselves against those qualities, using a scale of 1 (lowest) to 10 (highest). This is essentially an extension of Kelly's original repertory grid. It is often displayed in a visual profile like the one in Figure 10.1.

In this example, I have included only psychological constructs. From this, we can see the constructs that have been identified as important by the performer. We can also determine that they

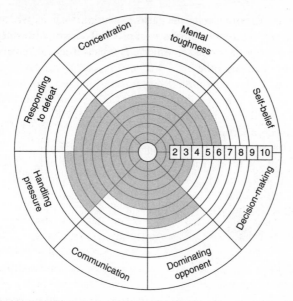

Figure 10.1 An example of a visual performance profile

believe that their strengths are in handling pressure, dominating opponents and self-belief. Conversely, decision-making, communication and concentration appear to be areas ripe for improvement.

The performance profiling method is used commonly in a variety of sports (Weston, 2008). From an interdisciplinary perspective, it has the advantage of being useful for a coach or other sport scientist. As stated, the constructs identified are not necessarily to be restricted to psychological factors. When shared, this profile can be used by coaches to structure training (Butler, 1995, 1997) and monitor performance (Doyle & Parfitt, 1997).

It may also be useful to gain other perspectives of the relative strengths and weaknesses of a performer. If it is agreed with the performer, their coach can be presented with the same constructs and asked to rate the client. This can provide some useful insight into the extent to which the coach and athlete have similar perceptions of their performance strengths, which often provokes some very interesting conversations.

A further elaboration on the performance profile is to ask the performer to rate the constructs in order of performance prior to identifying their self-assessment. This can be useful because it is not necessarily the highest or lowest scoring self-assessment scores that should be targeted for intervention. For example, take table 10.1. If we subtract the athlete's self-assessment from the potential maximum score (10) and multiply this by their perceived importance, we generate a discrepancy value. In our example, we can see that although the lowest self-assessment score was a 4 for decision-making, the performer only values the importance of this as a 7, providing a discrepancy of 42. Although scoring a 5 for concentration, the performer has identified the importance of this as a 10, which provides a discrepancy score of 50.

Table 10.1 Example performance profile table with perceived importance and self-assessment

Construct	Athlete's Perceived Level of Importance (API)	Athlete's Self-assessment (ASA)	Discrepancy (10-ASA) × API
Concentration	10	5	50
Mental toughness	9	6	36
Self-belief	9	7	27
Decision-making	7	4	42
Dominating opponent	8	7	24
Communication	7	5	35
Handling pressure	9	8	18
Responding to defeat	8	7	24

It is important to stress to the athlete that they must consider the relative importance of each construct and not simply note 10 for each. In all sports, some skills are more important than others. For example, it is important for a 100-metre sprinter to be flexible to maximize muscle contraction, but it is more important to have raw speed. The same is true in mental skills. For example, a golfer needs many mental skills, but few are as important as handling pressure.

Although this provides some insight for the sport psychology practitioner, it does not necessarily mean that they will now work solely on interventions to develop the concentration skills of the performer. Rather, this can be more of a conversation starter. What this does not tell us is when concentration is an issue and what the client does about it. Some follow-up questions could be to ask when the client finds maintaining concentration to be an issue. In training or competition? Against stronger or weaker opposition? When winning or losing? When fatigued? There is a whole host of potential answers here. The key is to refine as much as possible to be able to identify at which moments we feel that we can be most effective.

To investigate athlete perceptions of performance profiling, Weston, Greenlees & Thelwell (2011) interviewed 8 athletes and then surveyed a further 191 to gain their insights. The results suggested that athletes considered profiling to be useful in raising their self-awareness, helping them to decide what they needed to work on, motivating them to improve, setting personal goals, monitoring and evaluating their performance, and taking more responsibility for their development. The same authors then further reviewed the effectiveness of profiling in a thorough review of all previous studies and again found support for performance profiling (Weston, Greenlees & Thelwell, 2013).

The method has been formally extended by some. For example, Gucciardi & Gordon (2009b) looked at range corollary, which was originally part of Kelly's construct theory (1955). Specifically, it was to identify that some constructs can be very broad and cover training, preparation, match, etc., while others are very specific to certain situations, such as taking a penalty. Gucciardi & Gordon encouraged athletes to identify the contexts in which each profile attribute was most applicable (e.g., in preparation for competition, during training, etc.). The argument therefore is that if a construct can be applied in more contexts/situations, then it is more important for performance development.

Key idea: Corollary

A proposition that follows another if the first one is true.

The importance of good assessment

Most consultancy models or practice frameworks regularly cite assessment and then evaluation/monitoring at every stage of the process. For example, Thomas (1990) identified seven stages:

▶ orientation

▶ sport analysis

▶ individual/team assessment

▶ conceptualization and clarify aims

▶ psychological skills training/implementation

▶ end of intervention

▶ follow-up.

Although the assessment component appears early in this process, it is actually referred to throughout because from the implementation onwards, there is evaluation. This means reviewing progress aims again and the easiest way to review progress is by having effective assessment initially.

> 'Yesterday is not ours to recover, but tomorrow is ours to win or lose.'
>
> Lyndon B. Johnson, former US president

Good assessment adds a layer of sophistication from the consultant but is a simple process from the athlete's perspective. As a nice example, consider that of Chris Harwood (2009), who was working with an elite male tennis player to develop his self-efficacy and achieve his aim of reaching the world's top 200. After speaking with the performer and observing practice and competition, Harwood asked him to identify the percentage of certainty to which he would achieve a ranking within the top 275, 250, 225 and 200. This is because self-efficacy is so bespoke to the person and the situation that an assessment should be likewise.

Table 10.2 Example of pre-intervention self-efficacy assessment

Ranking level	Percentage of certainty (%)										
(Units	1	2	3	4	5	6	7	8	9	**10**	11)
Inside the top:											
275	0	10	20	30	40	50	60	70	80	**90**	100	10 × 275 = 2750
250	0	10	20	30	40	50	60	70	*80*	90	100	9 × 250 = 2250
225	0	10	20	30	40	50	60	*70*	80	90	100	8 × 225 = 1800
200	0	10	20	30	40	50	60	**70**	80	90	100	8 × 200 = 1600

Total efficacy score (pre-intervention) = 8400 (2750 + 2250 + 1800 + 1600)
Maximum possible efficacy score = 10450
Pre-intervention efficacy index = 8400/10450 × 100 = <u>80.3%</u>

To obtain a pre-intervention self-efficacy score that could later be referred to, Harwood multiplied the percentage by a 1–11 unit, added these and compared this to the maximum possible score to create an overall percentage. This process is illustrated in Table 10.2. This enables the sport psychologist and performer to identify progress in self-efficacy for each ranking goal and overall for achieving the main goal.

Another benefit of good assessment is that it enables the performer to zoom out a little bit and see the bigger picture. When consumed by a particular goal, it is easy to become so immersed that we do not see progress. For example, imagine that you are a golfer trying to reduce your handicap. Over a few years it may have come down from the mid-20s to the teens to single figures. With progress, though, comes diminishing returns. When your handicap was 23, there was a lot of room for improvement so it was easier to improve. Now your handicap is six, there is much less room for improvement. This means that it takes longer and is harder to make progress. Perhaps you go out, have a bad day and shoot a round of 83. At this point, it is easy to feel like you are not improving. You go out for another round and shoot an 82 and still feel the same. If you have kept good records, though, you will be able to consult them to zoom out and see this improvement. To explain further, consider Figure 10.2.

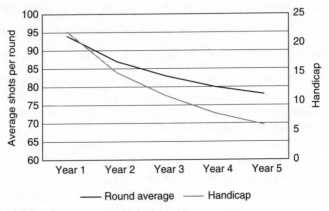

Figure 10.2 Hypothetical golf score tracking

The overall picture here is clearly a positive one but if we were able to zoom in to individual weeks of even rounds, we would find that it goes up and down in a much more inconsistent style. In these moments, it is necessary to zoom out to see the big picture – something that is made easier with good assessment. More sophisticated assessments here could be evaluations of self-efficacy in different components of the game, such as short game, driving, iron play, course management, hazard play and putting.

Psychometric assessment of psychological skills

The thing we are most interested in assessing is, of course, performance. But performance is made up of several different facets. There is objective performance, such as games or races won; physical performance, such as speed or strength; tactical, technical and mental performance. Here, we will consider the assessment of mental skill in more detail.

The most common assessment of an athlete's psychological skills is the Test of Performance Strategies (TOPS; Thomas, Murphy & Hardy, 1999). If interested in this area, you may also want to look up the Psychological Skills Inventory for Sport (PSIS; Mahoney, Gabriel & Perkins, 1987), the Athletic Coping Skills Inventory (ACSI-28; Smith, Schultz, Smoll & Ptacek, 1995) and the Ottawa Mental Skills Assessment Tool (OMSAT-3; Durand-Bush, Salmela & Green-Demers, 2001).

The TOPS measures eight psychological skills and was recently refined to create the TOPS 2 (Hardy, Roberts, Thomas & Murphy, 2010). This second version has demonstrated greater validity than the earlier version. The eight skills assessed are goal setting, relaxation, activation, imagery, self-talk, attentional control, emotional control and automaticity. These are measured at practice and in competition, with the exception that during competition negative thinking is included rather than attentional control.

Case study: Devil in the detail

Noting the predominance and (often) necessity for psychological inventories in sport psychology, Anshel & Brinthaupt (2014) provided some useful advice on best practice. Referring to other research, Anshel & Brinthaupt found that between 63 and 75 per cent of sport psychology consultants report using psychological inventories. Before providing recommendations for best practice, they identified some common errors. These included an over-reliance on experience (rather than relying on individualized assessment), not using an inventory for its intended purpose (i.e., some inventories are developed for research purposes only), an overdependence on inventory scores (they are not always correct!), failing to establish a relationship with an athlete (anyone can hand out a questionnaire) and neglecting to take into account athlete attitudes (some hate questionnaires).

To get the most from inventories in practical assessments, Anshel & Brinthaupt (2014) identified eight pre-administration considerations and eight during-and-after administration considerations. Prior to administering the inventory, they recommended that sport psychology consultants: (1) determine the purpose, (2) confirm the internal validity, (3) determine the theory behind it, (4) determine if it has norm values to compare against, (5) determine the external validity, (6) assess the role in the consultation, (7) detect multiple applications of the data, and (8) obtain written consent. During and after administration, consultants should: (1) establish trust with the athlete, (2) be sensitive to cultural differences, (3) determine the client's reading level, (4) obtain confirmation from the athlete of the scores, (5) ensure accuracy, (6) interpret with norms, (7) have a data disclosure plan and (8) document the experience. This just goes to show how much goes into what seems like such a simple process.

Using something like the TOPS 2 could be useful for a quick assessment to inform further discussion. Alternatively, if you were working with a large squad, it is much more efficient than performance profiling, so, again, this could be a useful tool. Even if you did not want to use a psychometric assessment, perhaps being aware of the contents can help in determining probing questions during interview.

'When we take time to notice the things that go right – it means we're getting a lot of little rewards throughout the day.'

Martin Seligman, US psychologist

Strengths-based approaches

Some of the assessments discussed in this chapter can instinctively lead to what might be called a **deficit model**. That is, look at where you need to be, look at where you are now, and find out how far off you are. Essentially, it identifies relative weakness (we normally say 'areas for development'). But we don't need to focus only on assessments in this way. Rather, we can adopt a strengths-based approach by looking at what the performer is good at and finding how to best make use of these mental strengths.

Key idea: Deficit model

Identifying areas of deficiency from an optimum level to inform practice.

For example, looking at the performance profile earlier in this chapter, we can see that handling pressure is a strength. As such, we can focus on making the most of pressured situations, such as a tennis player winning games that reach deuce, or a team gaining late victories. A second strength from the chart is dominating the opponent. It is worthwhile focusing on developing this even further. To use a tennis example again; try looking at body language and aggression when in a good position. There could be opportunities to really pile pressure on to the opponent when in a commanding position.

Key idea: Positive psychology

A branch of psychology intended to use theory and intervention to achieve greater life satisfaction.

Generally, strengths-based approaches take their lead from the broad area of positive psychology. Much of the development of positive psychology is attributed to Martin Seligman, who identified that a lot of psychology was focused on the treatment of mental illness. Rather, positive psychology focuses on how to further develop life satisfaction. It is not my intention to provide a complete discussion of positive psychology in this book, but further detail is offered when referring to flow in Chapter 12.

Positive, not necessarily popular

Positive psychology is a branch of psychology informed by rigorous empirical research. Popular psychology (or 'pop psych') normally appears in a self-help section, often (but not always) written by people with limited qualifications. It is 'popular' because it is the populous who perceive it as psychology, not because it really is. So when you head into a book store and reach for a psychology book, do check the author and be aware of books that claim they will dramatically change things about your life, or have 'easy steps'.

Dig deeper

Grenville-Cleave, B. (2012), *Introducing Positive Psychology: A Practical Guide*. London: Icon Books.

Harwood, C. (2009), *Enhancing Self-Efficacy in Professional Tennis: Intensive Work for Life on the Tour*. In Hemmings, B. & Holder, T. (Eds.), *Applied Sport Psychology: A Case-Based Approach* (pp. 7–32). Oxford: Wiley-Blackwell.

Kremer, J. & Moran, A. (2013), *Pure Sport: Practical Sport Psychology*. London: Routledge.

Seligman, M. E. P. (2003), *Authentic Happiness: Using the New Positive Psychology to Realize Your Potential for Lasting Fulfillment*. London: Nicholas Brealey Publishing.

Turner, M. & Barker, J. (2014), *Tipping the Balance: The Mental Skills Handbook for Athletes*. Stoke: Bennion Kearny.

Fact check

1 Performance profiling derives from…?
- **a** interpersonal content theory
- **b** personal concept theory
- **c** personal construct theory
- **d** constructed theory

2 Constructs in performance profiling should come from…?
- **a** the athlete
- **b** the coach
- **c** the psychologist
- **d** a book

3 The performance profile discrepancy is calculated by…?
- **a** $(10 + \text{ASA}) \times \text{API}$
- **b** $\text{ASA} \times (10 + \text{API})$
- **c** $\text{API} / (10 - \text{ASA})$
- **d** $(10 - \text{ASA}) \times \text{API}$

4 Focusing on areas of weakness is a…?
- **a** strengths-based approach
- **b** positive psychology
- **c** deficit model
- **d** counselling approach

5 A strengths-based approach…?
- **a** utilizes existing strengths to improve performance
- **b** identifies ways to improve
- **c** turns weakness into strength
- **d** turns strength into weakness

11

Psychological skills training

In this chapter you will learn:

▶ *what psychological skills training is*
▶ *common interventions in PST*
▶ *the importance of teaching*
▶ *the power of practice*
▶ *the basics of imagery*
▶ *how goal setting is used*

Psychological skills training (PST) is a sport psychologist's toolkit. I use the phrase in the broadest possible sense to mean anything that the sport psychologist does to effect a positive change. It is a huge area. The purpose of this chapter is to introduce PST and provide some examples of how it works. Further information on interventions can be found by using the Dig deeper reading list below. To give you an idea of how big this subject is, I will provide a brief overview of imagery within this chapter; there are complete books that concentrate solely on using imagery in sport.

A toolkit needs to include tools. If PST is the sport psychologist's toolkit, then interventions and practices are the tools. These include: goal setting, imagery, self-talk, thought stopping relaxation methods, and many more. Psychological skills training, which is also sometimes referred to as mental skills training, is the systematic process of developing psychological skills. It is helpful to keep this analogous to physical skills training, as I will do throughout this chapter.

Key idea: PST

Educationally based intervention to improve sport performance by developing mental skills.

Often, PST is divided into three stages: education, acquisition and practice. The education phase aims to achieve buy-in from the performer. It is important that they understand what the purpose is and how the programme is going to look. Key to the education phase is teaching.

Teaching

Psychological skills are exactly that – skills. That means that they need to be taught in order to be effective. One's ability to solve maths equations is a psychological skill also. Learning that skill is so much easier if it is taught well. Physical skills, too, are much easier to master when well taught. One of the most important components in effecting change is taking the time to ensure interventions are appropriately taught before they are practised.

Teaching something well ensures that when the client practises their new skill, they are doing so correctly so it can have the greatest effect. Moreover, though, if it is well taught, the client is more likely to understand how and why it will work. Their belief in the effectiveness of the intervention grows, which means they will expend more energy and persistence to ensure that it is useful.

Good teaching is necessary for an intervention to be successful, but good teaching alone is not sufficient. Good learning is at the centre of the acquisition phase. Acquisition refers to how the athlete is able to grasp the new skills, understanding how they can impact on performance. In particular, the programme is individualized so it meets the specific needs of the performer. To acquire and develop skills requires practice, which is the third phase of PST.

The power of practice

Imagine that you want to run a marathon in 12 months' time… Do you go for a quick three-mile run now and then expect to be fine for the big day? Of course not. It is clearly not enough. Practice needs to be appropriately planned and carried out with dedication. Periodized training schedules would be prepared and you would stick to your new regime, monitoring your progress all the way. To improve your psychological skills, you must also plan, practise and remain dedicated to it.

An intervention would be practised at certain times. This could be before, during or after training or competition. It could be at a training ground or at home. It might be once a week or every day. The structure of a PST programme really does depend on the client's needs, attitude towards PST, ability to learn psychological skills, and time. For example, if a performer is not sure about its usefulness, it is unlikely that they will want to devote much time to practising psychological skills. In this case, rather than burdening them with something they are unlikely to do, provide them with simple skills that can be practised in very short periods of time to start with.

Some skills, such as relaxation, can be quite simple and quick to learn. Other skills however, such as imagery, can be quite complex and challenging to learn. As such, it is important to test the ability of the imager and to spend a significant amount of practice time for it to be effective.

Imagery

The brain is a powerful thing, but it is not good at detecting the difference between real and imaginary experiences. Although this sounds like a deficiency, it is actually great for PST. Imagery exploits this by mimicking a real-life experience in order to gain practice without actually having to perform the activity. For example, a Formula 1 racing driver will typically race the course around hundreds of laps prior to actually driving around it.

There are several different ways that imagery is used. People often refer to visualization, which is a type of imagery where the performer creates an imagery picture of an experience, usually in the future, and visualizes performing a skill successfully. Generally, imagery is distinct from visualization becomes it uses several or even all of the senses. As an example, read the imagery script below about entering a swimming pool and try to imagine it.

The example imagery script provided uses several senses. The most prominent in most imagery is sight. Here, the focus is also on smell, touch, and hearing though. A swimming pool is quite a unique environment and one where these senses are perhaps even more heightened than sight. By using a greater range of senses, the imagery experience becomes closer to a lived one.

There are two main perspectives that people adopt when practising imagery: internal and external. An internal perspective is one where the imager sees things through their own eyes. In an external perspective, the imager can see themselves, as though they are a movie camera watching the event. People tend to naturally favour one over the other.

> *You are walking out of the changing room to the poolside. Take a moment to look around and notice the flags above the lanes and the audience watching from the sides. You can smell the chlorine, and as you walk you can feel the dramatic drop in temperature on your skin. You can feel the contours of the floor press against your feet as you step. There is plenty of noise from conversations around the pool and they echo. It is noisy but not possible to make out any specific words. As you make your way towards the pool, you can feel the adrenaline begin to rush through your body. You become aware of your heart rate increasing. You take a couple of deep breaths. As you breathe out, you tell yourself to relax.*

Figure 11.1 Example imagery script

The internal perspective is useful for relating to thoughts and physiological feelings. For example, thinking that you will succeed, or feeling energized in your legs are things that you would not identify with an external perspective so much. An external perspective though can be beneficial if you were aiming to focus more on your strategic play, such as positioning.

Not quite how I pictured it

In the same way that practising physical skills does not guarantee success, practising imagery is no guarantee of success either. Stepping up to take an important penalty is something that many will have imagined doing thousands of times, yet history is littered with high-profile slips, scuffs and ballooned efforts. It is unlikely that Chelsea captain John Terry imagined slipping as he struck his penalty in the 2009 Champions League final or that Texas Rangers outfielder Jose Canseco imagined the ball bouncing off his head for a home run to the opposition in a 1993 match against the Cleveland Indians.

There are many, many studies that demonstrate how effective imagery is. I will refer to some of them in this chapter. Most debate on imagery concerns why it actually works. There are many different theories to explain this. For example, **psychoneuromuscular theory** suggests that tiny muscular movements provide the nervous system with feedback, which helps refine movement patterns. **Dual code theory** explains how the memory recalls images or words and can use these memories effectively. **Attention-arousal set** focuses on how imagery prepares an optimum arousal level. Some researchers have suggested that the main benefit of imagery is a boost of self-efficacy.

Perhaps the most used explanation in recent sport psychology is **functional equivalence**. This theory has a lot of supporting research identifying that imaginary and real movements both recruit the same structures from the central nervous system. In effect, if you imagine doing something, then from a brain and nerve point of view it is the same as actually doing it. Think now about a movement; the physical bit is really just the tip of an iceberg. The decision is made in the brain, this travels through the nervous system to motor neurons attached to muscle, and the actual movement is the final part. Therefore, by practising imagery, you are practising most of the skill.

Key idea: Functional equivalence

Theory explaining that imaginary and real movements show similar central nervous system recruitment patterns, which create a training effect from imagined experience.

Some of the research around functional equivalence, including the use of brain scans, is fascinating but beyond the scope of this book. For now, I will focus on how imagery is used to improve performance. In particular, the focus is on different functions of imagery and practical approaches for implementing imagery training.

> 'Before every shot I go to the movies inside my head. Here is what I see. First, I see the ball, white and sitting up high on the bright green grass. Then, I see the ball going there; its path and trajectory and even its behaviour on landing. The next scene shows me making the kind of swing that will turn the previous image into reality. These home movies are key to my concentration and my positive approach to every shot.'
>
> Jack Nicklaus, golfer, winner of 18 Major titles

Functions of imagery

Allan Paivio (1985) recognized that imagery could be used to serve several different functions. He noted that these functions could be cognitive or motivational. Further, he recognized that some uses of imagery helped perform specific tasks proficiently, while other uses were more general. As a result, he constructed an imagery framework, which is now understood within sporting domains as illustrated in Table 11.1.

Table 11.1 Adaptation of Paivio's (1985) imagery framework

	Motivational	Cognitive
Specific	Goal-oriented responses	Skills
General	Arousal	Strategy
	Mastery	

Paivio's framework cites that imagery can be motivational or cognitive, specific or general. Motivational imagery is when the practice is designed to elicit positive responses to make the athlete feel more positive about an upcoming performance. A specific version (MS) of this would be something goal-oriented, such as imagining winning a race or match, or lifting a trophy.

Motivational general imagery originally contained only arousal but has since included a mastery element after research by Martin, Moritz & Hall (1999). Motivation–arousal (MG–A) is about using imagery to manipulate physiological arousal levels. This means psyching yourself up or relaxing to suit the desired state. Motivational general–mastery (MG–M) involves the athlete using imagery to improve their confidence in performing well or winning. For example, they might use experiences of previous success to increase the extent to which they feel they can go and win.

Cognitive functions of imagery are more about thought processes. Cognitive specific (CS) imagery is about imagining particular skills that make up a performance. For example, a cricketer imagining playing the perfect cover drive. Cognitive. general (CG) imagery, however, involves rehearsing a whole game plan. An example could be sticking to a baseline game in tennis and moving the opponent into particular positions.

All forms of imagery have been shown to be effective in a variety of studies. The important thing to take from this is understanding that it is essential to know what you want to achieve from using imagery. This will dictate the type of imagery used and, ultimately, the success of the intervention.

Doing effective imagery

So far we have focused on why we do imagery more than how we do it. There is one overriding model at the moment to guide practitioners in implementing imagery. This is known as the PETTLEP model (Holmes & Collins, 2001). PETTLEP stands for the following:

▶ *Physical* movement

▶ *Environmental* specifics

▶ *Task* undertaken

▶ *Timing* of the movement

▶ *Learning* of the movement

▶ *Emotion* associated with the movement

▶ *Perspective* of the individual.

The *physical* component of PETTLEP means that imagery should be performed in the correct position. Traditionally, imagery used to be done lying down but if you were to be imagining driving a car, for example, it would be easier if you were sitting in a car with your hands on the steering wheel. The use of equipment such as rackets, bats and balls is common in PETTLEP imagery. The *environment* refers to where imagery takes place. If possible, it is best to have this in the same place where the performance occurs. The *task* means that it must be identical to the real task. If you are a full back in football, it is no use imagining taking on ten players and scoring. Instead, you should imagine closing down an opponent and winning the ball.

Key idea: PETTLEP imagery

A checklist of elements to ensure effective imagery use.

Timing is very important and elicits a common mistake when people begin using imagery. The imagined experience should be the same, and therefore take the same amount of time as the real experience. So if you are imagining performing a three-minute gymnastics floor routine, the imagery should last this length of time. *Learning* refers to the current ability of the athlete. Typically, performance will improve as we learn. As such, the imagery content should change to meet these. For example, at early stages of learning we are often focused on basic technical instructions, such as keeping an eye on the ball. At an expert level, the eye focuses on teammates or opponents as we search for space. *Emotion* should reflect how a performer feels during the skill. This is often an opportunity to include some positive phrases. *Perspective* refers to whether the imagery is performed from an internal or external perspective.

Case study: Gain without the pain

Wright & Smith (2009) were interested in examining the effects of PETTLEP imagery compared to traditional imagery and physical practice. To do so, they took 50 sport science students and measured their one repetition max (1RM) on a bicep curl machine. This means, identifying the maximum weight that a person can curl just once. After the initial test, all participants were placed in one of five groups.

The first group was a physical practice group. These people trained twice a week, performing two sets of 6–10 reps for six weeks on the bicep curl machine. The second group was a traditional imagery group, who practised imagery at home for the equivalent time. The third group was a PETTLEP imagery group, who practised PETTLEP imagery at the machine twice a week but never actually lifted the weight. The fourth group conducted half of the repetitions and imagined doing the other half at the machine (PETTLEP). The final group was the control group and was given a biography on Arnold Schwarzenegger to read.

At the end of the six weeks, the physical practice group improved its performance by 26.56 per cent; the traditional imagery group improved by just 13.75 per cent and the control group improved by 5.12 per cent. The PETTLEP group improved its performance by a staggering 23.29 per cent, despite never actually lifting a weight during this time. The combined physical practice and PETTLEP group improved its performance by 28.03 per cent. With results like that, it is impossible to ignore the effects that well-conducted imagery can have on performance.

Goal setting

You probably already use goal setting. We all use goal setting in one form or another. If you make 'to do' lists, or ponder your upcoming day over breakfast, or talk about the future, you are setting goals. Much of this is probably very informal and not recorded, but it is natural to do it. We all want things, whether it is a new skill, a holiday, material goods, or a particular job. Once we identify that we want something, we have set a goal. What do we do next? We identify ways of achieving said goal by identifying smaller goals along the way. Here, we will look at how we can formalize this process a bit more to ensure that we keep making strides towards achieving the things that we want to achieve.

If you have ever done anything related to goal setting, here is an acronym that you will undoubtedly be familiar with: SMART. Depending on who you listen to or read will depend on what you consider SMART stands for. It is a simple guide that provides criteria for setting goals, targets or objectives. Most commonly, SMART stands for the following:

Specific   Targeting a specific area for improvement
Measureable   Can be quantified as an indicator of success
Achievable   Can realistically be attained
Relevant   Make a useful and notable impact
Time-bound   Identify when the results can be achieved

As stated, you may well have come across variations of this model. Specific and measureable tend to stay the same, as does time-bound (allowing for some changes in phrasing such as 'time-phased' or 'timely'). The 'A' in the SMART model is sometimes referred to as 'agreed', 'attainable', 'actionable', 'ambitious' or, as was originally proposed by George Doran (1981), 'assignable'. The 'R' can be 'results-based', 'reasonable' or, quite often, 'realistic'. I guess it fits well as 'realistic' as long as 'A' does not stand for 'achievable' or 'attainable', as it would not be sufficiently distinct. For all intents and purposes, it doesn't really matter exactly what the SMART acronym stands for and it doesn't matter that there are small differences in interpretation. The important thing is that practitioners are guided by some sort of criteria to ensure the quality of goals set.

From experience, I would offer some advice to perhaps muddy the waters a little here. The measureable element can be more flexible than you might at first think. For example, in sport psychology it is common that we may want to assess the extent to which the performer felt that a certain technique that we had taught them was effective or not. A goal could be set here to improve the skills of this technique. To do so, we need to identify a measure to satisfactorily note progress towards the goal and know when it has been achieved. We can therefore make this measurable by providing some sort of subjective judgement from the athlete. They might rate the extent to which they felt that the new technique was effective in their latest performance and we take a three-game average for example.

TYPES OF GOAL

Some goals that we set are very outcome based. For example, let's assume that we are working with an Olympic athlete. What is their main goal likely to be? To win an Olympic gold medal. That is a perfectly appropriate goal for an Olympian. This is what we call an outcome goal because it focuses entirely on the final outcome. While this is great because it recognizes a clear ambition, it has some potential stumbling blocks as well. Mainly, that is because it is norm-referenced, it is not under control of the individual. To explain this further, by norm-referenced I mean that the success of the goal is based on comparing performance to a norm group (i.e., other athletes). The problem here is that we are not in control of what other athletes do and therefore do not know what standard is required to achieve our goal. This makes training towards this very difficult.

To highlight this, consider the 1996 200m men's Olympic sprint final in Atlanta, Georgia. Before the final, the world record stood at 19.66 seconds, having been broken from 19.72 seconds two months earlier. Frankie Fredericks of Namibia stormed to the finish line in 19.68 seconds – an incredible time. The only problem for Fredericks was that Michael Johnson of the United States had crossed the line way ahead of him in 19.32 seconds. So when we are training, we tend to focus on more self-referenced goals.

Key idea: Norm- and self-referenced

Norm-referenced comparisons refer to an external source; self-referenced comparisons are internal.

Self-referenced goals come in two forms: performance goals and process goals (Kingston & Hardy, 1994, 1997). Performance goals are typically concerned with numerical measures of performance. For example, rather than aiming to win a race, which is in part determined by the performances of other competitors, a performance goal might be to identify a particular time, such as a personal best, or a time that the coach believes will be good enough to achieve an outcome goal. The advantage of this is that it is under the control of the individual. This can reduce anxiety, because we only need to focus on our own performance and not worry about how others will perform. As more numerical measures of performance become evident, the opportunity to set performance goals increases. Setting performance goals is helpful because it is possible to continuously monitor progress in training and they can be very clear. The danger is that it can only assure relative success because an opponent can always exceed everyone's expectations.

Key idea: Performance goals

Numerical, self-referenced targets related to effective performance.

The main difficulty with performance goals is the selection of the numerical measure of performance. For example, many team sports include an enormous amount of statistics. Some sports are entirely governed by statistics. For example, in baseball there is a plethora of statistics to judge the quality of an individual player. This includes batting average, gross production average, base runs and slugging average to name only a few. This seems to work quite well because analysts can be confident that the data in baseball is a good representation of performance and a likely predictor of success. In some sports, though, few statistics appear to accurately predict the outcome. A case in point is football.

We always see statistics that are somehow used as key performance indicators. The most common one is possession. We could easily say that we want to achieve a certain percentage of possession in a match or over a season. This would represent a performance goal. But the thing is, in the 2013/14 Premier League season, the team with the most possession only won 55 per cent of matches. If possession were such an important indicator of success, this statistic would be much higher. Even more misleading is the number of corners. Crowds often get excited when their team gets a corner. This is despite the correlation between corners gained and goals scored ranging between less than 0.01 in Italy's Serie A and Spain's La

Liga and 0.06 in the Premier League. Essentially, this means that the chances of scoring because a team win a corner have increased by practically zero. I don't want to go into too many match statistics here – other books do that very well – but the point is that while performance goals can be very useful, it is important that the numerical measure of performance is a worthwhile one.

> 'Set your goals high and don't stop until you get there.'
> Bo Jackson, American football and baseball player

The final type of self-referenced goal is a process goal. Here, we concern ourselves with the processes that generate the performance, which in turn generate the outcome. Process goals are normally rooted in technique or strategy. For example, a tennis player may think about wrist rotation in order to create sufficient top spin, or movement close to the baseline to dictate a rally. We don't want performers thinking about every small technical detail during a movement though; that would result in a more jerky and uncoordinated movement. Rather, we use process goals holistically. Often, cue words are used that the performer associates with a technical part of the movement. For example, a golfer may use the holistic cue word 'push' to trigger the muscle memory for gently transferring weight into the club head and ball. To remember to use the hips to generate greater rotation in a movement, an off-spinner in cricket may use the holistic cue word 'whip'. These are just examples, but you can probably think of several that relate to appropriate movements in your preferred sports.

Egotistical little people

People with high egos love outcome goals, which can be a problem because of the lack of control. Some of the most egotistical people are children. Children's goals often include wanting to score more than friends, win a trophy for something or score the winner. For children, seeing the effects of other people is a very difficult task.

Various research has supported the use of different types of goal. Burton (1992) claimed that because sport is socially competitive, it naturally led to outcome goals. This is difficult to argue with and certainly we would expect to find that performers naturally set outcome goals. Jones & Hanton (1996) argued that performance goals are preferable, however, because the self-referenced nature of them allows for a greater degree of control and, therefore, reduced anxiety. Kingston & Hardy (1997), among others, have promoted the use of process goals because of the highest levels of control. It is generally accepted, as Weinberg, Butt, Knight & Perritt (2001) suggest, that a hierarchy of goals works best. As such, when working with a performer, consider how you can integrate process, performance and outcome goals.

Key idea: Process goals

Self-referenced, holistic goals referring to an individual understanding of technique or strategy.

PRACTICALITIES IN GOAL SETTING

Think about goals in time phases. It is normal to include short-term, medium-term and long-term goals. You might find it easier to work backwards though. Think about what your dream goal would be. Now consider what you could achieve this year, this month, this week, today... Once you have done this look at it – do you have a hierarchy of goals in there? There should be some process, performance and outcome goals. Now think about whether they are SMART goals and, if not, consider how you could reword them so they are. It may also be worth thinking about how you could prioritize your goals.

So you take your time and come up with a goal-setting programme that has been carefully considered. But the problem is, nothing ever goes entirely according to plan does it? So before we plough on full of enthusiasm and vigour, stop to think of any contingencies that we might need. Inevitably, things will go wrong from time to time. Perhaps a missed goal through a bad decision, an off performance, luck, injury or illness. For each goal, consider how you could adjust this goal if necessary and, if so, is the next goal still achievable?

This is very important because we know that if someone has a set goal that they are not progressing towards, they are likely to experience stress. What is required here is known as **goal adjustment**. Goal adjustment requires the individual to constantly monitor and change goals to maintain motivation towards achieving them. Sometimes it is necessary to scrap a goal altogether and set a new one. People who are good at this tend to maintain focus and cope better with anxiety. This is a very new area to sport psychology, but studies in health (e.g., Wrosch, Amir & Miller, 2011; Wrosch, Scheier & Miller, 2013) have demonstrated greater wellbeing and physical health in people who adjust their goals better.

Key idea: Goal adjustment

Refining set goals in order to maintain relevance, motivation and wellbeing.

Dig deeper

Afremow, J. (2015), *The Champion's Mind: How Great Athletes Think, Train, and Thrive.* Emmaus, PA: Rodale Books.

Blumenstein, B. & Weinstein, Y. (2010), *Psychological Skills Training: Application to Elite Sports Performance.* Michigan, MI: Ultimate Athlete Concepts.

Karageorghis, C. & Terry, P. (2010), *Inside Sport Psychology.* Champaign, IL: Human Kinetics.

Morris, T., Spittle, M. & Watt, A. P. (2005), *Imagery in Sport: The Mental Approach to Sport.* Champaign, IL: Human Kinetics.

Weinberg, R. S. & Gould, D. (2014), *Foundations of Sport and Exercise Psychology* (6th ed.). Champaign, IL: Human Kinetics.

Fact check

1 The three stages of PST are education, acquisition, and what?
- **a** implementation
- **b** practice
- **c** action
- **d** challenge

2 CS imagery normally focuses on...?
- **a** skills
- **b** strategy
- **c** goal-oriented responses
- **d** mastery

3 MS imagery normally focuses on...?
- **a** skills
- **b** arousal
- **c** goal-oriented responses
- **d** mastery

4 Which of the following imagery theories suggests that memory recalls images and patterns?
- **a** self-efficacy
- **b** functional equivalence
- **c** dual code
- **d** psychoneuromuscular

5 Identical central nervous system recruitment patterns between imagined and real experience forms which theory?
- **a** psychoneuromuscular
- **b** attention-arousal
- **c** dual code
- **d** functional equivalence

6 PETTLEP imagery takes place...?
- **a** in an office
- **b** on a couch
- **c** in the sporting environment
- **d** anywhere

7 Which type of goal is norm-referenced?
   a process
   b performance
   c outcome
   d all of the above

8 Which of these goals are usually holistic?
   a process
   b performance
   c outcome
   d all of the above

9 Goal adjustment is...?
   a good for wellbeing
   b bad for wellbeing
   c an easy way out
   d ill-advised

10 How is imagery different from visualization?
   a it isn't
   b it uses all of the senses
   c it is written down
   d it focuses on just one sense

12

Concentration

In this chapter you will learn:

- ▶ *that we don't 'lose' concentration*
- ▶ *how we use attentional resource*
- ▶ *about positive and negative self-talk*
- ▶ *how to control distractions*
- ▶ *how to develop a focus plan*
- ▶ *what flow is*
- ▶ *how to enhance the number of flow experiences*

Scenario

Olivia is a young footballer who is a second-year professional. She is on the fringes of the first team, often making the match-day squad as a substitute and performing well in the reserves. She is eager to improve so she talks to the first team coach to ask how he thinks she can develop.

The coach tells Olivia that she needs to make more of an impact in the game. She appears to fade out of games at times and loses that intensity required to perform well for longer periods in a match, and more often.

She agrees with this and says that at times she switches off when not involved in the game and it passes her by for a while.

Here's a common phrase: 'lost concentration'. Rather than viewing concentration as something that we have an amount of (or none of), we should consider it to be something that we always have, but it is not necessarily directed where we would like it to be. Instead of losing concentration we just concentrate on the wrong thing – we become distracted.

Think of concentration as a spotlight that is always on. Sometimes this spotlight is exactly where it should be, which is great. Sometimes, though, it drifts to something less helpful... or even harmful. For example, if preparing to return a serve in tennis, it is helpful for our spotlight to be focused on the ball. It is unhelpful to be focused on the crowd, or on our own level of fatigue. This spotlight might be very narrow and focused intently on the ball, to the point where everything else is in darkness. Alternatively, it could be very broad, with its light shared among a whole host of relevant and irrelevant things. As well as the breadth of our spotlight, its focus can be internal or external. So far, examples such as the ball, the opponent or the crowd are all external. Our perceived level of fatigue would be an internal focus. Other internal things we focus on include thoughts, which can often be distractions. When the spotlight is internal, it could be on positive thoughts but it could also be on negative ones. Both have the potential to be distractions. It is also useful to imagine a timeline that our light moves between – the past, present and future. Of course, it is best when it is focused on the present.

Key idea: Concentration

Selective attention that maintains focus and awareness of the situation, shifting attention when necessary to avoid performance errors.

In our scenario, Olivia doesn't actually switch off, she just allows her spotlight to drift either to the wrong thing, or it becomes too broad, which is creating a loss of intensity and the game passes her by.

Is concentration becoming harder?

British comedian Dave Gorman's recent book, *Too Much Information*, explains that in writing a book, the computer is the workstation. This also contains the internet, or, access to almost all of the information in the world. How can you not get distracted? With a wealth of information available to people now, including digital technologies with secondary functions, the idea of intense concentration on a single stimulus could become very rare.

The fields of concentration here, in terms of both broad/narrow and internal/external, was explained by Nideffer (1976, 1981; Nideffer & Segal, 2001). Nideffer referred to this as **attentional focus**. In short, it is the width and direction of our attention. A broad attentional focus is like pulling the spotlight back to have a wide view. This takes in lots of information. A broad internal focus could be on an individual's overall game plan, whereas a broad external focus will likely be on using a wide range of visual cues, which might be to seek out a teammate in space to pass to. A narrow focus is when we turn the spotlight into a powerful thin beam on few objects or thoughts. A narrow internal focus is normally zoning in on one thought, such as using self-talk to mentally prepare. A narrow external focus is on an object, such as a target.

A skilled performer is able to switch attentional focus. Olivia has not sufficiently developed this skill. She needs some internal things to focus on, some specific cues to attend to, and to be aware of when her spotlight is drifting out of her control.

> 'Concentration is a fine antidote to anxiety.'
> Jack Nicklaus, US golfer, winner of 18 Major titles

Attentional resource

There is only so much attention that we can hold at one time. Think of the mind being like a pie here. If you start thinking about incidents in the past, the future, irrelevant topics, things that you cannot do anything about, or start doubting yourself, each of these thoughts takes up part of the pie, leaving less room for attention on the stuff that matters.

Key idea: Attentional resource

The limited capacity to direct attention to several things at once.

That sounds easy enough – we rid the mind of unwanted thoughts and have lots of room left over to focus on relevant cues. There are some difficulties with this though. First, competitive sport includes much disguise and deception. An opponent will deliberately withhold information or present incorrect information about what they are going to do to ensure that the thing you are concentrating on is actually irrelevant. Second, as we identified very early in this book, sport induces stress. When we become stressed, this not only takes up a significant portion of our attentional resource, it creates what we call **attentional narrowing**. This means that our focus becomes much narrower because we attempt to block out the stress. In doing so, we can also block out some relevant cues.

Case study: (Un)welcome distraction?

There are minor distractions and real distractions, right? To explore this further, let's consider a two-part study from Buodo, Sarlo & Palomba (2002). In the first study, they recruited 53 volunteers, who were left in front of a computer screen and randomly shown images of a threat (guns, knives, attacks), sport (used as pleasure items) and household objects (neutral). At random intervals, a sound was played and participants were required to press the space bar. Their reaction time to this demonstrates how distracted they are by the image. The more distracted they are, the longer it would take them to react.

At first, there was no measurable difference in reaction time, but as the pictures went on (there were 32 images shown), reaction time decreased for threat. This is probably because we are evolutionarily advantaged by spotting threats quicker. In the second study, a further 54 volunteers were selected to view 48 images, but this time the images were of two unpleasant scene categories (threats and blood/mutilated bodies), two pleasant scene categories (sport and nude couples having sex) and neutral (household objects). To make reaction time choice-based, this time there were two tones (high and low) with corresponding keys to press.

The results were much more striking than for the first study. Little difference existed between the sport and threat images, even though they represented pleasant and unpleasant scenes, but reaction time was significantly slower for sex and blood images. One explanation for this is the emotional response is much greater and therefore the distraction is also greater. So if you really want to distract someone, get them either aroused or disgusted.

The key is to recognize when distraction occurs. It is inevitable that at times all performers will become distracted, or concentration will be too broad or too narrow. The more aware the performer is of this, the quicker they can recognize it and change it. A very simple but useful exercise is to make a list of helpful and harmful focuses. Helpful focuses are those things that the athlete attends to that are beneficial for performance. This could be an external object or an internal thought. Anything that is not helpful is considered as harmful because, even if it does not directly negatively affective performance, it takes up attentional resources, which makes our spotlight less bright.

Positive self-talk

This sounds like common sense. If you talk more positively to yourself you become more immersed in positive feelings, enhance your confidence and perform better. If you talk negatively to yourself, the opposite happens. So why do so many performers use negative self-talk more than positive self-talk? Van Raalte, Cornelius, Brewer & Hatten (2000) recorded the self-talk of 18 tennis players and found that negative self-talk was demonstrated at least six times in a match by 94 per cent of players. This was almost nine times more frequently than positive self-talk.

> 'If you hear a voice within you saying "You are not a painter", then by all means paint and that voice will be silenced.'
> Vincent van Gogh, Dutch artist

Short, memorable and repeated phrases are very effective for improving concentration and staying positive. To go back to our scenario, let's assume that Olivia just missed an opportunity to score. Consider the emotional consequence of the phrase 'I can't believe I messed that up' compared to 'be lively, there are chances here'. Both of these are options for Olivia. The difference is that the former is negative and based in the past. The latter is positive, filled with optimism, and based in the present. The emotion that will follow the first phrase is likely to be regret, anger or frustration. This will impact concentration and have physiological impacts on muscle tension and, ultimately, behavioural impacts on performance. The second phrase is designed to strengthen focus and elicit feelings of excitement and relaxation.

Key idea: Positive self-talk

Short, memorable and positively worded phrases used by the individual to maintain or regain concentration, intensity or self-belief.

In practice it is good to develop several self-talk phrases. These should be personalized to the athlete. As such, it is good to let the performer come up with some key words. Perhaps a reflective interview to describe their best-ever performances is a good way to do this naturally. Use the vocabulary from the responses. It is sometimes possible to develop a mnemonic to make sure this is memorable. For example, imagine that you are talking with Olivia and she uses the word 'smashed' a lot when describing good performances. A host of short, positive phrases rooted in the present could be developed using the letters of this cue word. For example, the following could be a negotiated mnemonic.

Stay lively
Meet the ball
Aerial winners
Second ball's mine
Head in the game
Each pass matters
Deliver quality

The majority of self-talk takes place in silence. Although people do express both positive and negative phrases out loud, this is likely a fraction of the conversation happening inside their head. We know that positive self-talk can lead to better self-concept, confidence, less doubt, less anxiety and greater concentration… but it is a skill. It is not as simple as just doing it, it must be learned.

Based on a large sample of Greek athletes, Zourbanos, Hatzigeorgiadis, Chroni, Theodorakis & Papaioannou (2009) identified eight categories of self-talk. These were:

▶ psyching up (e.g., 'let's go')

▶ confidence ('I can do this')

- instruction ('bend knees and get low')
- anxiety control ('relax')
- worry ('I'm not good enough')
- disengagement ('I give up')
- somatic fatigue ('I'm tired')
- irrelevant thoughts ('I'm hungry').

These are typical of thoughts during a performance. The key is to focus on the positive ones but be aware of the negative ones so they can be recognized and stopped quickly. A good way of being aware of self-talk is to use a reflective log after performance to note the self-talk that occurred.

Controlled distraction

There are all sorts of numbers thrown around about how long an individual can concentrate for. Seven minutes, 20 minutes, an hour… Whichever you buy into, the one common thing researchers agree on is that distraction is inevitable. Once we accept that we will all get distracted at some point, the next step is to think about how we can control this distraction.

To be able to control distraction it is necessary to have a pre-performance routine. Essentially, this is a way of intentionally increasing intensity and focus as appropriate. This is particularly important in intermittent sports, such as cricket. When batting in cricket, it is possible to bat for a two-hour session (sometimes longer) before having a sustained break. There is no way that a performer can maintain intense concentration for such a period. Instead, they will likely use pre-performance routines to get into the zone for short periods, such as an over, or even just one ball.

Key idea: Controlled distraction

Intentionally shifting attention to an alternative stimuli in order to restart a pre-performance routine.

To control distraction requires letting yourself become distracted when it is ok to do so. So when a cricketer is between overs, they can adopt a broad attentional focus, or even a narrow one on something completely different. This allows them to release intense concentration. When taking their mark to face the next ball, they will often go through a routine of feeling the bat with their hands or the ground with their feet, using a breathing technique, or using self-talk. This is to redirect concentration towards the very narrow external focus that is the ball.

Thought stopping and focus plans

Thoughts are internal and therefore, to a greater or lesser extent, controllable at some level. If a performer has made a list of helpful and harmful focuses, some of these will be specific thoughts. Another way of obtaining such information is to go through a process of thinking out loud. In thinking out loud, an athlete verbalizes thoughts as they encounter them. This is much easier to do in self-paced activities, such as golf. Other sports might require this to be done reflectively after the event.

Once a list of unhelpful thoughts are identified, the performer is now aware of them and can recognize when these thoughts appear. Once recognized, they must then be stopped. Thought stopping is a way of imagining a visual cue to remove a thought. This is often a large stop sign.

The magic little red dot

A famous example of thought stopping is from South African golfer Louis Oosthuizen, who was the surprise winner of the 2010 Open. Oosthuizen did not set an objective of winning The Open that week, but to follow his pre-shot routine perfectly and execute each shot. He had identified that concentration was a key area that he could develop. As such, he drew a red dot on to his golf glove. The red dot became a symbol for stopping thoughts and moving into the pre-shot routine. It worked, and he won the championship.

Often, the key to effective psychological performance is to actually think very little. To reach an elite level of performance, technical skills and decision-making have been over-learned to the point where they happen automatically. As such, our thoughts are largely governed by emotions and are less rational than simply allowing our trained behaviour to take over. It is for this reason why thought stopping is effective. It is a form of cognitive inhibition. This means stopping thoughts permeating and lingering. It is a very useful skill.

Key idea: Cognitive inhibition

The mind's ability to tune out irrelevant stimuli.

So how can we help Olivia? For those who struggle with visual cues, a physical action can be incorporated into thought stopping. For example, in football the ball is actually only in play for around 60 of the 90 minutes. This means a lot of short breaks in play. These are all opportunities to improve psychological performance. Olivia could use thought stopping here and by including a physical action, such as adjusting her shin pad, she is removing himself from all current conditions, taking an opportunity to relax and use self-talk, and then re-entering the match mentally ready to go – all in the space of a few seconds.

Key idea: Thought stopping

Using simple imagery or physical cues to attend to a neutral stimulus and therefore stop current cognitive processes.

The addition of self-talk means that we have implemented more than just thought stopping. We might call this a focus plan. It is difficult to simply change a negative thought into a positive one, but by removing the thought, we are in a neutral position. We can then attend to positive self-talk more fully, as we have our whole attentional resource to devote to this. Other options for the middle part of a focus plan include **centring**, which involves focusing all energy towards the navel while exhaling, and grounding. **Grounding** is used by feeling the ground beneath as a reminder of being in the present. This stimulus is neither positive nor negative, it is simply a way of bringing the spotlight into the present.

Flow

Think about your best-ever performance. A time when everything you tried worked. You seemed to have loads of time, yet time flew by. Everything seemed so easy and you were never in any doubt. You were absolutely 'in the zone', but you didn't really think about it. This optimal performance state is what we are chasing. We cannot do it every time, of course, but we can work hard to put everything in place to maximize how often these states are experienced. This state is known as **flow**.

> 'I just kept going. Suddenly I was nearly two seconds faster than anybody else, including my teammate with the same car. And suddenly I realized that I was no longer driving the car consciously. I was driving it by a kind of instinct, only I was in a different dimension. It was like I was in a tunnel.'
>
> Ayrton Senna, Brazilian Formula 1 world champion

Flow was popularized by leading positive psychology researcher Mihaly Csíkszentmihályi (1990). In sport, Jackson & Csíkszentmihályi (1999) identified ten essential elements for achieving a flow state. These are presented below:

Table 12.1 Essential flow elements in sport

Flow element	Meaning
Challenge-skill balance	High perceived ability but also pushed to perform to maximum
Complete absorption	Nothing else matters
Clear goals and feedback	Knowing exactly what is required and what to do to achieve it
Merging of action and awareness	Awareness of actions but not of the awareness itself
Total concentration on task at hand	Absolute and intense focus
Loss of ego and self-consciousness	Forget who you are and what it means
Paradox of control	A feeling of total control without trying to control
Complete intrinsic motivation (autotelic)	External rewards or consequences are entirely insignificant
Transformation of time	Time speeds up or slows down
Effortless movement	Performance seems easy

The most significant element to take note of is the balance between challenge and skill. Low challenge and low skill leads to apathy and withdrawal. High challenge but low skill creates anxiety. High skill but low challenge generates boredom and complacency, but high levels of perceived skill and a difficult challenge bring out the best in people. Complete absorption is when performing in the moment is the only thing that seems to matter. Players sometimes report having personal problems or injuries that they simply forgot about during performance. This is an example of complete absorption.

Key idea: Flow

A mental state in which the individual is entirely immersed in the activity and performing optimally.

To experience flow, a lack of thinking is required. As such, there can be no room for ambiguity. Clear goals and feedback encourage this. This forms part of what is sometimes referred to as an autotelic experience. This experience is conducted for its own sake and considerations of the self and efforts to control outcomes are non-existent. Or at least, these kind of considerations are not consciously existent. The transformation of time and effortless movement creates an autopilot type experience, where performers cannot often explain what they did, how they did it, or how long it took, but they are aware of enjoying the experience.

Flow comes, flow goes

Golf is one of the most frustrating sports in terms of flow. A typical round lasts about four hours with lots of thinking time. This makes flow really difficult to maintain. There are lots of examples but I'll point to one from Ryder Cup star Ian Poulter in the 2014 China Open. On his second round he was in the zone – six-under par after 11 holes. We've seen him get into flow states before at the Ryder Cup. This time, though, he made an error on the 12th to double-bogey. On the next hole, he drove into the trees, took a drop but did so illegally and received a two-shot penalty. He ended up with a triple-bogey and his round had gone from a brilliant five under after 11 to par after 13.

Poulter's other three rounds were good and he finished tied for fifth in the tournament, but it goes to show how flow is great, but don't count on it lasting.

Flow is a fickle beast, though. Someone can be in the zone, experiencing flow, but when they stop and reflect on the fact that they are having such an experience, it is no longer subconscious and no longer flow. Imagine playing tennis. You are playing brilliantly, leading the first set 4–1 at the change of ends and you have a moment to sit and reflect on how well you are playing. By doing so, that experience ends and a new one begins. You strive to try to get it back but you are now trying too hard to force flow. Stoppages in play can be great when playing poorly, but really disrupt flow. This is why football managers sometimes make substitutions in the last minute. Not because they think the substitute will influence the match, but because it will disrupt the flow for the other team.

Dig deeper

Bailey, R. & Browne, E. (2015), *Improving Concentration: A Professional Resource for Assessing and Improving Concentration and Performance.* London: Speechmark Publishing.

Csíkszentmihályi, M. (2008), *Flow: The Psychology of Optimal Experience.* New York: Harper Perennial.

Jackson, S. & Csíkszentmihályi, M. (1999), *Flow in Sports.* Champaign, IL: Human Kinetics.

Kahneman, D. (2012), *Thinking, Fast and Slow.* London: Penguin Books.

Moran, A. P. (1996), *The Psychology of Concentration in Sport Performers: A Cognitive Analysis.* Abingdon: Psychology Press.

Fact check

1 Focusing on an object, such as a target or ball is an example of...?

   a   a broad, internal focus

   b   a broad, external focus

   c   a narrow, internal focus

   d   a narrow, external focus

2 Focusing on the run of a teammate to pass to is an example of...?

   a   a broad, internal focus

   b   a broad, external focus

   c   a narrow, internal focus

   d   a narrow, external focus

3 Focusing on a game plan is an example of...?

   a   a broad, internal focus

   b   a broad, external focus

   c   a narrow, internal focus

   d   a narrow, external focus

4 Focusing on breathing and emotional control is an example of...?

   a   a broad, internal focus

   b   a broad, external focus

   c   a narrow, internal focus

   d   a narrow, external focus

5 The amount that we are capable of concentrating is known as...?

   a   attentional resource

   b   attentional focus

   c   concentration avoidance

   d   distraction

6 'Bend knees' is an example of which type of self-talk?

   a   irrelevant

   b   anxiety control

   c   instruction

   d   psyching up

7 To experience flow...?

    a challenge must be high but perceived skill low

    b challenge must be low but perceived skill high

    c challenge and perceived skill must be low

    d challenge and perceived skill must be high

8 During flow, what appears to happen to time?

    a it speeds up

    b it slows down

    c nothing

    d it can speed up or slow down

9 How is control an element of flow?

    a There is a feeling of no control or attempt to

    b There is a feeling of total control without trying to control

    c Efforts are made to ensure complete and total control

    d There is no control in flow

10 What is cognitive inhibition?

    a Not being able to think of something

    b The mind's ability to focus on relevant stimuli

    c The mind's ability to tune out irrelevant stimuli

    d Difficulty in remembering

Coping techniques

In this chapter you will learn:

▶ *methods people use to cope with stress*

▶ *the best way to cope with stress*

▶ *how to tackle stressors rather than hide from them*

▶ *how to use social support*

▶ *how to teach coping strategies*

▶ *about relaxation methods*

Scenario

Annette is a professional tennis player on the tour. She has made good progress so far and is ranked at a career high of 80 in the world. She is now competing regularly against the top players in the world. She knows that this is the stage of her career that will dictate whether she breaks into the world's elite or not.

In her last tournament, she was performing well and made it through to the third round and had been serving particularly well. However, when she was facing a match point in the final set she served a double-fault and therefore lost the match.

She met up with a sport psychologist she occasionally works with the following week to discuss how to improve her performance in big matches.

When asked what she did in training the day after her defeat, she laughed ironically and said: 'I practised my serve of course!'

The thing is, Annette didn't lose the match because of her serving ability. She had served well all tournament until that point. She lost the match because she was unable to cope with the pressure she was experiencing. The next day, she should have been practising how to better cope with pressure. In this chapter, we will discuss some of the ways she could do this.

Coping has been defined as:

'Constantly changing cognitive and behavioural efforts to manage specific external and/or internal demands that are appraised as taxing or exceeding the resources of a person.'
Lazarus & Folkman (1984), p. 141

Coping strategies can range in type and effectiveness. In terms of types of coping strategies, we generally understand most forms of coping to fall into problem-focused, emotion-focused or avoidance-focused coping.

PROBLEM-FOCUSED COPING

Problem-focused coping refers to attempts to cope with stress by managing or adjusting the stressor. In effect, we are trying to change the thing that is causing stress. Problem-focused coping is most effective in controllable situations. This means when we are able to affect the stressor. Examples include strategies like planning, information seeking, goal setting, time management and problem-solving. All of these are ways of managing the stressor. For example, if being rushed or late is a stressor, managing time better is a very obvious coping strategy. Seeking more information and planning can help to alleviate fears about an upcoming tournament or opposition. If we feel like we are entering known territory, we tend to be more comfortable. Sometimes, however, we cannot control the stressor. In these situations, we are better off employing emotion-focused coping.

Key idea: Problem-focused coping

Attempts to cope by managing or adjusting the stressor.

EMOTION-FOCUSED COPING

When we cannot manage or change the thing that is causing stress, we consider how we can better regulate our internal states to cope with it. Common emotion-focused coping strategies include relaxation, acceptance, meditation, wishful thinking and cognitive efforts to change the meaning of the stressor. Relaxation is an obvious method and one that we will consider in a little more depth later in this chapter. It doesn't make the stressor go away, it simply makes you feel better about it. By changing the meaning, I am referring to what researchers call **centrality**. If the stressor is considered as something that is extremely important, it is central to our perception of success and therefore creates vulnerability. We become protective over things that are more important to us. By changing the meaning, we normally try to add some perspective. While it may seem like something that is incredibly important, this is probably an exaggerated view.

Key idea: Emotion-focused coping

Attempts to cope by managing internal states.

AVOIDANCE-FOCUSED COPING

We can all identify with this coping method at times. We sometimes call it the 'ostrich impression', which refers to how an ostrich buries its head in the sand. When faced with a stressor, one response is to ignore it. This is because we strive for immediate gratification and an easy option. By avoiding an issue, we can immediately feel better because we focus on something that makes us feel happier instead. The problem is, it doesn't normally go away. There are two types of avoidance coping: **cognitive avoidance** and **behavioural avoidance**. Cognitive avoidance is sometimes called blocking and is exactly how it sounds – blocking out unwelcome thoughts. Behavioural avoidance refers to physically removing ourselves from a situation or not going in the first place.

Key idea: Avoidance-focused coping

Cognitively and behaviourally distancing oneself from a stressor by ignoring or blocking it.

CONTROL THE CONTROLLABLES

Imagine that you have an important exam coming up. Which type of coping strategy could you use? You could employ avoidance-focused coping. Cognitive avoidance would mean not thinking about it. Perhaps do something else instead to distract yourself. Behavioural avoidance could mean not attending the exam. You would avoid those feelings of nerves, though neither of these options are likely to ultimately lead to the ideal outcome.

Remember that we said that problem-focused coping is more effective in controllable situations and that emotion-focused coping is more effective in uncontrollable situations. Whether this is controllable depends on how we identify what the stressor is. If we believe that the stressor is the exam, then it is uncontrollable. However, it is unlikely that the fact an exam is taking place is the real stressor. I would suggest that in this situation the stressor is that an exam is taking place that you have deemed success in as being of significance to you personally. Success in the exam is a controllable stressor because much of it is dependent on preparation. Preparation then would be a problem-focused approach to coping.

> 'It's not stress that kills us, it is our reaction to it.'
> Hans Selye, psychologist

Now imagine that it gets to the morning of the exam. There is little that is controllable about this now, since extra preparation is likely to be futile. At this point, emotion-focused coping would be best employed. Largely, this refers to efforts to stay relaxed and remain positive.

Some of the methods used by sport psychologists include:

▶ conditioned practice

▶ mapping current coping

▶ relaxation

▶ social support

I'll get to it, but I must do this first...

Distraction coping techniques can be very useful, particularly if trying to avoid stress in incontrollable situations. For example, if an upcoming task such as a match, a test or an evaluation were impending, distraction can be an effective method to reduce anxiety. The key is to know when distraction is being used as a genuine coping strategy or as avoidance.

Conditioned practice

The purpose of practice is to prepare for competition. In doing so, we perform the same actions required in competition many times to hone our skill. It makes sense, then, that the skills we practise in training are the same skills that we need to be successful in competition. But the thing is, we often don't practise the same skills in training. Often, we practise the same skill, minus pressure.

Case study: Banter

'Banter' must be the most overused phrase of the past few years. Sports performers, especially those in team sports, love it. There is limited research on banter itself, but there is a significant amount on playfulness. This is predominantly in children but Magnuson & Barnett (2013) tested university students aged 18–27. They examined how playful participants were through a questionnaire requiring them to respond to personality characteristics such as 'spontaneous', 'energetic' and 'clowns around'. Also through a questionnaire, the researchers measured perceived stress and coping styles.

Their results found that the least playful reported significantly higher levels of perceived stress than their more playful counterparts. The low playfulness group also demonstrated less adaptive/effective coping strategies (e.g., active coping, positive reframing, humour, emotional support) than the more playful students.

There is limited research around playfulness in adult sport, but perhaps this is one of the reasons why sports performers so regularly cite banter as being so important – it reduces stress.

I once observed a golfer practising his short putts. He was frustrated because he had missed several short putts in competition. I watched him expertly roll balls into the hole from 6 feet, one after another from his bucket of 50 balls. He was dumbfounded as to why he missed them on a proper round. I said that he should try taking 49 of the balls away. What he was practising was the technical requirements of putting without any psychological requirements. It was entirely inconsequential. It mattered not a jot if the balls went in or not. By using only one ball, we immediately transformed this practice into one that had a preparation and reflection stage either side of the actual putt. This, I believe, is more like the skill that he wants to improve. He wouldn't putt a ball without lining it up on a round so why do it in practise? When you miss a short putt, you take a moment to experience the annoyance and reflect on what went wrong. Our golfer was also removing this from practice.

This golf example is very simple. There are many ways that we can condition practice to induce pressure. A boxer or tennis player might consider how to take charge and dominate in training rather than focus on technique. The best performers enjoy competitive arenas and have an aura about them. For some it comes naturally, but you can train yourself. You can condition your practice to better train those psychological attributes that you wish to develop.

Mapping current coping

A useful way to gain insight into times of anxiety for an individual and into existing coping mechanisms is to perform a simple mapping exercise. There are a number of ways this can be done but the table identified below presents a simple way of doing it. Performers are asked to complete the left-hand column first, which identifies the incidents where anxiety was experienced. Ask them to think back to their recent performances and when they felt anxious. Next, ask them to note down (in the right-hand column, as shown) what they did about it.

Of course, it does not have to be in a table like I have shown here. You could draw it out as a spider diagram to identify times of anxiety, or just write notes down on a blank piece of paper or a flipchart. It depends on the expected preferences of the client and how you like to work.

Often, we find that when people have identified times of anxiety and they are asked to say what they did about it, they look blankly, shrug their shoulders and say 'nothing'. That is fine. In fact, it is very useful because it highlights to the performer that they are experiencing anxiety but not doing anything about it. This can be a useful way to get them to see that sport psychology can be of significant value to them. So in our example above, Annette didn't do anything about recovering from a mistake. Having this information really helps us to discuss what she should do next time after a mistake. Perhaps reframing and refocusing. After all, thinking about it isn't going to change the past.

'There is nothing either good or bad, but thinking makes it so.'
William Shakespeare, English playwright

The mapping exercise also allows us to identify instances of **maladaptive coping**. That is, coping that is not effective. In particular, this could be instances of avoidance or disengagement coping. For example, Annette's response to a missed opportunity was to vent emotions. She seems to have identified her coping mechanism in a positive sense, but the venting of unpleasant emotions is typically considered as maladaptive and unhelpful. Here, we could review alternative methods, such as focusing on the technical lessons from the error to feel confident that the performer will be successful at the next opportunity.

Why always last minute?

If you still are, or have been, a student you are likely to have left an assignment until the last moments, therefore creating stress for yourself. You tell yourself that you won't do this again and then the next semester comes and guess what? You've done it again. Why?

I normally observe students with several assignments due and rather than selecting the one we need the most support and time on, we pick the one we are most confident about, using problem-focused coping on one but avoidance coping on the other. Really, of course, we should do this the other way around.

Table 13.1 Example table of mapping current coping

What stress or anxiety did you experience and when?	What did you do about it?
Immediately before the match I started to feel sick	Just told myself I'd be fine
When I made a mistake, I felt like I'd messed up and my coach looked disappointed	Nothing
In a really long game in the final set I felt like I was going to make a mistake	I told myself that I am good enough and I made sure to give 100% effort
I had a big opportunity and kept second-guessing myself. This led to a missed chance that I should have taken.	I shouted at myself to get my head back in the game

Often, clients identify instances of **adaptive coping**. This can be seen in Annette's response to feeling that she was going to make a mistake. Increasing effort expenditure is often a way of using energy in a positive way. Performers often also employ this method when feeling angry. Anger is a negative emotion that has a detrimental effect on performance. By reframing the boost of adrenaline from the emotion, we can believe it to be a surge of energy that can be channelled into a positive. The first example in Table 13.1 identifies a coping response that attempts to be positive, but is not as effective as it could be. Positive self-talk, as identified in Chapter 11, is a very simple and effective way of overcoming anxiety. However, it works much better when it is properly structured. Annette's response to feeling sick was simply to tell herself that she would be fine. If we were to spend more time structuring a self-talk intervention, we could significantly improve this. This is also an area where she could use social support, which is discussed later.

The examples provided here relate to an individual sport. When working in a team sport it is also useful to consider how an individual's coping mechanisms can have an effect on their teammates. For example, by coping with an individual stressor by venting unpleasant emotions, they are creating a stressor for the rest of the team. Perhaps a more adaptive coping strategy could be to raise team efficacy by remaining more positive.

Relaxation

Relaxation is a sensible way to combat stress and anxiety. Effective relaxation can reduce both cognitive and somatic anxiety. There are various ways to achieve this, some of which are more cognitive, some physiological and some a bit of both.

'The ideal attitude is to be physically loose and mentally tight.'
Arthur Ashe, US tennis player and three times a Grand Slam singles winner

RATIO BREATHING

Ratio breathing is a simple and effective way to relax by reducing heart rate and blood pressure while also managing cognitive processes. The core principle of this method is that you should breathe out for longer than you breathe in. A common ratio is to breathe in and count to four, and then breathe out and count to seven. Don't take huge breaths, breathe in through your nose comfortably and when breathing out, it should be through your mouth and with enough strength that if there were a candle six inches in front of you, the flame would flicker but not extinguish. Repeat this until you feel more relaxed. The more you practise ratio breathing the better you will get at it. The real beauty of this method is that you can practise it anywhere. Nobody will be aware that you are doing it.

Need some convincing that ratio breathing can be effective for you? When we breathe in, our diaphragm is raised and our sympathetic nervous system is stimulated. This causes the adrenaline glands to release the hormone adrenaline. Adrenaline causes heart rate to increase. As heart rate increases, oxygenated blood is pumped to the muscles. The result of this is that we sense an increase in heart rate, blood pressure and redness, as the volume of red blood cells are increased near the surface of the skin. When we breathe out, our diaphragm is lowered and the parasympathetic nervous system is stimulated. This causes the adrenal glands to release the hormone noradrenaline. Noradrenaline causes heart rate to reduce, which in turn reduces the volume of blood being pumped to the muscles.

As such, blood pressure and redness reduce. So by using ratio breathing, we are breathing out for longer than we breathe in, which will reduce heart rate and blood pressure. Try it – you will get better with practice.

Not the best coping strategy

Tennis can be a frustrating game, though for most it is not as frustrating as it was for American Jeff Tarango. At the 1995 Wimbledon championships, Tarango felt that he had had some rough decisions from the line judges and umpire (this was before the Hawk-Eye system was implemented). As he became frustrated, the crowd heckled and he responded by telling them to 'shut up'. The umpire, Bruno Rebeuh, issued a code violation and this seemed to be the last straw for Tarango. He protested, demanding Rebeuh be removed and accused him of being corrupt. For this, Rebeuh calmly issued another code violation and Tarango went into meltdown, swearing and muttering, he packed up his rackets and left the court, forfeiting the match. To cap a less than glorious day for the Tarango family, his then-wife proceeded to twice slap Rebeuh in the face. Tarango was banned from the following year's championships.

I also mentioned that cognitive anxiety can be affected. This is because previous thoughts, such as worry, doubt or concern have been replaced with numbers, as we count to four and seven. The numbers represent a neutral stimulus. They are neither positive nor negative and, as such, will not be appraised in either way. This means that we can no longer interpret this to be something negative, like anxiety.

PROGRESSIVE MUSCULAR RELAXATION

A good way to relax is to reduce muscle tension. An effective way to achieve this is through progressive muscular relaxation (PMR). PMR has two steps: tension and relaxation. To tense, you should focus on an area of the body, such as your toes, take a slow deep breath and squeeze the muscles hard for around five seconds. In step two, you quickly relax the tensed muscles. Take a moment to recognize the difference in tension after relaxation.

You should remain relaxed before progressing to the next set of muscles, for example the calf, and then gradually work your way up the body.

It is important to tense only the targeted muscles. This takes a bit of skill, as surrounding muscles will contract a little at first. With practice though, you will become better. At first, it is advised to spend around 15 minutes on PMR but as you develop your skill, you can practise tensing and relaxing large muscle groups quickly. This means that it can be done during brief breaks in play.

MINDFULNESS

Mindfulness is now incredibly popular and is strongly associated with mental health. It is the intentional, non-judgemental focus of attention to thoughts, emotions and sensations occurring in the present moment. There is a host of mindfulness methods, including **meditation**. Essentially, mindfulness practice is about recognizing and accepting physiological, emotional and cognitive states. It is an awareness of how you feel at a moment in time.

I will not go into mindfulness in any more depth here but there are many resources on it and studies identify the effectiveness of mindfulness as stress relief. There are also plentyof apps that can be downloaded to phones and tablets to support mindfulness practice – some better than others naturally.

Key idea: Mindfulness

Intentional, non-judgemental focus on attention, thoughts, emotions and sensations experienced in the moment.

Social support

Seeking support from others is an effective coping strategy but requires planning to maximize its effectiveness. Some people are good at offering problem-focused support and others are good at offering emotional support. It is important that the performer can approach the right person for the right type of support.

To work with Annette, her sport psychologist may first ask her to list all of the people she can go to for support when she is feeling stressed. Next, she would be asked to consider whether the people in her list are good problem solvers or better at providing emotional support. An example of how her list might look is presented below.

Table 13.2 Example of a social support network

People	Problem	Emotion
Steven (coach)	✓	
Michelle (physio)	✓	✓
Matt (boyfriend)		✓
Chris (friend)		✓
Mum		✓
Sally (friend)	✓	
Geoff (fitness coach)	✓	

Annette has identified that her coach is good for problem solving but not for emotional support. Conversely, her boyfriend is good for emotional support but not for problem solving. Her physio, Michelle, is a good source of social support for both.

As identified earlier, some stressors are within our control and some are outside of our control. When a stressor is within our control it means that we can change it. When it is out of our control, it means that we cannot change it. When faced with controllable stressors, performers should seek problem-focused support. If the stressor is uncontrollable, then our performer is better advised to seek emotional support. By conducting this simple activity, we can recommend that Annette seeks support from Steve, Michelle, Sally or Geoff when faced with a controllable stressor and Michelle, Matt, Chris and her mum when faced with an uncontrollable stressor.

Dig deeper

Collard, P. (2014), *The Little Book of Mindfulness: 10 Minutes a Day to Less Stress, More Peace*. London: Gaia Books.

Mellalieu, S. & Hanton, S. (Eds.) (2015), *Contemporary Advances in Sport Psychology: A Review*. London: Routledge.

Nicholls, A. R. (2010), *Coping in Sport: Theory, Methods, and Related Constructs*. New York: Nova Science Inc.

Thatcher, J., Jones, M. & Lavallee, D. (Eds.) (2011), *Coping and Emotion in Sport* (2nd ed.). London: Routledge.

Weinberg, R. S. & Gould, D. (2015), *Foundations of Sport and Exercise Psychology* (6th ed.). Champaign, IL: Human Kinetics.

Fact check

1 Managing or changing a stressor is...?
   a   emotion-focused coping
   b   avoidance-focused coping
   c   problem-focused coping
   d   being too stressed

2 How much a stressor means to someone is known as...?
   a   anxiety
   b   centrality
   c   avoidance
   d   threat

3 Emotion-focused coping is...?
   a   managing internal states to feel better about the stressor
   b   changing the size of the stressor
   c   adjusting what the stressor is
   d   avoiding the stressor

4 Inducing pressure in practice is an example of...?
   a   pressure practice
   b   conditioned practice
   c   hard practice
   d   competitive practice

5 What does PMR stand for?
   a   positive muscular relaxation
   b   progressive mind relaxation
   c   particular muscular relaxation
   d   progressive muscular relaxation

6 Ratio breathing of 4 in and 7 out...?
   a   decreases heart rate
   b   releases more noradrenaline
   c   triggers the parasympathetic nervous system
   d   all of the above

7 Emotion-focused coping is most effective...?

    a   in uncontrollable situations

    b   in controllable situations

    c   in all situations

    d   never

8 Mindfulness...?

    a   ignores how the body feels

    b   increases awareness of physiological state

    c   decreases awareness of thought

    d   a and c

9 Time management is an example of...?

    a   problem-focused coping

    b   emotion-focused coping

    c   avoidance-focused coping

    d   distraction-coping

10 Acceptance is an example of...?

    a   problem-focused coping

    b   emotion-focused coping

    c   avoidance-focused coping

    d   not coping

14

Working with coaches and teams

In this chapter you will learn:

- ▶ *about leadership in sport*
- ▶ *how to implement leadership theory*
- ▶ *how groups form and evolve*
- ▶ *what social loafing is*
- ▶ *what cohesion is*
- ▶ *how to develop team cohesion*

Scenario

You're working as a sport psychology consultant and you are invited to work with a full-time professional sports team. They had experienced mixed fortunes of late after continued success under the previous management. The existing coaching team has been in place for one year and a new season is about to begin.

On your first day, you meet the coaching staff in the morning and the playing staff in the afternoon. In your morning meeting, the head coach presents a compelling argument to show that they have great plans to develop and achieve their aims, but they need to move out a few of the old players and bring in some fresh faces.

You meet the playing staff in the afternoon, who present a different perspective. They talk of a lack of organization and imagination. You notice that there seems to be three or four cliques in the group.

Scenarios like the above can provide great challenges, especially if it is the head coach who asked you to come in. There are two issues here: the coaches and the team. The aim of this chapter is to introduce some basic approaches to leadership and team cohesion. It is intentionally focused more on application rather than theory. That said, I will start with a brief introduction to leadership.

Leadership

Every sport (and especially team sports) has many examples of great leaders. Usually, we tend to identify those who win the most as great leaders. To achieve this, the leader needs to know how to achieve success and then be able to influence a group in order to achieve a common goal (Northouse, 2010). To be able to do this, they also need to be able to do all of the things we have discussed earlier in this book – to motivate, cope with stress and to manage emotion of themselves and others.

'Leadership is getting someone to do what they don't want to do, to achieve what they want to achieve.'

Tom Landry, American football player and coach

Many leaders in sport started out as what we call **emergent leaders**. These are people who are not officially appointed to leadership positions prior to adopting and demonstrating leadership characteristics. They are then appointed to positions of leadership such as captaincy and then when their playing days end, they are appointed to coaching and management positions. By this point, they are known as prescribed leaders. **Prescribed leaders** normally get respect based on previous accomplishments at other teams, whereas emergent leaders often already have the respect of the team when they are appointed. The danger for them is the transition from being one of the group to leading the group.

Key idea: Emergent leaders

Leaders who emerge from a group, often in informal roles before being appointed in a formal role.

There are several theoretical models of leadership but the most frequently referred to in sport is Chelladurai's (1978, 1990, 2007) multidimensional model of sport leadership (Figure 14.1). The model identifies how the behaviour of leaders has antecedents that go before it, and consequences. The consequence is performance and satisfaction. This is the end point of the model and identifies how well the team performs but also how satisfied

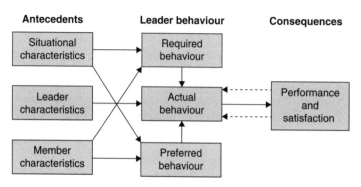

Figure 14.1 Multidimensional model of sport leadership

it is. This is influenced by, and in turn influences, actual leader behaviour.

Actual leader behaviour is the result of many factors. Impacting on this is the situation, such as the league position and short-term goals, and the personality traits and ambitions of the leader and the members (players). The model also identifies that the situation and the members lead to required behaviour. Leaders must be aware of what works for the personalities within the team. There is also a preferred behaviour. One of the challenges here is that when a leader is changed, it is likely that they have been appointed because they are different from their predecessor. This is likely to meet some difficulty somewhere along the line.

So looking at the scenario, how can we work with the coaching staff? Looking at the model, the situation must be acknowledged, which will include identifying what they believe is achievable in the coming season. It will be interesting to see if this is similar to what the players believe is achievable. Next, it is important to understand the people in the coaching team – their communication style, their personalities, their existing relationships among themselves and with the players. In an initial meeting, a glimpse of these components would be useful and they could be followed up as necessary from then on. We then need to consider the playing staff. It seems that we have cliques within the group and some different views on the effectiveness and organization of the leadership.

Transaction or transformation?

Times have changed in leadership style in elite sport. Once upon a time the leader was the boss and it was their role to say what was going to happen. The role of the group/team was to comply with this order. Compliance was rewarded, while rebellion was punished. This is essentially a description of transactional leadership.

Key idea: Transactional leadership

Encouraging group members to comply with instructions through reward and punishment.

For many years in many contexts transactional leadership has been successful. It includes setting goals and using extrinsic rewards as an outcome. Alternatively, a lack of compliance leads to punishment. Consider a traditional, and perhaps stereotypical military setting. If it is the leader's job to implement a strategy prescribed to them from elsewhere, transactional leadership appears to work well. Real change though is achieved through transformational leadership. Best described by Bass (1999), transformational leadership is based on fostering a social unit, whereby the leader raises member awareness, understanding of moral values and inspiring visions, and encourages team members to transcend their own interests for the collective good.

Bass (1985) described four dimensions of transformational leadership: idealized influence, inspirational motivation, intellectual stimulation and individualized consideration.

Idealized influence is about the leader acting as a role model, setting high expectations for behaviour to meet the overall team mission. By meeting their own high expectations, this is likely to set a precedent for group members. **Inspirational motivation** is about setting a clear and attractive vision, while presenting absolute confidence that this can be achieved. This is very common in transformational leaders. In a team sport context, a transformational leader sets out an ambitious vision, normally beyond what the team believes it will achieve and gets the team members to start believing. **Intellectual stimulation** is about the involvement of group members in the decision-making process. More involvement means empowerment and buy-in to the vision. **Individualized consideration** is where a leader demonstrates that they are aware of and have considered the relative strengths and weaknesses of individual group members. For example, if one player is nearing retirement, their role in a five-year plan will be different from a young performer.

Key idea: Transformational leadership

Inspiring change in groups and members by encouraging them to prioritize team goals and appeal to ideals.

Given the scenario here, the coaching staff could perhaps benefit from a greater understanding of transformational leadership and how to implement this. When Sir Alex Ferguson took charge of a fairly mediocre Manchester United side, he set out to build a club, citing that most managers just concentrated on the first team. This foresight and vision provided something that others could buy into and was a large part of the longevity of his success. The other key element, acknowledged by Ferguson himself, was his acceptance of change. This is another strength of a transformational leader, that they are prepared to create change when necessary, which in football is regularly. So after building some enthusiasm among the coaching staff as leaders, the focus turns to the playing staff.

Group dynamics

When we put individuals together, the extent to which the combined efforts are equal to the individual skills (or lower or greater) can be strikingly different. What we hope to achieve is synergy, where the whole is greater than the sum of its parts. To achieve this, it is necessary to look at how groups come together and establish roles.

The most identifiable model in group dynamics is Bruce Tuckman's (1965) linear perspective of group development. This identified four stages: forming, storming, norming, performing. In simple terms, this model suggests that new groups pass through these stages, which include some jostling for position and argument before settling down and working effectively. In 1977, Tuckman & Jensen added a fifth stage; adjourning in recognition of the end of a group's life cycle. There are several other models that develop this further but the notion of cycles is important in sport settings, as teams change regularly. In the scenario at the start of this chapter, the coaches refer to wanting to move on some of the older players. Perhaps these are strong characters and the coaching staff feel the links to previous versions of the team are unhelpful. It is important for coaches to recognize that teams must evolve and sometimes performers who have been great servants need to move on or take a back seat.

Established players in teams often create group norms. That is, the extent to which certain behaviours are considered as acceptable or not. This can be very difficult for a new coach to change without changing the personnel in the group. For example, if the group norm dictates that it is appropriate to go for a few drinks two days before a match, it is likely to be adopted by the newer members of the squad in an attempt to fit in. Establishing norms that are healthy for the team goals is essential.

SOCIAL LOAFING

I mentioned synergy, where the whole is greater than the sum of its parts. Well, social loafing is the opposite. When groups of people come together they generally reduce their individual effort, as responsibility is diffused among others. This is not to say that it is a conscious lowering of effort, but it occurs almost all of the time. The first experiment into this was by Max Ringelmann (1913, cited in Kravitz & Martin, 1986). Ringelmann asked a group of men to pull a rope, with the group sizes varying. He found that rope pulling decreased in a linear fashion from an individual pulling alone to a group of eight. At the time, one of the explanations was the decrease in coordination as the group becomes larger. However, follow-up studies noticed that this alone did not account for the large performance drops. Motivational causes have since been identified, such as by Latané, Williams & Harkins (1979).

Case study: Diminishing returns

To examine social loafing while learning from some of the methodological issues from Ringelmann's (1913) study, Latané et al (1979) conducted two experiments. In the first experiment, they recruited six male students on eight separate occasions and told them that they were interested in seeing how much noise people make in social settings. They told the participants that there would be 36 trials where they were required to clap or to cheer as loudly as they could for five seconds. On these occasions, there was sometimes just one person, sometimes two, four, or all six people involved. What they found was that although the noise created increased with group size, the increase was not proportional. In fact, the more people that were involved, the less noise each individual contributed in both clapping and cheering trials.

To address Ringelmann's contention that the group effect was largely down to coordination, in the second experiment the researchers conducted a similar study to the first. This time, all participants wore headphones and were blindfolded and asked to shout. This meant that they did not know if others were required to shout. At times, they were told that one, two or six people would shout. The results showed that when they believed others would be shouting, they were quieter than when they believed they were shouting on their own. The authors concluded by stating how important it is to work on improving group performance by reducing social loafing.

To prevent social loafing it is necessary to ensure accountability. To do this without performers feeling as if they are being picked on, a group norm must be created whereby reduced effort is simply not acceptable. A head coach consistently lamenting a player's work rate without the support of the team can appear like a bully or a tyrant. If, however, the responsibility for identifying and rectifying the reduced effort of a player is with the rest of the team, a strong work ethic is established as a group norm. One exercise to achieve this can be to identify the qualities of a successful team. For example, the table below shows how this might look for a cricket team.

To undertake this exercise, teams are gathered into groups and asked to discuss and report back what they believe to be the qualities of the most successful teams or the teams they admire. Responses are collated and then an overall list of qualities is produced. At this stage, each group can be asked to rate their current team out of ten against each of these qualities. To gain the overall judgement, an average score is used. You can also use a coaching group, or disperse the coaches among the player groups.

Key idea: Social loafing

Reduced individual effort to achieve a goal when working in a group

Table 14.1 Qualities of a successful cricket team example

Quality	Score
Dominating early Description: Getting out of the blocks right from the start of the match and beginning with high intensity to put the opposition under immediate pressure	6
Pressing home advantage Making sure that when in a good position, we continue to attack and take the opposition out of the game. Not allowing the opposition's tail to wag	4
Digging in when under pressure Recovering from bad positions, such as losing early wickets	8
Making something happen Changing the momentum of the game, especially in the field. Creating pressure and wickets when nothing is happening	6
Being feared Commanding a lot of respect from the opposition and being the team that makes the others respond	5

SHARED GOALS

Imagine you are part of a rowing team in the same boat. You all have the same goal to reach the finishing line as quickly as possible and know that to do so you must be able to row at the same speed in a coordinated fashion – simple. But in many team sports, such as football, rugby, hockey and netball, it is much more complicated. The large amount of decision-making involved means that there is more variability in coordination. Even greater than this, though, the variability means that practice must be together to be effective. This means that the importance of relationships within teams becomes much more of a factor in contributing to success.

> 'Talent wins games, but teamwork and intelligence wins championships.'
>
> Michael Jordan, US basketball player

To enhance this and the leadership of the team, it is recommended to set and share goals among a group. An effective way of doing this is to undertake the qualities of a successful team task, explained above, and then set goals related to the categories. For example, for making something happen, a goal could be to ensure that a new attacking fielding position is adopted every 20 minutes if there is no fall of wicket. Taking wickets is, to an extent, uncontrollable, but changing the field is entirely controllable, so this is a realistic goal that can contribute to the quality. There may be several goals per quality and there may be some for subgroups, such as bowlers, top-order batting, middle order, etc. The key is that they are shared and this process includes input from the team, influenced by the coaching staff. This can form part of transformational leadership.

We did our bit

Factions within teams can be very damaging. I observed this in a football team where arguments would regularly ensue between the defensive players and attackers. After a poor 0–0 draw, a defender stated that the attack needed to do more: 'We kept a clean sheet. We did our bit,' he said. The manager was livid – understandably so. They are all on the same team with the aim of winning a match.

Cohesion

Shared goals are a good way to get the team working in the same direction. This forms part of what we call cohesion. **Cohesion** is defined by Carron & Eys (2012, p. 213) as:

> 'a dynamic process that is reflected in the tendency for a group to stick together and remain united in pursuit of its instrumental objectives and/or for the satisfaction of member affective needs'

The crazy gang

Wimbledon Football Club historically rose from the fourth tier of English football to the top division in four years between 1982/83 to 1985/86 and beat the much more illustrious Liverpool in the FA Cup Final of 1987/88. As well as their success, though, they were known for their antics and togetherness as a squad. Stories include Chairman Sam Hammam forcing players to eat sheep testicles as an initiation, setting fire to one of the players' cars as a joke, and regularly cutting each other's clothing. There were some darker stories, also, but there can be no doubt that the cohesion of the group was a significant part of their success.

This essentially identifies two components of cohesion: instrumental objectives and member affective states. **Instrumental objectives** means working together towards the same goal. This is known as **task cohesion**. Alternatively, the **member affective states** is about how well the group serves individual members from an emotional point of view. This is known as **social cohesion**. Social cohesion is great for helping team members stay together and be a happy team. This is linked to notions of camaraderie and dressing room atmosphere. The extent to which teammates socialize beyond what they need to provides a sense of social cohesion. Cohesion is complex though. Carron (1982) proposed a model to explain how cohesion is affected by various factors and creates group and individual outcomes (Figure 14.2).

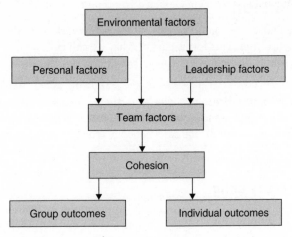

Figure 14.2 Model for cohesion in team sports

Ultimately, though, especially in elite sport, it is about maximizing performance. A happy team can contribute towards this, but in terms of our scenario the initial focus would be on task cohesion. This is about each individual taking accountability for team performance and working their hardest to contribute. Shared goals is an effective way of doing this. Other approaches to developing cohesion can be through taking pride and accountability, group identity, avoiding turnover and establishing a positive climate.

Key idea: Task cohesion

The extent to which a group works together in an effective manner to achieve shared objectives.

Pride and accountability is a key way of enhancing cohesion and reducing social loafing. As mentioned earlier, it is essential that team members understand that they are responsible for the team meeting goals. For professional clubs, taking pride in the shirt can connect the team with the supporters and the club as a whole. This increases group identity. At any level, wearing the same badged clothing, having a common team nickname, and various songs can all help to achieve a group identity. The life cycle of a team means that change will inevitably occur, but proper succession planning can reduce mass turnover and ensure that this happens smoothly. Finally, as discussed with motivation, a positive, mastery climate can make players look forward to coming into training.

Dig deeper

Bass, B. M. & Riggio, R. E. (2005), *Transformational Leadership* (2nd ed.). Abingdon: Psychology Press.

Beauchamp, M. R. (2007), *Group Dynamics in Exercise and Sport Psychology: Contemporary Themes.* London: Routledge.

Carron, A. V. & Eys, M. A. (2012), *Group Dynamics in Sport* (4th ed.), West Virginia, United States: Fitness Information Technology.

Nicholls, A. R. & Jones, L. (2012), *Psychology in Sports Coaching: Theory and Practice.* London: Routledge.

O'Boyle, I., Murray, D. & Cummins, P. (Eds.) (2015), *Leadership in Sport.* London: Routledge.

Fact check

1 An emergent leader...?

   a is normally the chairperson

   b is prescribed

   c comes from within a group

   d comes from outside the group

2 According to Chelladurai's leadership model, member characteristics is...?

   a a consequence

   b an antecedent of leader behaviour

   c an antecedent of preferred behaviour

   d b and c

3 Leading with reward and punishment is typical in...?

   a transactional leadership

   b transformational leadership

   c multidimensional leadership

   d simple leadership

4 Setting ambitious and attractive vision forms...?

   a idealized influence

   b inspirational motivation

   c intellectual stimulation

   d individualized consideration

5 Which of these does *not* form part of Tuckman's model of group development?

   a forming

   b storming

   c striving

   d performing

6 Social loafing refers to...?

   a increased effort in larger group sizes

   b decreased effort in larger group sizes

   c increased tension in large groups

   d avoiding taking part in groups

7 Attraction to a group based on affective states refers to…?
  a social cohesion
  b social facilitation
  c social loafing
  d task cohesion

8 According to Carron's model of cohesion: personal, environmental and which factor influence team factors?
  a social cohesion
  b task cohesion
  c teamwork
  d leadership

9 A way to develop cohesion is by enhancing…?
  a shared goals
  b group identity
  c a mastery climate
  d all of the above

10 A team that works together well but elements of the group don't particularly like each other has…?
  a low task but high social cohesion
  b high task and high social cohesion
  c high task but low social cohesion
  d low task and low social cohesion

Afterword

In this book I have reviewed some key topics in sport psychology from a theoretical perspective in Part One and in Part Two looked at some of the applied work that a sport psychology consultant does. Hopefully, this introductory book is able to spark enthusiasm to want to learn more about what I believe to be a fascinating subject. I genuinely believe that a huge amount of sport performance is psychological and that it is knowledge of sport psychology that can help performers to reach their potential and enjoy their career more.

The best bit is that we are still early in our journey. There are many areas of sport psychology not covered in this book, simply because it would be enormous if it were to cover everything. Even the topics that we have discussed are in development. Research in sport psychology is growing rapidly and with it so is our knowledge. There is a huge upward trend in those registering to train as sport psychology consultants also, and over the next years and decades I expect this to grow as both a research area and as a profession.

References

Allport, F. H. & Allport, G. W. (1921), 'Personality traits: Their classification and measurement', *The Journal of Abnormal and Social Psychology*, Vol. 16 Issue 1 pp. 6–40.

Allport, G. W. (1937), *Personality: A psychological interpretation*. New York: Henry Holt and Company.

Ames, C. (1992), 'Classrooms: Goals, structures, and student motivation', *Journal of Educational Psychology*, Vol. 84 Issue 3 pp. 261–71.

Ames, C. & Archer, J. (1988), 'Achievement goals in the classroom: Students' learning strategies and motivation processes', *Journal of Educational Psychology*, Vol. 80 Issue 3 pp. 260–7.

Anshel, M. H. & Brinthaupt, T. M. (2014), 'Best Practices for the Use of Inventories in Sport Psychology Consulting, *Journal of Clinical Sport Psychology*, Vol. 8 Issue 4 pp. 400–20.

Bandura, A. (1977), 'Self-efficacy: Toward a unifying theory of behavioral change', *Psychological Review*, Vol. 84 Issue 2 pp. 191–215.

Bandura, A. (1986), 'The explanatory and predictive scope of self-efficacy theory', *Journal of Social and Clinical Psychology*, Vol. 4 Issue 3 pp. 359–73.

Bandura, A. (1991), 'Social cognitive theory of moral thought and action'. In: Kurtines, W. M. & Gewirtz, J. L. (Eds.), *Handbook of moral behavior and development*, Vol. 1: Theory; Vol. 2: Research; Vol. 3: Application (pp. 45–103). Hillsdale, NJ: Lawrence Erlbaum Associates.

Bandura, A. (1997), *Self-efficacy: the exercise of control*. New York: W.H. Freeman.

Bandura, A. (1999), 'Moral disengagement in the perpetration of inhumanities', *Personality and Social Psychology Review*, Vol. 3 No. 3 pp. 193–209.

Bandura, A., Barbaranelli, C., Caprara, G. V. & Pastorelli, C. (1996), 'Mechanisms of moral disengagement in the exercise of moral agency', *Journal of Personality and Social Psychology*, Vol. 71 No. 2 pp. 364–74.

Bandura, A. & Locke, E. A. (2003), 'Negative self-efficacy and goal effects revisited', *Journal of Applied Psychology*, Vol. 88 No. 1 pp. 87–99.

Bandura, A., Ross, D. & Ross, S. A. (1961), 'Transmission of aggression through imitation of aggressive models', *Journal of Abnormal and Social Psychology*, Vol. 66 Issue 1 pp. 575–82.

Bandura, A. & Walters, R. H. (1963), *Social learning and personality development*. New York: Holt, Rinehart, & Winston.

Bass, B. M. (1985), *Leadership and performance beyond expectations*. New York: The Free Press.

Bass, B. M. (1999), 'Two decades of research and development in transformational leadership', *European Journal of Work and Organizational Psychology*, Vol. 8 Issue 1 pp. 9–32.

Baumeister, R. F., Campbell, J. D., Krueger, J. I. & Vohs, K. D. (2003), 'Does high self-esteem cause better performance, interpersonal success, happiness, or healthier lifestyles?', *Psychological Science in the Public Interest*, Vol. 4 No. 1 pp. 1–44.

Beaumont, C., Maynard, I. W. & Butt, J. (2015), 'Effective ways to develop and maintain robust sport-confidence: strategies advocated by sport psychology consultants', *Journal of Applied Sport Psychology*, Vol. 27 Issue 3 pp. 301–18.

Boardley, I. D. & Kavussanu, M. (2007), 'Development and validation of the Moral Disengagement in Sport Scale', *Journal of Sport & Exercise Psychology*, Vol. 29 Issue 5 pp. 608–28.

Boardley, I. D. & Kavussanu, M. (2008), 'The moral disengagement in sport scale – short', *Journal of Sports Sciences*, Vol. 26 Issue 14 pp. 1507–17.

Boardley, I. D. & Kavussanu, M. (2009), 'The influence of social variables and moral disengagement on prosocial and antisocial behaviours in field hockey and netball', *Journal of Sports Sciences*, Vol. 27 Issue 8 pp. 843–54.

Boardley, I. D. & Kavussanu, M. (2010), 'Effects of goal orientation and perceived value of toughness on antisocial behavior in soccer: The mediating role of moral disengagement', *Journal of Sport & Exercise Psychology*, Vol. 32 Issue 2 pp. 176–92.

Boardley, I. D. & Kavussanu, M. (2011), 'Moral disengagement in sport', *International Review of Sport and Exercise Psychology*, Vol. 4 No, 2 pp. 93–108.

Bolter, N. D. & Weiss, M. R. (2012), 'Coaching for character: Development of the Sportsmanship Coaching Behaviors Scale (SCBS)', *Sport, Exercise, and Performance Psychology*, Vol. 1 Issue 2 pp. 73–90.

Bolter, N. D. & Weiss, M. R. (2013), 'Coaching behaviors and adolescent athletes' sportspersonship outcomes: Further validation of the Sportsmanship Coaching Behaviors Scale (SCBS)', *Sport, Exercise, and Performance Psychology*, Vol. 2 Issue 1 pp. 32–47.

Brand, S., Kalak, N., Gerber, M., Clough, P. J., Lemola, S., Pühse, U. & Holsboer-Trachsler, E. (2014), 'During early and mid-adolescence, greater mental toughness is related to increased sleep quality and psychological functioning', *Journal of Health Psychology*.

Bredemeier, B. J. L. (1994), 'Children's moral reasoning and their assertive, aggressive, and submissive tendencies in sport and daily life', *Journal of Sport and Exercise Psychology*, Vol. 16 pp. 1–14.

Bredemeier, B. J. L. (1997), 'Character in action: promoting moral behavior in sport. In: *Innovations in sport psychology: linking theory and practice: proceedings* (pp. 25–7) Netanya (Israel), The Zinman College of Physical Education and Sport Sciences, The Wingate Institute for Physical Education and Sport.

Bredemeier, B. J. L. & Shields, D. L. (1984), 'Divergence in children's moral reasoning about sport and everyday life', *Sociology of Sport Journal*, Vol. 1 pp. 348–57.

Bredemeier, B. J. L. & Shields, D. L. (1985), 'Values and violence in sports today. The moral reasoning athletes use in their games and in their lives', *Psychology Today*, Vol. 19 pp. 22–32.

Bredemeier, B. J. L. & Shields, D. L. (1986), 'Game Reasoning and interactional morality', *The Journal of Genetic Psychology*, 147, 257–75.

Bredemeier, B. J. L. & Shields, D. L. (2001), 'Moral growth among athletes and non-athletes: A comparative analysis', *The Journal of Genetic Psychology*, Vol. 147 pp. 7–18.

Brown, I., Jr. & Inouye, D. K. (1978), 'Learned helplessness through modeling: The role of perceived similarity in competence', *Journal of Personality and Social Psychology*, Vol. 36 pp. 900–8.

Buckels, E. E., Trapnell, P. D. & Paulhus, D. L. (2014), 'Trolls just want to have fun', *Personality and Individual Differences*, Vol. 67 pp. 97–102.

Buodo, G., Sarlo, M. & Palomba, D. (2002), 'Attentional resources measured by reaction times highlight differences within pleasant and unpleasant, high arousing stimuli', *Motivation and Emotion*, Vol. 26 pp. 123–38.

Burton, D. (1992), 'The Jekyll/Hyde natures of goal: Reconceptualizing goal setting in sport'. In Horn, T. (Ed.), *Advances in sport psychology* (pp. 267–97). Champaign, IL: Human Kinetics.

Burton, D. & Naylor, S. (1997), 'Is anxiety really facilitative? Reaction to the myth that cognitive anxiety always impairs sport performance', *Journal of Applied Sport Psychology*, Vol. 9 pp. 295–302.

Butler, R. J. (1995), 'Athlete assessment: The performance profile', *Coaching Focus*, Vol. 29 pp. 18–20.

Butler, R. J. (1997), 'Performance profiling: Assessing the way forward'. In Butler, R. J. (Ed.), *Sports psychology in performance* (pp. 33–48). Oxford: Butterworth-Heinemann.

Butler, R. J. & Hardy, L. (1992), 'The performance profile: Theory and application', *The Sport Psychologist*, Vol. 6 pp. 253–64.

Campbell, W. K., Goodie, A. S. & Foster, J. D. (2004), 'Narcissism, confidence, and risk attitude', *Journal of Behavioral Decision Making*, Vol. 17 pp. 297–311.

Carron, A. V. (1982), 'Cohesiveness in sport groups: Interpretations and considerations', *Journal of Sport Psychology*, Vol. 4 pp. 123–38.

Carron, A. V. & Eys, M. (2012), *Group dynamics in sport* (4th ed.), West Virginia, United States: Fitness Information Technology.

Chelladurai, P. (1978), 'A contingency model of leadership in athletics'. Unpublished doctoral dissertation, University of Waterloo, Canada.

Chelladurai, P. (1990), 'Leadership in sports: A review', *International Journal of Sport Psychology*, Vol. 21 pp. 328–54.

Chelladurai, P. (2007), 'Leadership in sports. In Tenenbaum, G. & Eklund, R. C. (Eds.), *Handbook of sport psychology* (pp. 113–135). New York: Wiley.

Ciani, K, D. & Sheldon, K. M. (2010), 'Evaluating the mastery-avoidance goal construct: A study of elite college baseball players', *Psychology of Sport and Exercise*, Vol. 11 pp. 127–32.

Clark, L., Li, R., Wright, C. M., Rome, F., Fairchild, G., Dunn, B. D. & Aitken, M. R. F. (2012), 'Risk-avoidant decision making increased by threat of electric shock', *Psychophysiology*, Vol. 49 No. 10 pp. 1436–43

Clough, P. J., Earle, K., Perry, J. L. & Crust, L. (2012), 'Comment on "Progressing measurement in mental toughness: A case example of the Mental Toughness Questionnaire 48" by Gucciardi, Hanton & Mallett', *Sport, Exercise, and Performance Psychology*, Vol. 1 pp. 283–7.

Clough, P., Earle, K. & Sewell, D. (2002), 'Mental toughness: the concept and its measurement'. In Cockerill, I. (Ed.), *Solutions in sport psychology*, (pp. 32-43). London: Thomson.

Clough, P., J., Newton, S., Bruen, P., Earle, F., Earle, K., Benuzzi, F., Gardini, S., Hiber, A., Lui, F. & Venneri, A. (2010), 'Mental toughness and brain structure'. Poster presented at the

16th Annual Meeting of the Organization for Human Brain Mapping, June 6-10, Barcelona.

Clough, P. & Strycharczyk, D. (2012), *Developing mental toughness: Improving performance, wellbeing and positive behaviour in others*. London: Karnac Books.

Colbert, S. D., Scott, J., Dale, T. & Brennan, P. A. (2012), 'Performing to a world class standard under pressure – Can we learn lessons from the Olympians?', *British Journal of Oral and Maxillofacial Surgery*, Vol. 50 pp. 291–7.

Connaughton, D. & Hanton, S. (2009), 'Mental toughness in sport: Conceptual and practical Issues'. In Mellalieu, S. D. & Hanton, S. (Eds.). *Advances in applied sport psychology: A review* (pp. 317–46). Abingdon, UK: Routledge.

Conroy, D. E., Elliot, A. J. & Hofer, S. M. (2003), '2 × 2 Achievement Goals Questionnaire for Sport: Evidence for Factorial Invariance, Temporal Stability, and External Validity', *Journal of Sport and Exercise Psychology*, Vol. 25 Issue 4 pp. 456–76.

Cooper, A. & Petrides, K. V. (2010), 'A psychometric analysis of the Trait Emotional Intelligence Questionnaire-Short Form (TEIQue-SF) using Item Response Theory', *Journal of Personality Assessment*, Vol. 92 pp. 449–57.

Corbetta, M. & Shulman, G. L. (2002), 'Control of goal-directed and stimulus-driven attention in the brain', *Nature Reviews Neuroscience*, Vol. 3 pp. 201–15.

Corrion, K., Long, T., Smith, A.L. & d'Arripe-Longueville, F. (2009), '"It's not my fault; it's not serious": Athlete accounts of moral disengagement in competitive sport', *The Sport Psychologist*, Vol. 23 pp. 388–404.

Costa, P. T., Jr., McCrae, R. R. & Dye, D. A. (1991), 'Facet scales for agreeableness and conscientiousness: A revision of the NEO Personality Inventory', *Personality and Individual Differences*, Vol. 12 pp. 887–98.

Costa, P. T. & McCrae, R. R. (1992), 'Revised NEO Personality Inventory (NEO-PI-R) and NEO Five-Factor Inventory

(NEO-FFI) professional manual. Odessa, FL: Psychological Assessment Resources.

Crawford, M. (1957), 'Critical incidents in intercollegiate athletics and derived standards for professional ethics (Doctoral dissertation, University of Texas, Austin). Dissertation Abstracts International, 18, 02, 489.

Crust, L. (2008), 'A review and conceptual re-examination of mental toughness: Implications for 16 future researchers', *Personality and Individual Differences*, Vol. 45 pp. 576–83.

Crust, L. & Clough, P. J. (2005), 'Relationship between mental toughness and physical endurance', *Perceptual & Motor Skills*, Vol. 100 pp. 192–4.

Crust, L. & Clough, P. J. (2006), 'The influence of rhythm and personality in the endurance response', *Journal of Sports Sciences*, Vol. 24 pp. 187–95.

Crust, L. & Clough, P. J. (2011), 'Developing mental toughness: From research to practice', *Journal of Sport Psychology in Action*, Vol. 2 pp. 21–32.

Crust, L. & Swann, C. (2011), 'Comparing two measures of mental toughness', *Personality and Individual Differences*, Vol. 50 pp. 217–21.

Csíkszentmihályi, M. (1990), *Flow: The psychology of optimal experience*. New York: Harper and Row.

Deci, E. L. & Ryan, R. M. (1985), 'The General Causality Orientations Scale: Self-Determination in Personality', *Journal of Research in Personality*, Vol. 19 pp. 109–34.

Deci, E. L. & Ryan, R. M. (1991), 'A motivational approach to self: Integration in personality'. In: Dienstbier, R. (Ed.), Nebraska Symposium on Motivation Vol. 38, *Perspectives on Motivation*, (pp. 237–88), Lincoln, NE: University of Nebraska Press.

Derakshan, N. & Eysenck, M. W. (2009), 'Anxiety, processing efficiency, and cognitive performance: New developments from attentional control theory', *European Psychologist*, Vol. 14 pp. 168–76.

Dewhurst, S. A., Anderson, R. J., Cotter, G., Crust, L. & Clough, P. J. (2012), 'Identifying the cognitive basis of mental toughness: Evidence from the directed forgetting paradigm', *Personality and Individual Differences*, Vol. 53 pp. 587–90.

Díaz, M. M., Bocanegra, O. L., Teixeira, R. R., Espindola, F. S. (2013), 'Salivary surrogates of plasma nitrite and catecholamines during a 21-week training season in swimmers'. PLoS One, Vol. 8 e640643.

Diaz, M., Bocanegra, O. L., Teixeira, R. R., Tavares, M., Soares, S. S. & Espindola, F. S. (2013), 'The relationship between the cortisol awakening response, mood states, and performance', *Journal of Strength and Conditioning Research*, Vol. 27 Issue 5 pp. 1340–8.

Dienstbier, R. A. (1989), 'Arousal and physiological toughness: Implications for mental and physical health', *Psychological Review*, Vol. 96 pp. 84–100.

Dienstbier, R. A. (1991), 'Behavioral correlates of sympathoadrenal reactivity: the toughness model', *Medicine and Science in Sports and Exercise*, Vol. 23 pp. 846–52.

Digman, J. M. (1990), 'Personality structure: Emergence of the five-factor model', *Annual Review of Psychology*, Vol. 41 pp. 417–40.

Doran, G. T. (1981), 'There's a S.M.A.R.T. Way to Write Management's Goals and Objectives', *Management Review*, Vol. 70 pp. 35–6.

Doyle, J. M. & Parfitt, G. (1997), 'Performance profiling and constructive validity', *The Sport Psychologist*, Vol. 11 pp. 411–25.

Duda, J. L. (1989), 'The relationship between task and ego orientation and the perceived purpose of sport among male and female high school athletes', *Journal of Sport and Exercise Psychology*, Vol. 11 pp. 318–35.

Duda, J. L. & Nicholls, J. (1992), 'Dimensions of achievement motivation in schoolwork and sport', *Journal of Educational Psychology*, Vol. 84 pp. 1–10.

Duda, J. L., Olson, L. K. & Templin, T. J. (1991), 'The Relationship of Task and Ego Orientation to Sportsmanship

Attitudes and the Perceived Legitimacy of Injurious Acts', *Research Quarterly for Exercise and Sport*, Vol. 62 pp. 79–87.

Dunn, J. G. H. & Causgrove Dunn, J. (1999), 'Goal orientations, perceptions of aggression, and sportspersonship in elite male youth ice hockey players', *The Sport Psychologist*, Vol. 13 pp. 183–200.

Durand-Bush, N., Salmela, J. H. & Green-Demers, I. (2001), 'The Ottawa Mental Skills Assessment Tool (OMSAT-3)', *The Sport Psychologist*, Vol. 15 Issue 1 pp. 1–19.

Elliot, A. J. (1999), 'Approach and avoidance motivation and achievement goals', *Educational Psychologist*, Vol. 34 Issue 3 pp. 169–89.

Epstein, J. (1988), 'Effective schools or effective students? Dealing with diversity'. In Haskins, R. & MacRae, B. (Eds.), *Policies for America's public schools* (pp. 89-126). Norwood, NJ: Ablex.

Epstein, J. (1989), 'Family structures and student motivation: A developmental perspective'. In Ames, C. & Ames, R. (Eds.), *Research on motivation in education* (Vol. 3 pp. 259–95). New York: Academic Press.

Ericsson, K. A., Chase, W. G. & Faloon, S. (1980), 'Acquisition of a memory skill', *Science*, Vol. 208 pp. 1181–2.

Eysenck, H. J. (1967), *The biological basis of personality.* Springfield: Thomas.

Eysenck, H. J. (2000), *Intelligence: A new look.* Piscataway, NJ: Transaction Publishers.

Flory, K., Lynam, D., Milich, R., Leukefeld, C. & Clayton, R. (2002), 'The relations among personality, symptoms of alcohol and marijuana abuse, and symptoms of comorbid psychopathology: Results from a community sample', *Experimental and Clinical Psychopharmacology*, Vol. 10 pp. 425–34.

Gardner, H. (1983), *Frames of Mind: The Theory of Multiple Intelligence.* New York: Basic Books.

Gerber, M., Brand, S., Feldmeth, A. K., Lang, C., Elliot, C., Holsboer-Trachsler, E. & Pühse, U. (2013b), 'Adolescents with high mental toughness adapt better to perceived stress: A longitudinal study with Swiss vocational students', *Personality and Individual Differences*, Vol. 54 pp. 808–14.

Gerber, M., Kalak, N., Lemola, S., Clough, P. J., Perry, J. L., Pühse, U., Elliot, C., Holsboer-Trachsler, E. & Brand, S. (2013a), 'Are adolescents with high mental toughness levels more resilient against stress?' *Stress and Health*, Vol. 29 pp. 164–71.

Gerber, M., Kalak, N., Lemola, S., Clough, P. J., Pühse, U., Elliot, C., Holsboer-Trachsler, E. & Brand, S. (2012), 'Adolescents' exercise and physical activity are associated with mental toughness', *Physical Activity and Mental Health*, Vol. 5 pp. 35–42.

Gibbons, S. L., Ebbeck, V. & Weiss, M. R. (1995), 'Fair play for kids: Effects on the moral development of children in physical education', *Research Quarterly for Exercise and Sport*, Vol. 66 pp. 247–55.

Glisky, M. L., Tataryn, D. J., Tobias, B. A., Kihlstrom, J. F. & McConkey, K. M. (1991, 'Absorption, openness to experience, and hypnotizability', *Journal of Personality and Social Psychology*, Vol. 60 pp. 263–72.

Gucciardi, D. F. & Gordon, S. (2009a), 'Development and preliminary validation of the Cricket Mental Toughness Inventory', *Journal of Sports Sciences*, Vol. 27 pp. 1293–1310.

Gucciardi, D. F. & Gordon, S. (2009b), 'Construing the athlete and exerciser: Research and applied perspectives from personal construct psychology', *Journal of Applied Sport Psychology*, Vol. 21 (Supp1), pp. S17–S33.

Gucciardi, D. F., Gordon, S. & Dimmock, J. A. (2008), 'Towards an understanding of mental toughness in Australian football', *Journal of Applied Sport Psychology*, Vol. 20 pp. 261–81.

Gucciardi, D. F., Hanton, S., Gordon, S., Mallett, C. J. & Temby, P. (2015), 'The concept of mental toughness: Tests of dimensionality, nomological network and traitness', *Journal of Personality*, Vol. 83 pp. 26–44.

Gucciardi, D. F., Hanton, S. & Mallett, C. J. (2012), 'Progressing measurement in mental toughness: A case example of the Mental Toughness Questionnaire 48', *Sport, Exercise and Performance Psychology*, Vol. 1 pp. 194–214.

Hanin, Y. L. (1997), 'Emotions and athletic performance: Individual zones of optimal functioning model', *European Yearbook of Sport Psychology*, Vol. 1 pp. 29–72.

Hanin, Y. L. (Ed.) (2000), *Emotions in sport*. Champaign, IL: Human Kinetics.

Hardy, L. (1996), 'Three myths about applied consultancy work in sport psychology', Coleman R. Griffith Lecture at the AAASP Conference. Williamsburg, October.

Hardy, L. & Fazey, J. (1987), 'The inverted-U hypothesis: A catastrophe for sport psychology?', Paper presented at the Annual Conference of the North American Society for the Psychology of Sport and Physical Activity. Vancouver, June.

Hardy, L., Roberts, R., Thomas, P. & Murphy, S. (2010), 'Test of Performance Strategies (TOPS): Instrument refinement using confirmatory factor analysis', *Psychology of Sport and Exercise*, Vol. 11 pp. 27–35.

Harwood, C. G. (2009), 'Enhancing self-efficacy in professional tennis: Intensive work for life on the tour'. In Holder, T. & Hemmings, B. (Eds.). *Applied sport psychology: A case-based approach* (pp. 7–32). Chichester: Wiley-Blackwell.

Hays, K., Maynard, I., Thomas, O. & Bawden, M. (2007), 'Sources and types of confidence identified by world class sport performers', *Journal of Applied Sport Psychology*, Vol. 19 pp. 434–56.

Hays, K., Thomas, O., Maynard, I. & Bawden, M. (2009), 'The role of confidence in world-class sport performance', *Journal of Sport Sciences*, Vol. 27 pp. 1185–99.

Heider, F. (1944), 'Social perception and phenomenal causality', *Psychological Review*, Vol. 51 Issue 6 pp. 358–74.

Hemmings, B. & Holder, T. (Eds.) (2009), *Applied sport psychology: A case-based approach*. Chichester: Wiley-Blackwell.

Higham, A., Harwood, C. & Cale, A. (2005), *Momentum in Soccer*. Leeds: Coachwise.

Holmes, P. S. & Collins, D. J. (2001), 'The PETTLEP approach to motor imagery: A functional equivalence model for sport psychologists', *Journal of Applied Sport Psychology*, Vol. 13 pp. 60-83.

Horsburgh, V. A., Schermer, J. A., Veselka, L. & Vernon, P. A. (2009), 'A behavioural genetic study of mental toughness and personality', *Personality and Individual Differences*, Vol. 46 pp. 100–5.

Hull, C. (1943), *Principles of behavior*. New York: Appleton-Century-Crofts.

Jackson, S. A. & Csíkszentmihályi, M. (1999), *Flow in sports: The keys to optimal experiences and performances*. Champaign, IL: Human Kinetics.

Jones, G. (1995), 'Competitive anxiety in sport'. In Biddle, S. (Ed.), *European Perspectives on Exercise and Sport* (pp. 128–47). Champaign, IL: Human Kinetics.

Jones, G. (2012), 'The role of superior performance intelligence in sustained success'. In Murphy, S. M. (Ed.), *The Oxford handbook of sport and performance psychology*. Oxford: Oxford University Press.

Jones, G. & Hanton, S. (1996), 'Interpretation of competitive anxiety symptoms and goal attainment expectations', *Journal of Sport and Exercise Psychology*, Vol. 18 pp. 144–58.

Jones, G., Hanton, S. & Connaughton, D. (2002), 'What is this thing called mental toughness?: An investigation with elite performers', *Journal of Applied Sport Psychology*, Vol. 14 pp. 211–24.

Jones, G., Hanton, S. & Swain, A. B. J. (1994), 'Intensity and interpretation of anxiety symptoms in elite and non-elite sports performers', *Personality and Individual Differences*, Vol. 17 pp. 657–63.

Jones, J. G. & Hardy, L. (1990), 'Stress in sport: Experiences of some elite performers'. In Jones. G. & Hardy, L. (Eds.), *Stress and performance in sport* (pp. 247-277). Chichester: Wiley.

Jones, G. & Swain, A. B. J. (1995), 'Predispositions to experience debilitative and facilitative anxiety in elite and non-elite performers', *The Sport Psychologist*, Vol. 9 pp. 201–11.

Jones, J. G., Swain, A. & Hardy, L. (1993), 'Intensity and direction dimensions of competitive state anxiety and relationships with performance', *Journal of Sports Sciences*, Vol. 1 pp. 525–32.

Kaiseler, M., Polman, R. & Nicholls, A. (2009), 'Mental toughness, stress, stress appraisal, coping and coping effectiveness in sport', *Personality and Individual Differences*, Vol. 47 pp. 728–33.

Kavussanu, M. & Boardley, I. D. (2009), 'The prosocial and antisocial behavior in sport scale', *Journal of Sport and Exercise Psychology*, Vol. 31 pp. 97–117.

Kavussanu, M., Boardley, I. D., Sagar, S. & Ring, C. (2013), 'Bracketed Morality Revisited: How do Athletes Behave in Two Contexts', *Journal of Sport and Exercise Psychology*, Vol. 35 pp. 449–63.

Kelly, G. A. (1955). The psychology of personal constructs (Vols. 1 & 2). New York: Norton.

Kerr, J. H. (1997), *Motivation and emotion in sport*. East Sussex: Psychology Press.

Kingston, K. & Hardy, L. (1994), 'Factors affecting the salience of outcome, performance, and process goals in golf'. In Cochran. A. & Farrally, M. (Eds.), *Science and golf* (pp. 144–9). London: Chapman Hill.

Kingston, K. & Hardy, L. (1997), 'Effects of different types of goals on processes that support performance', *The Sport Psychologist*, Vol. 11 No. 3 pp. 277–93.

Kobasa, S. C. (1979), 'Stressful life events, personality, and health: An inquiry into hardiness', *Journal of Personality and Social Psychology*, Vol. 37 pp. 1–11.

Kohlberg, L. (1958), 'The Development of Modes of Thinking and Choices in Years 10 to 16', Ph.D. Dissertation, University of Chicago.

Kohlberg, L. (1976), 'Moral stages and moralization'. In: Lickona, T. (Ed.), *Moral Development and Behavior* (pp. 31–53) New York: Holt, Rinehart and Winston.

Kravitz, D. A. & Martin, B. (1986), 'Ringelmann rediscovered: The original article', *Journal of Personality and Social Psychology*, Vol. 50 pp. 936–41.

Latané, B., Williams, K. & Harkins, S. (1979), 'Many hands make light the work: The causes and consequences of social loafing', *Journal of Personality and Social Psychology*, Vol. 37 pp. 822–32.

Laursen B., Pulkkinen L. & Adams R. (2002), 'The antecedents and correlates of agreeableness in adulthood', *Journal of Developmental Psychology*, Vol. 38 pp. 591–603.

Lazarus, R. S. & Folkman, S. (1984), *Stress, appraisal, and coping.* New York: Springer.

Levy, A., Polman, R., Clough, P., Marchant, D. & Earle, K. (2006), 'Mental toughness as a determinant of beliefs, pain, and adherence in sport injury rehabilitation', *Journal of Sports Rehabilitation*, Vol. 15 pp. 246–54.

Long, T., Pantaléon, N., Bruant, G. & d'Arripe-Longueville, F. (2006), 'A qualitative study of moral reasoning of young elite athletes', *The Sport Psychologist*, Vol. 20 pp. 330–47.

Magnuson, C. D. & Barnett, L. A. (2013), 'The playful advantage: How playfulness enhances coping with stress', *Leisure Sciences: An Interdisciplinary Journal*, Vol. 35 pp. 129–44.

Mahoney, M. J., Gabriel, T. J. & Perkins, T. S. (1987), 'Psychological skills and exceptional athletic performance', *The Sport Psychologist*, Vol. 1 pp. 181–99.

Mallett, C. J., Kawabata, M., Newcombe, P., Otero-Forero, A. & Jackson, S. (2007), 'Sport Motivation Scale-6 (SMS-6): A revised six-factor sport motivation scale', *Psychology of Sport and Exercise*, Vol. 8 pp. 600–14.

Manzo, L. G., Silva, J. M. & Mink, R. (2001), 'The Carolina Sport Confidence Inventory', *Journal of Applied Sport Psychology*, Vol. 13 Issue 3 pp. 260–74.

Marchant, D. C., Polman, R. C. J., Clough, P. J., Jackson, J. G., Levy, A. R. & Nicholls, A. R. (2009), 'Mental toughness in the work place: Managerial and age differences', *Journal of Managerial Psychology*, Vol. 27 pp. 428–37.

Markland, D. & Tobin, V. (2004), 'A modification of the Behavioral Regulation in Exercise Questionnaire to include an assessment of amotivation', *Journal of Sport and Exercise Psychology*, Vol. 26 pp. 191–6.

Marsh, H. W. (1990), 'The structure of academic self-concept: The Marsh/Shavelson model', *Journal of Educational Psychology*, Vol. 82 pp. 623–36.

Martens, R. (1977, *Sport Competition Anxiety Test*. Champaign, IL: Human Kinetics.

Martens, R., Burton, D., Vealey, R. S., Bump, L. A. & Smith, D. E. (1990), 'Development and validation of the Competitive State Anxiety Inventory-2'. In Martens, R., Vealey, R. S. & Burton, D. (Eds.), *Competitive anxiety in sport* (pp. 117–90). Champaign, IL: Human Kinetics.

Martin, K. A., Moritz, S. E. & Hall, C. R. (1999), 'Imagery use in sport: A literature review and applied model', *The Sport Psychologist*, Vol. 13 pp. 245–68.

Masters, R. S. W. (1992), 'Knowledge, knerves and know-how: The role of explicit versus implicit knowledge in the breakdown of a complex motor skill under pressure', *British Journal of Psychology*, Vol. 83 pp. 343–58.

Mayer, J. D., Salovey, P., & Caruso, D. R. (2000), 'Models of emotional intelligence'. In Sternberg, R. J. (Ed.), *Handbook of human intelligence* (pp. 396–420). New York: Cambridge University Press.

Mayer, J. D., Salovey, P. & Caruso, D. R. (2002), 'Mayer–Salovey–Caruso Emotional Intelligence Test (MSCEIT): User's manual'. Toronto, Ontario: Multi-Health Systems, Inc.

McClelland, D. C. (1962), 'Business drive and national achievement'. *Harvard Business Review*, Vol. 40 pp. 99–112.

McCown, K., Keiser, R., Mulhearn, S. & Williamson, D. (1997), 'The role of personality and gender in preference for exaggerated bass in music', *Personality and Individual Differences*, Vol. 23 pp. 543–7.

McCutcheon, L. E. (1999), 'The multidimensional sportspersonship orientations scale has psychometric problems', *Journal of Social Behavior and Personality*, Vol. 14 pp. 439–44.

McNair, D. M., Lorr, M. & Droppleman, L. F. (1971), 'Manual for the Profile of Mood States'. San Diego, CA: Educational and Industrial Testing Services.

Merton, R. K. (1948), 'The self-fulfilling prophecy', *Antioch Review*, Vol. 8 pp. 193–210.

Middleton, S. C., Marsh, H. W., Martin, A. J., Richards, G. E. & Perry, C. (2004), 'Developing a test for mental toughness: The mental toughness inventory'. AARE Conference, Sydney.

Miller, B. W., Bredemeier, B. J. & Shields, D. L. (1997), 'Sociomoral education through physical activity with at-risk children'. *Quest*, Vol. 49 pp. 114–29.

Mischel, W. & Ebbesen, E. B. (1970), 'Attention in delay of gratification', *Journal of Personality and Social Psychology*, Vol. 16 pp. 329–37.

Morgan, W. P. (1979), 'Prediction of performance in athletics'. In Klavora, P. & Daniel, J. V. (Eds.), *Coach, athlete, and the sport psychologist* (pp. 173–86). Champaign, IL: Human Kinetics.

Morgan, W. P. (1980), 'The trait psychology controversy', *Research Quarterly for Exercise and Sport*, Vol. 51 pp. 50–76.

Mullan, E., Markland, D. & Ingledew, D. K. (1997), 'A graded conceptualisation of self-determination in the regulation of exercise behaviour: Development of a measure using confirmatory factor analytic procedures', *Personality and Individual Differences*, Vol. 23 pp. 745–52.

Musek, J. (2007), 'A general factor of personality: Evidence for the Big One in the five-factor model', *Journal of Research in Personality*, Vol. 41 Issue 6 pp. 1213–33.

Nelis, D., Quoidbach, J., Mikolejczak, M. & Hansenne, M. (2009), 'Increasing emotional intelligence: (How) is it possible?', *Personality and Individual Differences*, Vol. 47 pp. 36–41.

Newton, M., Duda, J.L. & Yin, Z. (2000), 'Examination of the psychometric properties of the Perceived Motivational Climate in Sport Questionnaire-2 in a sample of female athletes', *Journal of Sport Sciences*, Vol. 18 pp. 275–90.

Nicholls, J. (1984), Conceptions of ability and achievement motivation. In Ames, R. & Ames, C. (Eds.), *Research on motivation in education: Student motivation* (Vol. 1, pp. 39–73). New York: Academic Press.

Nicholls, A. R., Perry, J. L., Jones, L., Sanctuary, C., Carson, F. & Clough, P. J. (2015), 'The mediating role of mental toughness in sport', *Journal of Sports Medicine and Physical Fitness*. Vol. 55 pp. 824–34

Nicholls, A. R., Polman, R. C. J. & Levy, A. R. (2012), 'A path analysis of stress appraisal, emotion, coping and performance satisfaction among athletes', *Psychology of Sport and Exercise*, Vol. 13 pp. 263–70.

Nicholls, A. R., Polman, R. C. J., Levy, A. R. & Backhouse, S. (2008), 'Mental toughness, optimism, and coping among athletes', *Personality & Individual Differences*, Vol. 44 pp. 1182–92.

Nicholls, A. R., Polman, R. C. J., Levy, A. R. & Hulleman, J. (2012), 'An explanation for the fallacy of facilitative anxiety: Stress, emotions, coping and subjective performance in sport', *International Journal of Sport Psychology*, Vol. 43 pp. 273–93.

Nideffer, R. M. (1976), 'Testing attentional and interpersonal style', *Journal of Personality and Social Psychology*, Vol. 34 pp. 394–404.

Nideffer, R. M. (1981), *The ethic and practice of applied sport psychology*. Ithaca, NY: Movement.

Nideffer, R. M. & Segal, M. (2001), 'Concentration and attention control training'. In Williams, J. M. (Ed.), *Applied sport psychology: Personal growth to peak performance* (4th ed.) (pp. 312–32). Mountain View, CA: Mayfield.

Northouse, P. G. (2010), *Leadership theory and practice.* Thousand Oaks, CA: Sage Publications.

Onley, M., Veselka, L., Schermer, J. A. & Vernon, P. A. (2013), 'Survival of the scheming: A genetically informed link between the dark triad and mental toughness', *Twin Research and Human Genetics*, Vol. 16 pp. 1087–95.

Orth, U. & Robins, R. W. (2014), 'The development of self-esteem', *Current Directions in Psychological Science*, Vol. 23 pp. 381–7.

Paivio, A. (1985), 'Cognitive and motivational functions of imagery in human performance', *Canadian Journal of Applied Sport Sciences*, Vol. 10 pp. 22–8.

Palmer, B. R., Gignac, G., Manocha, R. & Stough, C. (2005), 'A psychometric evaluation of the Mayer–Salovey–Caruso Emotional Intelligence Test Version 2.0', *Intelligence*, Vol. 33 pp. 285–305.

Pavlov, I. P. (1897), 'The work of the digestive glands. London: Griffin. Syed, M. (2011). Bounce: *The myth of talent and the power of practice*. London: 4th Estate.

Pelletier, L. G., Fortier, M. S., Vallerand, R. J., Tuson, K. M., Brière, N. M. & Blais, M. R. (1995), 'Toward a new measure of intrinsic motivation, extrinsic motivation, and amotivation in sports: The Sport Motivation Scale (SMS)', *Journal of Sport & Exercise Psychology*, Vol. 17 pp. 35–53.

Pelletier, L. G., Rocchi, M. A., Vallerand, R. J., Deci, E. L. & Ryan, R. M. (2013), 'Validation of the revised sport motivation scale (SMS-II)', *Psychology of Sport and Exercise*, Vol. 14 pp. 329–41.

Perry, J. L. (2014), 'Sport and its role in developing young people'. In Strycharczyk, D. & Clough, P. J., *Developing mental toughness in young people: Approaches to achievement, well-being and positive behaviour* (pp. 181–90). London: Karnac Books.

Perry, J. L., Clough, P. J. & Crust, L. (2013), 'Psychological approaches to enhancing fair play', *Athletic Insight*, Vol. 5 No. 2

Perry, J. L., Clough, P. J., Crust, L., Nabb, S. & Nicholls, A. R. (2015), 'Development and validation of the compliant and principled sportspersonship scale', *Research Quarterly for Exercise and Sport*, Vol. 86 pp. 71–80.

Perry, J. L., Clough, P. J., Earle, K., Crust, L. & Nicholls. A. R. (2013), 'Factorial validity of the Mental Toughness Questionnaire 48', *Personality and Individual Differences*, Vol. 4 pp. 587–92.

Peters, S. (2012), *The chimp paradox: The mind management programme to help you achieve confidence, success and happiness.* London: Vermilion.

Petrides, K. V. (2009), 'Technical manual for the Trait Emotional Intelligence Questionnaires (TEIQue)', London: London Psychometric Laboratory.

Petrides, K. V. (2011), 'Ability and trait emotional intelligence'. In Chamorro-Premuzic, T., Furnham, A. & von Stumm, S. (Eds.), *The Blackwell-Wiley handbook of individual differences.* New York: Wiley.

Petrides, K. V., Pita, R. & Kokkinaki, F. (2007), 'The location of trait emotional intelligence in personality factor space', *British Journal of Psychology*, Vol. 98 pp. 273–89.

Ravel, S. & Richmond, B. J. (2006), 'Dopamine neuronal responses in monkeys performing visually cued reward schedules', *European Journal of Neuroscience*, Vol. 24 pp. 277–90.

Rentfrow, P. J. & Gosling, S. D. (2003), 'The do re mi's of everyday life: The structure and personality correlates of music preferences', *Journal of Personality and Social Psychology*, Vol. 84 pp. 1236–56.

Rest, J. R. (1984), 'The major components of morality'. In: Kurtines, W. & Gewirtz, J. (Eds.) *Morality, moral behavior and moral development* (pp. 24–40). New York: Wiley.

Roberts, G. C., Treasure, D. C. & Balague, G. (1998), 'Achievement goals in sport: The development and validation of the Perception of Success Questionnaire', *Journal of Sports Sciences*, Vol. 16 pp. 337–47.

Rowley, A., Landers, D., Kyllo, L. & Etnier, J. (1995), 'Does the iceberg profile discriminate between successful and less successful athletes? A meta-analysis', *Journal of Sport and Exercise Psychology*, Vol. 17 pp. 185–99.

Rushton, J. P. & Irwing, P. (2011), 'The general factor of personality: Normal and abnormal'. In Chamorro-Premuzic, T., van Stumm, S. & Furnham, A. (Eds.), *The Wiley-Blackwell Handbook of Individual Differences*. Oxford: Blackwell Publishing Ltd.

Sage, L. & Kavussanu, M. (2007), 'The effects of goal involvement on moral behavior in an experimentally manipulated competitive setting', *Journal of Sport and Exercise Psychology*, Vol. 29 pp. 190–207.

Salovey, P. & Mayer, J. D. (1990), 'Emotional intelligence', *Imagination, Cognition, and Personality*, Vol. 9 pp. 185–211.

Salovey, P., Brackett, M. A. & Mayer, J. D. (Eds.), (2004), *Emotional intelligence: Key readings on the Mayer and Salovey model*. New York: National Professional Resources Inc.

Schmitt, D. P., Realo, A., Voracek, M. & Allik, J. (2008), 'Why can't a man be more like a woman? Sex differences in Big Five personality traits across 55 cultures', *Journal of Personality and Social Psychology*, Vol. 94 pp. 168–82.

Seifriz, J. J., Duda, J. L. & Chi, L. (1992), 'The relationship of perceived motivation climate to intrinsic motivation and beliefs about success in basketball', *Journal of Sport and Exercise Psychology*, Vol. 14 pp. 375–91.

Seligman, M. E. P. (1975), *Helplessness: On depression, development, and death*. San Francisco: W. H. Freeman.

Selye H. (1976), *The Stress of Life*. New York: McGraw-Hill.

Sharp, L. & Hodge, K. (2014), 'Sport psychology consulting effectiveness: The athlete's perspective, *International Journal of Sport and Exercise Psychology*, Vol. 12 pp. 91–105.

Sheard, M. & Golby, J. (2006), 'Effect of a psychological skills training program on swimming performance and positive psychological development', *International Journal of Sport Psychology*, Vol. 4 pp. 149–69.

Sheard, M., Golby, J. & van Wersch, A. (2009), 'Progress toward construct validation of the sports mental toughness inventory (SMTQ)', *European Journal of Psychological Assessment*, Vol. 25 pp. 186–93.

Shields, D. L. L. & Bredemeier, B. J. L. (1995), *Character development and physical activity*. Champaign, IL: Human Kinetics.

Shields, D. L. L., Bredemeier, B. J. L., LaVoi, N. M. & Power, C. F. (2005), 'The sport behavior of youth, parents, and coaches: The good, the bad & the ugly', *Journal of Research on Character Education*, Vol. 3 pp. 43–59.

Short, S. E., Sullivan, P., & Feltz, D. L. (2005), 'Development and preliminary validation of the Collective Efficacy Questionnaire for Sports', *Measurement in Physical Education and Exercise Science*, Vol. 9 pp. 181–202.

Skinner, B. F. (1938), *The behavior of organisms: An experimental analysis*. Acton, MA: Copley.

Slaney, R. B., Rice, K. G. & Ashby, J. S. (2002), 'A programmatic approach to measuring perfectionism: The almost perfect scales'. In Flett, G. L. & Hewitt, P. L. (Eds.), *Perfectionism: Theory, research, and treatment* (pp. 63–88). Washington, D.C. American Psychological Association.

Smith, E. R. & Mackie, D. M. (2007), *Social psychology* (3rd ed.). Hove: Psychology Press.

Smith, R. E., Schultz, R. W., Smoll, F. L. & Ptacek, J. T. (1995), 'Development and validation of a multidimensional measure of sport-specific psychological skills: The Athletic Coping Skills

Inventory-28', *Journal of Sport and Exercise Psychology*, Vol. 17 pp. 379–98.

Smith, R. E., Smoll, F. L., Cumming, S. P. & Grossbard, J. R. (2006), 'Measurement of multidimensional sport performance anxiety in children and adults: The Sport Anxiety Scale-2', *Journal of Sport and Exercise Psychology*, Vol. 28 pp. 479–501.

Smith, R. E., Smoll, F. L. & Schutz, R. W. (1990), 'Measurement and correlates of sport-specific cognitive and somatic trait anxiety: The Sport Anxiety Scale', *Anxiety Research*, Vol. 2 pp. 263–80.

Spence, J. T. & Spence, K. W. (1966), 'The motivational components of manifest anxiety: Drive and drive stimuli'. In Spielberger, C. D. (Ed.), *Anxiety and behavior*. New York: Academic Press.

Spielberger, C. D. (1966), 'Theory and research on anxiety'. In Spielberger, C. D. (Ed.), *Anxiety and behavior* (pp. 3–19). New York: Academic Press.

Spray, C. M., Wang, C. K. J., Biddle, S. J. H. & Chatzisarantis, N. L. D. (2006), 'Understanding motivation in sport: An experimental test of achievement goal and self determination theories', *European Journal of Sport Science*, Vol. 6 pp. 43–51.

Stoeber, J., Otto, K. & Dalbert, C. (2009), 'Perfectionism and the big five: Conscientiousness predicts longitudinal increases in self-oriented perfectionism', *Personality and Individual Differences*, Vol. 47 pp. 363–8.

Swain, A. B. J. & Jones, G. (1993), 'Intensity and frequency dimensions of competitive state anxiety', *Journal of Sport Sciences*, Vol. 11 pp. 533–42.

Swain, A. B. J. & Jones, G. (1996), 'Explaining performance variance: The relative contribution of intensity and direction dimensions of competitive state anxiety', *Anxiety, Stress and Coping: An International Journal*, Vol. 9 pp. 1–18.

Terry, P. C. & Karageorghis, C. I. (2011), 'Music in sport and exercise'. In Morris, T. & Terry, P. C. (Eds.), *The new sport and exercise psychology companion* (pp. 359–380). Morgantown, WV: Fitness Information Technology.

Thomas, P. (1990), 'An overview of the performance enhancement process in applied psychology'. Unpublished manuscript, United States Olympic Training Center at Colorado Springs.

Thomas, O., Lane, A. & Kingston, K. (2011), 'Defining and contextualizing robust sport-confidence', *Journal of Applied Sport Psychology*, Vol. 23 pp. 189–208.

Thomas, P. R., Murphy, S. M. & Hardy, L. (1999), 'Test of Performance Strategies: development and preliminary validation of a comprehensive measure of athletes' psychological skills', *Journal of Sports Sciences*, Vol. 17 pp. 697–711.

Thorndike, E. L. (1901), 'Animal intelligence: An experimental study of the associative processes in animals', *Psychological Review Monograph Supplement*, Vol. 2 pp. 1–109.

Tuckman, B. W. (1965), 'Developmental Sequence in Small Groups', *Psychological Bulletin*, Vol. 63 pp. 384–99.

Tuckman, B. W. & Jensen, M. A. C. (1977), 'Stages of small group development revisited', *Group and Organization Studies*, Vol. 2 pp. 419–27.

Vallerand, R. J., Deshaies, P., Cuerrier, J. P., Briere, N. M. & Pelletier, L. G. (1996), 'Toward a multidimensional definition of sportsmanship', *Journal of Applied Sport Psychology*, Vol. 8 pp. 89–101.

Vallerand, R. J., Brière, N. M., Blanchard, C. M. & Provencher, P. (1997), 'Development and validation of the multidimensional sportspersonship orientations scale', *Journal of Sport and Exercise Psychology*, Vol. 19 Issue 2 pp. 197–206.

van der Linden, D., te Nijenhuis, J. & Bakker, A. B. (2010), 'The general factor of personality: A meta-analysis of Big Five intercorrelations and a criterion-related validity study', *Journal of Research in Personality*, Vol. 44 pp. 315–27.

Van Raalte, J. L., Cornelius, A. E., Brewer, B. W. & Hatton, S. J. (2000), 'The antecedents and consequences of self-talk in competitive tennis', *Journal of Sport and Exercise Psychology*, Vol. 22 pp. 345–56.

Vancouver, J. B., Weinhardt, J. M. & Schmidt, A. M. (2010), 'A formal, computational theory of multiple-goal pursuit: integrating goal-choice and goal-striving processes', *Journal of Applied Psychology*, Vol. 95 pp. 985–1008.

Vealey, R. S. (1986), 'Conceptualization of sport-confidence and competitive orientation: Preliminary investigation and instrument development', *Journal of Sport Psychology*, Vol. 8 pp. 224–46.

Vealey, R. S. (2001), 'Understanding and enhancing self-confidence in athletes'. In Singer, R., Hausenblaus, H. & Janelle, C. (Eds.), *Handbook of sport psychology* (2nd ed.), (pp. 550–63). New York: McMillan.

Vealey, R. S. & Chase, M. A. (2008), 'Self-confidence in sport: Conceptual and research advances'. In Horn, T. S. (Ed.), *Advances in Sport Psychology* (3rd ed.), (pp. 65–97). Champaign, IL: Human Kinetics.

Vealey, R. S., Hayashi, S. W., Garner-Holman, M. & Giacobbi, P. (1998), 'Sources of sport-confidence: Conceptualization and instrument development', *Journal of Sport and Exercise Psychology*, Vol. 20 pp. 54–80.

Vealey, R. & Knight, B. (2002), 'Conceptualization and measurement of multidimensional sport-confidence'. Paper presented at the Association for the Advancement of Applied Sport Psychology Conference, Tucson, AZ.

Weinberg, R., Butt, J., Knight, B. & Perritt, N. (2001), 'Collegiate coaches' perceptions of their goal-setting practices: A qualitative investigation', *Journal of Applied Sport Psychology*, Vol. 13 pp. 374–98.

Weiner, B. (1974), *Achievement motivation and attribution theory*. Morristown, NJ: General Learning Press.

Weiner, B. (1979), 'A theory of motivation for some classroom experiences', *Journal of Educational Psychology*, Vol. 71 pp. 3–25.

Weiner, B. (1985), 'An attributional theory of achievement motivation and emotion', *Psychological Review*, Vol. 92 pp. 548–73.

Weiner, B. (1992), *Human motivation: Metaphors, theories and research*. Newbury Park, CA: Sage Publications.

Weston, N. J. V. (2008), 'Performance profiling'. In Lane, A. M. (Ed.), *Topics in applied psychology: Sport and exercise psychology* (pp. 91–108). London: Hodder Education.

Weston, N. J. V., Greenlees, I. A. & Thelwell, R. C. (2011), 'Athlete perceptions of the impacts of performance profiling', *International Journal of Sport and Exercise Psychology*, Vol. 9 pp. 173–88.

Weston, N., Greenlees, I. & Thelwell, R. (2013), 'A review of Butler and Hardy's (1992) performance profiling procedure within sport', *International Review of Sport and Exercise Psychology*, Vol. 6 pp. 1–21.

Wiggins, J. (1996), *The Five-Factor Model of Personality* (1st ed.). New York: The Guildford Press.

Wilson, P. M., Rodgers, W. M., Loitz, C. C. & Scime, G. (2006), '"It's who I am...really!" The importance of integrated regulation in exercise contexts', *Journal of Biobehavioral Research*, Vol. 11 pp. 79–104.

Woodman, T., Akehurst, S., Hardy, L. & Beattie, S. (2010), 'Self-confidence and performance: A little self-doubt helps', *Psychology of Sport and Exercise*, Vol. 11 Issue 6 pp. 467–70.

Woodman, T. & Hardy L. (2003), 'The relative impact of cognitive anxiety and self-confidence upon sport performance: A meta-analysis', *Journal of Sports Sciences*, Vol. 21 pp. 443–57.

Wright, C., J. & Smith, D. (2009), 'The effect of PETTELP imagery on strength performance', *International Journal of Sport and Exercise Psychology*, Vol. 7 pp. 18–31.

Wrosch, C., Amir, E. & Miller, G. E. (2011), 'Goal adjustment capacities, coping, and subjective well-being: The sample case of caregiving for a family member with mental illness', *Journal of Personality and Social Psychology*, Vol. 100 pp. 934–46.

Wrosch, C., Scheier, M. F. & Miller, G. E. (2013), 'Goal adjustment capacities, subjective well-being, and physical health', *Social and Personality Psychology Compass*, Vol. 7 pp. 847–60.

Yerkes, R. M. & Dodson, J. D. (1908), 'The relation of strength of stimulus to rapidity of habit-formation', *Journal of Comparative Neurology and Psychology*, Vol. 18 pp. 459–82.

Zourbanos, N., Hatzigeorgiadis, A., Chroni, S., Theodorakis, Y. & Papaioannou, A. (2009), 'Automatic self-talk questionnaire for sports (ASTQS): Development and preliminary validation of a measure identifying the structure of athletes' self-talk', *The Sport Psychologist*, Vol. 23 pp. 233–51.

Answers

CHAPTER 1
1 b
2 c
3 a
4 d
5 d
6 b
7 b
8 d
9 a
10 b

CHAPTER 2
1 b
2 a
3 c
4 d
5 c
6 b
7 a
8 c
9 c
10 b

CHAPTER 3
1 b
2 b
3 d
4 a
5 c
6 c
7 d
8 a
9 c
10 a

CHAPTER 4
1 b
2 a
3 c
4 c
5 d
6 d
7 b
8 a
9 b
10 c

CHAPTER 5
1 b
2 a
3 d
4 d
5 d
6 b
7 a
8 b
9 c
10 a

CHAPTER 6
1 b
2 d
3 d
4 c
5 a
6 a
7 d
8 b
9 d
10 c

CHAPTER 7

1 d

2 c

3 b

4 c

5 a

6 d

7 c

8 d

9 b

10 a

CHAPTER 8

1 b

2 a

3 c

4 b

5 a

6 b

7 a

8 b

9 c

10 b

CHAPTER 9

1 d

2 c

3 a

4 b

5 c

CHAPTER 10

1 c

2 a

3 d

4 c

5 a

CHAPTER 11

1 b

2 a

3 c

4 c

5 d

6 c

7 c

8 a

9 a

10 b

CHAPTER 12

1 d

2 b

3 a

4 c

5 a

6 c

7 d

8 d

9 b

10 c

CHAPTER 13

1 c

2 b

3 a

4 b

5 d

6 d

7 a

8 b

9 a

10 b

CHAPTER 14

1 c

2 d

3 a

4 b

5 c

6 b

7 a

8 d

9 d

10 c

Index

emotions, 125–40
  facilitating thought, 128
  managing, 129–30
  perception of, 127–8
  understanding of, 129
endocrine system, 29
Ericsson, K. Anders, 20–1
ethics in consultancy, 198–9
euphemistic labelling, 152–3
euphoria, 137–8
experiential emotional intelligence, 128–9
extroversion, 6, 11–12
Eysenck, Hans, 6

facial expressions, 127–8
facilitative anxiety, 39
failure, 69, 106–7
fair play, 160–1
fear of failure, 41
fear, ruling by, 120
fight or flight, 139, see also, alarm reaction stage
five-factor model, 7–15
five myths, xiv–xv
flexibility with clients, 194–5
Flintoff Andrew, 159–60
flow, 245–7
focus groups, 180–1
focus plans, 244
Ford, Doug, 109–10
Freud, Sigmund, 4
functional equivalence, 222

GAS model, see general adaptation syndrome
GBC, see Graduate Basis for Chartered membership (GBC)
gender differences, 174
general adaptation syndrome, 29–30
goal adjustment, 232
goal setting, 226–32
Gorman, Dave, 237

Graduate Basis for Chartered membership (GBC), 196
grounding, 244
group dynamics, 272–7
group life cycle, see group dynamics
group norms, see group dynamics
Gucciardi's seven indicators of mental toughness, 61

hardiness, 65
hard work, 20–1
Harwood, Chris, 208–9
HCPC, see Health and Care Professions Council (HCPC)
Health and Care Professions Council (HCPC), 197
Heinz dilemma, 148–9, 151

iceberg profile, see Profile of Mood States
idealized influence, see transformational leadership
identified regulation, 116
'IKEA' psychology, 190–1
imagery, 220–6
  effective, 224–6
  functions of, 223
immoral acts, 152
indemnity insurance, 190
individualized consideration, see transformational leadership
individualized zone of optimal functioning (IZOF), 31–2, 82
inhibitive morality, 147
innate sources of confidence, 88–9
inspirational motivation, see transformational leadership
instrumental objectives, 277
integrated regulation, 116
integrity, 162
intellectual stimulation, see transformational leadership
intelligent emotions, 133